Praise for

ESCAPE FROM PARIS

"Stephen Harding has done it again. With this well-researched, well-written and genuinely exciting account of American airmen shot down over Occupied France and hidden by the French Resistance in Paris, he has proved that he has an extraordinary feel for the hitherto untold stories of World War II."

—Andrew Roberts, bestselling author of
Churchill: Walking with Destiny

"*Escape from Paris* is a thrilling, brilliantly told true tale of heroism, love, and escape, set in the dark shadows of Nazi Paris. Tense and compulsively readable from beginning to end."

—Alex Kershaw, bestselling author of *The First Wave*

"*Escape from Paris* has the emotional pull of a great thriller, yet it's a true and memorable account of the interlinked heroism of courageous American bomber crews downed in enemy territory and intrepid French resisters who risked everything to spirit them to safety. History of a high order rendered with verve and riveting authenticity."

—Donald L. Miller, bestselling author of *Masters of the Air*

"From the first exhilarating moments of a fierce air battle over France, Stephen Harding delivers page-after-page of high adventure, intrigue and drama. He paints a vivid, unforgettable portrait of Nazi-occupied Paris and the efforts of a band of resistance fighters who risk everything to secret downed Allied airmen to freedom. Bravo!"

—Neal Bascomb, author of *The Escape Artists*

"From Stephen Harding, a brilliant and thrilling recreation of a great World War II story, a story of love in time of war. Harding is a scrupulous and knowledgeable author and, caution; you will not put *Escape from Paris* down until you've finished it. Very highly recommended."

—Alan Furst, *New York Times* bestselling author of *Mission to Paris*

"Stephen Harding's *Escape from Paris* is fascinating and a terrific read. I honestly could not turn the pages fast enough. It is thrilling and terrifying in equal measure; an amazing story of love and resistance that—almost unbelievably—happens to be true."

—Anne Sebba, award-winning author of *Les Parisiennes*

"In this thrilling WWII history...Harding masterfully recreates thrilling details of air combat, the intrigue of the French Resistance, and the horrors of war. This masterfully told and dramatic tale will keep readers spellbound until the final page."

—*Publishers Weekly*

"A poignant World War II saga of the relationship between an American gunner shot down over France and the French family who helped him...an engaging human story."

—*Kirkus Reviews*

ESCAPE FROM PARIS

ESCAPE
FROM PARIS

A True Story of Love and Resistance
in Wartime France

STEPHEN HARDING

New York

Hachette Books
Hachette Book Group
1290 Avenue of the Americas
New York, NY 10104
HachetteBooks.com
Twitter.com/HachetteBooks
Instagram.com/HachetteBooks

Printed in the United States of America

First Paperback Edition: October 2021

Published by Hachette Books, an imprint of Perseus Books, LLC, a subsidiary of Hachette Book Group, Inc. The Hachette Books name and logo is a trademark of the Hachette Book Group.

The Hachette Speakers Bureau provides a wide range of authors for speaking events. To find out more, go to www.hachettespeakersbureau.com or call (866) 376-6591.

The publisher is not responsible for websites (or their content) that are not owned by the publisher.

Print book interior design by Trish Wilkinson.

Library of Congress Cataloging-in-Publication Data has been applied for.

ISBNs: 978-0-306-92216-9 (hardcover), 978-0-306-92215-2 (paperback),
        978-0-306-92214-5 (ebook)

LSC-C

Printing 1, 2021

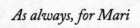

As always, for Mari

Contents

Think not only of their passing, remember the glory of their spirit.

—Inscription on the wall of the
Normandy American Cemetery Chapel

PROLOGUE

FROM 22,000 FEET ABOVE THE ENGLISH CHANNEL, GERMAN-OCCUPIED France appeared remarkably serene on the morning of July 14, 1943.

Out the left waist gun position of his B-17 Flying Fortress, Staff Sergeant Joe Cornwall could trace the coast of Normandy as far north as Dieppe, the thin white ribbon of breaking surf clearly discernable from the sun-dappled greens and browns of farm fields farther inland. Buffeted by the forty-below-zero winds that poured in through both of the bomber's waist windows and cold despite his heavy, sheepskin-lined flying clothes, thick gloves, and leather helmet, the twenty-eight-year-old airman readjusted his oxygen mask and daydreamed briefly of how warm it must be on the sandy beaches four miles below.

Gazing upward, Cornwall took in a less tranquil but equally stirring sight. Barely fifty feet off the Fortress's left wing, two other B-17s droned along in formation, one slightly ahead and higher, the other somewhat lower, offset and in trail. And though he could not see them from his position, the gunner knew that two additional bombers were right where they were supposed to be—one directly forward of and slightly above his aircraft, and the other ahead and off to the right. Together, the five Fortresses—a sixth had turned back to England with mechanical problems—constituted the low squadron of the U.S. Army Air Forces' 94th Bomb Group. Out fellow gunner Frank Santangelo's right waist window, Cornwall could see the six B-17s of the unit's lead squadron, highlighted by the bright morning sunlight. Farther up and directly to the right were the eight bombers that constituted the group's high squadron; there should have been a ninth, but the lead machine had also been forced to return to base.

Nor was the 94th alone in the sky that morning, because stacked upward and to the right of the group's formation were the thirty-six other B-17s of the 95th, 96th, and 100th Bomb Groups. Together the fifty-five Fortresses comprised the 4th Bombardment Wing, and the four contrails that streamed from each machine looked, Joe thought, like long, slender skeins of wispy cotton candy—though his tinted goggles turned the white vapor trails an ethereal, golden yellow. Above and to either side of the bomber stream dozens of nimble Spitfire fighters of the Royal Air Force (RAF) spun their own interwoven webs of condensation as they ranged back and forth, their pilots alert for the first sign of German interceptors.

The enemy fighters would almost certainly not descend until after low fuel reserves forced the Spits to turn for home, but the ragged blossoms of dirty black-gray smoke that had just begun to appear ahead of the ponderous Fortresses clearly indicated the Germans were aware of the aerial armada's progress. While the antiaircraft fire was still relatively light and inaccurate—in their dry postmission reports the 94th's intelligence officers classified such barrages as "meager"—every man in the bomber stream knew that would certainly change the nearer the formation got to its target. That objective—the commercial airport–turned–Luftwaffe base at Le Bourget, outside Paris—was heavily defended by flak batteries, and Cornwall briefly mused about how ironic it would be to get shot down during a raid on the place where Charles Lindbergh had received a hero's welcome after his solo flight across the Atlantic sixteen years earlier. Even more ironic, the young gunner thought, would be to die bombing France on this particular day—the 154th anniversary of a key event in the now subjugated nation's history: Bastille Day.

SOME FORTY MILES TO THE SOUTHEAST OF THE AMERICAN BOMBER STREAM, Major Egon Mayer was just lifting his Focke-Wulf Fw 190 off from the Luftwaffe airfield at Beaumont-le-Roger. The twenty-six-year-old was one of Germany's most successful fighter pilots, and as of that morning had sixty-eight confirmed aerial victories—the majority of them RAF Spitfires downed over France or the Channel. But the start of American daylight bombing raids in the fall of 1942 had brought about a gradual change in the nature of Mayer's victims, from nimble fighters to what Luftwaffe pilots called *Viermots,* the four-engine B-17s and B-24 Liberators of the fledgling U.S. VIII Bomber Command.

The change in prey had also necessitated a change in tactics for the German pilots tasked with intercepting the heavy bombers. The American formations could throw out a deadly stream of defensive fire in all directions, and the attacks that worked so well against fighters—a relatively slow, overtaking approach from the side or rear that allowed a concentration of hits on the enemy's control surfaces and cockpit—were vastly more dangerous and notably less successful when attempted against a *Viermot* bristling with machine guns. Mayer himself had helped develop a new way to engage the American heavies—a high-speed, head-on attack that took advantage of the relatively weak nose armament of early model B-17s and B-24s and concentrated the attacker's fire on the bomber's cockpit. The tactic demanded a high degree of skill and considerable courage on the part of the attacker; with the fighter and its target closing at a combined speed of nearly 500 mph, even the slightest miscalculation on the Luftwaffe pilot's part could spell disaster for him as well as his quarry. But when executed correctly the head-on attack could be devastatingly effective, as Mayer proved the first time the new technique was used in combat. During a U.S. raid on the German submarine pens at Saint-Nazaire, France, on November 23, 1942, he shot down two Fortresses and a Liberator in less than thirty minutes.

By the summer of 1943 Mayer was not only among the Luftwaffe's highest-scoring fighter pilots, he was the commander of one of the service's most renowned units—Jagdgeschwader (Fighter Wing) 2. Bearing the honorific title "Richthofen" after Germany's leading World War I ace, JG 2 was the first line of defense against the Allies' increasingly vigorous strategic-bombardment campaign. The unit's three groups of heavily armed and highly lethal Messerschmitt Bf 109 and Fw 190 fighters—some 120 aircraft in all—were in action almost every day, rising from airfields across western France to engage the bomber streams. And Mayer, a pilot arguably as skilled and certainly as determined as the man for whom JG 2 was named, flew as many missions as his administrative duties allowed.

On this Bastille Day, as always, Mayer was leading from the front, the other aircraft of his headquarters flight already in tight formation on either wing as he raised his fighter's nose and clawed for altitude. He and his comrades would have to be thousands of feet above and several miles ahead of the American bombers for the head-on tactic to work as planned. And Mayer was determined that it would, for he intended to mark France's special day in his own ironic fashion—with the funeral pyres of burning *Viermots* littering the idyllic countryside of Basse-Normandie.

WHILE EGON MAYER AND HIS COMRADES WERE BENT ON DESTRUCTION THAT Bastille Day, a family in the heart of Paris was prepared to risk everything to aid those Allied aviators whose aircraft might fall victim to the German fighters. In an irony Mayer himself might well have appreciated, the downed airmen would find refuge on the grounds of a national monument that is home to what is arguably the most revered tomb in the French capital.

Set on some thirty acres just south of the River Seine in Paris's fashionable 7th arrondissement, the seventeenth-century Hôtel des Invalides was built by order of King Louis XIV as a hospital and retirement home for military veterans. Over the decades the sprawling complex's former Chapelle royale became the final resting place for scores of France's most honored military and political leaders, their compact tombs and memorial stones dotting the narrow-walled corridors radiating outward from the former church's rotunda. And it is there that Napoléon Bonaparte—general, emperor, and the sanctuary's most famous occupant—passes eternity in a massive granite and marble sarcophagus set beneath a lofty golden dome.

While Invalides and Napoléon's Tomb have long been among Paris's most famed and often-visited landmarks, in that difficult and dangerous summer of 1943 the complex was also home to the Morin family—Georges and his wife, Denise, both forty-five, and their twenty-two-year-old daughter, Yvette. The family occupied a small, two-bedroom apartment on the grounds because both parents worked within the complex.

Georges was a senior official in l'Office nationale des mutilés et réformés (National Office for the Wounded and Discharged), an Invalides-based government organization tasked with, among other things, caring for men who, like himself, had been left disabled by their service in World War I. His time in the trenches had left Georges with a false eye, a permanent limp, and an intense hatred for all things German. The latter was an emotion shared by Denise, a slight woman whose stature and outward calm belied the intensity of her love for Georges and her devotion to Invalides, where she oversaw the safety and maintenance of the statuary and other works of art scattered among the complex's many buildings and across its open spaces. And though Yvette worked outside Invalides as a secretary, she aided her parents when she could. That assistance was made easier by the fact that the severe housing shortage in Paris caused by an influx of refugees and by the presence of thousands of occupying German troops ensured that she returned home each evening to the cramped family home in time for dinner.

Except, that is, on the nights when the petite, vivacious, and striking young Frenchwoman joined other twenty-something Parisians to socialize in impromptu gatherings organized by the "Zazou" movement—like-minded young people who sought to express their individuality and distaste for the strict traditionalism of France's collaborationist Vichy regime through a devotion to "swing" music, frenetic dance competitions, and often flamboyant clothes. Yvette's brilliant green eyes, engaging smile, and the mass of brunette hair she wore in an avant-garde style ensured that she was always a welcome participant.

Georges, Denise, and Yvette Morin jokingly referred to themselves as the "caretakers" of Invalides, but it was an apt description—both in terms of the labor they undertook and as an expression of the dedication they brought to their varied tasks. As essential as they knew their work to be, however, caring for the famous complex was not their most important responsibility that summer.

By all appearances the family was a typical working-class Parisian family trying to make the best of life under Nazi rule. But the Morins had a secret—one that if revealed to the wrong person would put them all before a German firing squad or aboard a train bound for the living hell of a concentration camp. They were all members of a resistance organization that specialized in helping downed Allied aviators and others evade capture and return to England. While similar networks existed throughout France, the "caretakers" of Invalides literally carried the keys to what was arguably one of the safest hiding places in the country—a sprawling complex within which those on the run could shelter while their escapes were being arranged. And in one of those great ironies of war, the evaders' security was enhanced by the fact that they were literally hiding among the enemy. More than half of Invalides had been taken over by the hated "Boche" as administrative offices and barracks, and German troops guarded every public entrance to the complex around the clock. Once smuggled in through concealed passages known only to the Morins and a few of their fellow résistants, the evaders were among the safest people in Paris—the Germans never thought to search what they assumed was a completely secure facility.

Invalides was a sanctuary that would soon prove particularly important to some of the B-17 crewmen who were about to encounter Egon Mayer and his fellow hunters on the way to Le Bourget that July 14. For the men of the inbound 94th Bomb Group were about to have a very bad day— one that would result in death for some, imprisonment for others, and harrowing escapes for a lucky few. In the monumental heart of a city full of implacable and relentless enemies—Gestapo agents and their French collaborationist allies determined to flush out the downed airmen and eliminate those who aided and protected them—young Americans on the run would find shelter, encouragement, and assistance on the difficult and dangerous road to freedom.

And, inexplicably, in the occupied City of Light in that dark summer of 1943, one aviator would not only find safety, he would find an unexpected love.

Chapter 1

A GUY NAMED JOE

J OE CORNWALL'S PRESENCE IN THE DANGEROUS SKIES ABOVE OCCUPIED France on Bastille Day 1943 was the direct result of a decision he'd made two and a half years earlier. On November 27, 1940—fourteen months after the outbreak of World War II and two months after the enactment of the Selective Training and Service Act launched the first peacetime draft in American history—the young man walked into a recruiting station in Tacoma, Washington, and enlisted in the U.S. Army Air Corps.[1]

Then a few months shy of his twenty-sixth birthday, Joe's decision to join up was in large part a pragmatic one. He was in good health, unmarried, and certain to get drafted, and he was convinced that the United States would soon become an active participant in the war that had been convulsing Europe since September 1939. He hoped that by volunteering he would have some say in how he'd spend what promised to be at least a few years in uniform, and assumed that flying would be a better way to go to war than walking. He'd always been interested in aviation, but had neither the education nor the desire to be a pilot, navigator, or bombardier. And while Joe was mechanically adept and good with machines, the possibility of spending years in oil-stained coveralls tinkering with balky aircraft engines in some drafty hangar struck him as both boring and decidedly less than heroic. The recruiter suggested that Joe might do well as an aerial gunner—a job title that hinted at a high-flying and adventurous way to do one's patriotic duty, but still promised a good meal and a warm bed at the end of the day instead of cold rations and a soggy blanket in a remote foxhole surrounded by Germans. It seemed a logical choice, and Joe happily signed on the dotted line.

But while enlisting in the Air Corps was an act both patriotic and practical, it was also something much more personal and necessary for Joe Cornwall. It was a means of escape.

JOSEPH ELLISON CORNWALL WAS BORN JULY 5, 1915, IN ELLENSBURG, Washington, a growing community in the Kittitas Valley just east of the rugged Cascade Range. The third child and second son of Frank and Grace Cornwall, Joe came into the world a few weeks earlier than expected, though without any complications. His safe arrival undoubtedly pleased his parents, but it did little to bridge the ever-widening gaps in their five-year marriage.

Just nineteen at the time of Joe's birth, Grace Elizabeth Cornwall had not had an easy life. A native of East Kittitas, a small farming community some six miles southeast of Ellensburg, Grace and her younger brother, Alexander, had been raised by their mother, Mary Jane Campbell. Her husband, Marion S. Campbell, had only been an occasional presence in the family home, and by the time Grace celebrated her tenth birthday her father was little more than a hazy memory. As a single mother trying to run a farm and make a living in what was still very much a male-dominated society, the redoubtable Mary Jane—known since childhood as Mollie—took to signing all important papers as "M.S. Campbell." This small subterfuge was undoubtedly meant to persuade people that her absent husband, Marion, was still part of the family.[2]

Running the small family farm in East Kittitas required more effort than a single mother and two children could handle by themselves, so in 1908 Mollie hired two local young people to help out. Twenty-one-year old Clara Pewees did the cooking and other household chores, while twenty-two-year-old Frank Cornwall helped Mollie in the fields and handled any other necessary heavy chores. Though born in Canada, Frank had come to Washington as a child with his extended family, and the Cornwall clan was widely known and greatly respected in the Kittitas Valley.

Unfortunately, Frank Cornwall seems to have overstepped the bounds of his employment. On Friday, July 1, 1910, the twenty-four-year-old took out a marriage license at the Kittitas County courthouse. Five days later in a civil ceremony held in the same building, Frank married Grace, whose age on the license was given as eighteen. She was, in fact, not yet fifteen. While it is entirely possible that the marriage was a love match, some five months after the wedding Grace was admitted to the Ellensburg hospital for what, in retrospect, appears to have been treatment for a miscarriage.

Whatever the origins of their union, Frank and Grace Cornwall stayed together and over the following five years had a daughter, Elva, and Francis, their first son. By the time of Joe's birth in 1915 his parents' marriage was on rough ground, and it continued to deteriorate during the first few years of his life. For reasons that remain unclear, in 1919 Grace sent her two older children to live with their grandmother, Mollie, who by that time was farming a plot of land in East Wenatchee, some forty miles northeast of Ellensburg. Joe stayed with his parents until their divorce in 1920, and thereafter lived with his mother, grandmother, and siblings in Wenatchee—but with occasional visits to his father's new home in Yakima. Frank Cornwall eventually remarried and had a son, Earl Ray Cornwall, and by 1930 Joe and his older brother Francis—by then also known as Frank—were living with their father, stepmother, and stepbrother in Yakima. Both older sons attended Yakima High School, and by the time Joe graduated in 1934 he'd earned a reputation as something of a ladies' man. Five feet eight inches tall, solidly built, with brown hair, piercing blue eyes, and an infectious sense of humor, Joe never had trouble securing a date for the school dances.

After high school Joe spent six years working at odd jobs around Washington. It seems he was looking for adventure as well as income, for his work included time on both a logging crew and on a Seattle-based fishing boat. The latter position gave him the occasional opportunity to visit his mother, who in early 1939 had moved to Juneau, Alaska, to manage the hair salon in one of the territorial capital's hotels. By early 1940 Joe had left the adventurous life behind and was working on his grandmother Mollie's farm in Wenatchee. It appears he sought out the solitude of farm life to help heal a broken heart, though the details of the relationship are lost to history. Mollie, now in her early sixties, was just glad to have her grandson's help. The two got along well, and when not tending to the crops or mending equipment Joe would listen to war news on the radio or hunt quail in the nearby grasslands.

Frank Cornwall had taught each of his sons to wing shoot when they were young, and by Joe's early teens his eye-hand coordination was excellent and he could handle a shotgun as though it were an extension of his arm. Without conscious thought he could estimate a fast-moving game bird's speed, direction of flight, and relative distance, effortlessly leading his target and pulling the trigger at the exact moment needed to put bird shot and his elusive quarry in the same small piece of sky at the same moment. Joe rarely missed, and just as rarely gave any thought to how unusual his talent was. But on hearing about the young man's wing-shooting experience, the Air Corps recruiter in Tacoma undoubtedly knew he was dealing with a born aerial gunner.

Joe underwent initial basic recruit training at McChord Field, south of Tacoma, after which he was assigned to the station's 44th Air Base Group. Somewhat to his own surprise, the young man discovered that he enjoyed the structure and predictability of Air Corps life. The camaraderie and feeling that he was a member of an elite organization were especially important to him, and his occasional familiarization flights on the Douglas B-18 medium bombers that undertook coastal patrols out of McChord whetted his appetite for more time in the air.

In late May 1941 a vacancy finally opened in the school that would transform Joe's lifelong wing-shooting hobby into a deadly wartime skill, and on June 1 he boarded a train in Seattle, bound for Colorado.

IN 1938 LOWRY ARMY AIRFIELD HAD BEEN ESTABLISHED ON THE GROUNDS of a former tuberculosis hospital in Aurora, and by the summer of 1941 the base was home to the Denver Branch of the Air Corps Technical School.[3] That institution consisted of two departments; one trained still and motion-picture photographers, while the other produced armament specialists. Joe reported to the latter school on June 3, 1941, because the aptitude tests he'd taken during basic training indicated that he would excel as what the Air Corps termed a "career gunner." While individuals so designated would man guns during combat missions, they received additional technical training that enabled them to also serve as airplane mechanics, radio operators, or armorers. Joe was slotted into the third track, and spent five months learning all there was to know about the offensive and defensive systems employed on each type of bombardment aircraft in the Army inventory. The training began with the operation and maintenance of .30- and .50-caliber machine guns and 20mm and 37mm aircraft cannons. Instruction then moved on to fuzing and maintaining aerial bombs, loading and unloading them on aircraft, and maintaining and repairing bomb racks, bomb bays, and power-operated gun turrets.

Joe completed his course on November 28, 1941, and was awarded the Military Occupational Specialty code 911, Airplane Armorer. As proud as he was of his accomplishment, he was eager to move on to what he considered to be the more important part of his training—the aerial gunnery course. The instruction was given at several bases around the United States, and Joe was initially scheduled to join the first class to be trained at the newly opened Las Vegas Army Airfield. The December 7, 1941, Japanese attack on Pearl Harbor put his plans on hold; in the wake of America's declaration of war against the Axis powers, the majority of Lowry's Armament Department instructors were hastily transferred to combat units. Joe and other top graduates of the armorer's course were of necessity selected to stay on as instructors—for a period that was initially described to them as "indefinite."

Being held at Lowry was a frustrating development for Joe and his classmates. They were eager to get into the war they all assumed America would win in short order. But the needs of the service came first, which in Joe's case meant that he spent nearly a year as an instructor at the technical school, watching his students graduate and move on while he himself seemed destined to spend the entire war in Colorado.

Joe's enforced stay at Lowry did have one positive aspect, however. Though the exact timing isn't clear, at some point Joe met Clara Kathryn Gypin, a twenty-seven-year-old mother of two young boys. Her husband, thirty-five-year-old Jesse Gypin Sr., was an Army sergeant undergoing treatment for tuberculosis at Fitzsimons Army Hospital in Aurora, just over three miles from Lowry Field. Though Clara had followed her husband to Colorado from their previous duty station at Fort Bragg, North Carolina, their marriage had been in trouble for some time. When Joe met Clara she was in the process of divorcing Jesse Gypin, and she and Joe soon formed a close relationship. Though certainly emotionally involved, they—like many couples during the war—were necessarily pragmatic and did not make long-term plans. They both knew that Joe could be sent overseas at any moment, and Joe made no secret of his desire to "get into the fight." Clara understood Joe's point of view—she had already been an Army wife and knew that well-trained soldiers all want to put their skills to the ultimate test—but she also had two sons to think about and did not want to marry someone who might well be dead within months of the wedding.

In the end, the fate of their relationship was decided for them, for in late October 1942 newly promoted Staff Sergeant Joe Cornwall finally received orders directing him to report to Las Vegas. Given that nearly all graduates of the Flexible Gunnery School were immediately sent to combat units overseas, the couple reluctantly decided to put their relationship on indefinite hold, pending Joe's return from wherever the Army Air Forces ultimately sent him. In a gesture of support for a woman who obviously meant very much to him, before leaving Colorado and without telling Clara, Joe did something that was quite common for deploying service members in those early years of World War II—he changed the beneficiary on his GI life insurance. Until that time the sole beneficiary had been his mother, for 100 percent of the $1,500 payout should Joe die while on active duty. On the revised form he stipulated that Clara should receive 25 percent, and as Clara's permanent address he gave that of her mother's home near San Antonio, Texas. Changing his life insurance form was a heartfelt gesture on Joe's part, but one that would soon result in widespread confusion and even erroneous newspaper stories.

A few days before the end of October Joe and Clara said goodbye at the Denver train station, unaware that both would undergo life-changing experiences before they saw each other again.

HOWEVER JOE MAY HAVE FELT ABOUT THE WAY HE AND CLARA PARTED company, over the six weeks he spent at the Flexible Gunnery School in Las Vegas he had a variety of other things to occupy his thoughts. In many ways the school struck Joe as a shortened and more simplified version of the armorer's course—except, that is, for the actual hands-on firing of .30- and .50-caliber machine guns both on the ground and in the air. The young man's shooting skills had not deserted him, and upon graduating near the top of his class in mid-November he proudly wore the silver wings of an aerial gunner.[4]

The whole purpose of Joe's extensive training, of course, was to enable him to ultimately join the war effort overseas. He took the next step in that journey on November 28 in downtown Las Vegas, when he boarded a train for the overnight trip to Utah. His destination was the Combat Crew Replacement Pool at Salt Lake City Army Air Base. As its name suggests, the facility was where newly trained aviators—both officers and enlisted men—were brought together and formed into crews, primarily for B-17 Flying Fortress and B-24 Liberator bombers. Pilots and flight engineers arrived already trained in one of the aircraft types, but the remaining crew members—navigators, bombardiers, radio operators, and gunners—could be assigned to either machine. Joe's training as an armorer-gunner had prepared him to operate and maintain the differing types of gun turrets and bombing equipment used on both of the Army Air Forces' heavy bomber types, but having flown on several B-17s during his training at Lowry and Las Vegas, he preferred the elegant and famously sturdy Fortress to its slab-sided and purportedly less robust counterpart.

There was nothing very sophisticated about the way the men were assigned to a crew. On Monday, November 30—the day after his arrival at Salt Lake AAB—Joe joined almost a thousand other aviators in a large, hangar-like building, where those present were divided into groups based on their occupational specialties. Pilots, copilots, and enlisted flight engineer/top turret gunners type-rated in the B-17 stood at one end of the room, those rated in the B-24 at the other. Members of the replacement pool staff then simply went down the line of other occupational specialty groups, alternately assigning the men in them to either a B-17 or B-24 crew. Joe was mildly disappointed when he was pointed toward the Liberator group. As he walked up, an enlisted clerk asked his name and service number, noted both on a clipboard, then motioned Joe to join a knot of men standing beneath a small, handwritten sign bearing the word "Purdy."

It was a name, of course, and it belonged to First Lieutenant Edward A. Purdy, a strapping twenty-six-year-old from Colorado who was the new crew's pilot. After shaking hands with Joe, he turned and introduced the gunner to the four other aviators who would compose the bomber's "front-office staff." Three of the four were officers: Second Lieutenant Carroll T. Harris Jr., twenty-one, the copilot; First Lieutenant Charles W. Lichtenberger, twenty-five, the navigator; and First Lieutenant Edward B. Jones, twenty-seven, the bombardier. The fourth man, twenty-six-year-old Technical Sergeant Russell E. Crisp, was the flight engineer and top turret gunner. The five remaining crew members joined Purdy and the others over the next few minutes—Technical Sergeant Charles M. Sprague, twenty-six, radio operator/gunner; Staff Sergeant John W. Smith, twenty, the diminutive ball turret gunner; Staff Sergeant Lawrence H. Templeton, twenty-seven, tail gunner; and Technical Sergeant Francis J. Santangelo, twenty-two, right waist gunner. Joe's position on the crew would be armorer and left waist gunner.

Over the following four days the newly assembled Purdy crew undertook several training flights in various B-24s, the first steps in developing the cohesion and trust that would bind them together as a team. They had not yet heard which unit they were to be assigned to, but rumor had it that the Liberator's ability to fly longer distances than the Fortress made the B-24 the bomber of choice in the vast Pacific. Joe and his crewmates therefore assumed that when they received their assignment they would be heading west to one of the major ports in California or Washington, there to take ship for Australia.

When their orders arrived on Friday, December 4, however, the men found out just how wrong their assumptions had been. The Purdy crew was ordered to Biggs Army Airfield, at Fort Bliss, Texas, where it would join the still-forming 331st Bombardment Squadron. The unit was one of four squadrons that would constitute the 94th Bombardment Group (Heavy), which the rumor mill said was headed to Great Britain to join the Eighth Air Force in the nascent bombing campaign against Germany and German targets in Occupied Europe. While the change in war theaters was a surprise to Ed Purdy and his crew, it was nothing compared with the lightning bolt that was contained in the second paragraph of the movement order. Despite having trained as a B-24 crew, the men were being assigned to a B-17 group and would have to convert to the Fortress following their arrival in Texas. While the news significantly upset pilots Purdy and Harris—both of whom had spent months learning to fly the

Liberator—and flight engineer Crisp, who'd spent just as long studying the B-24's mechanical and power plant systems inside and out, Joe was rather pleased that he'd be able to go to war in a Fortress.

Early on Saturday, December 5, Ed Purdy and the nine other members of his crew boarded a train bound for El Paso. Whether the men liked it or not, they were about to become members of the 94th Bomb Group.

THE ORGANIZATION THAT JOE AND HIS CREWMATES WERE ABOUT TO JOIN had been activated on June 15, 1942, at MacDill Field in Tampa, Florida, with forty-year-old Colonel John G. Moore as the organization's first commander.

"Dinty" Moore, as he was inevitably and respectfully known, was a West Point graduate who'd received his wings in 1928 and had gone on to operational tours in pursuit, attack, and reconnaissance units.[5] His assignment as the 94th's top officer was an acknowledgment of both his flying skills and his organizational acumen. While the former would be of immense value later in the group's operational life, it was the latter talent that was most in demand in the early days. Moore's undeniably daunting task was to turn a completely "paper" unit into a functioning military organization capable of taking thirty-six B-17 Flying Fortresses into combat over Occupied Europe, and to achieve the required "operational readiness" with all possible dispatch. The unit's transformation would require many things—the acquisition of personnel and aircraft; the long hours of exhausting and often dangerous training required to meld men and machines into an effective fighting force; and the inevitable need to compete for essential resources and materiel with scores of other USAAF units that were all undertaking their own metamorphoses. Fortunately for Moore, he was ably assisted in his mission by a staff of ten subordinate officers, ranging in rank from second lieutenant to major.

Central Florida may have been the 94th Bomb Group's birthplace, but the unit's adolescence was spent far to the west, initially in the equally sunny but far less humid landscape of southern Arizona. By mid-October 1942 Moore and his growing staff had been ordered to Davis-Monthan Field, outside Tucson, where their bare-bones unit began to be fleshed out with the additional officers who would hold leadership positions in its four constituent bombardment squadrons—the 331st, 332nd, 333rd, and 410th. The ten members of each combat crew—who would actually man the group's Fortresses—also began arriving at this point. Those trained from the start to fly Fortresses had already attended the five-week B-17 Combat Crew School at Hendricks Field, Florida, and then been sent to the replacement pool in Salt Lake City.

Although it would be the combat crews who would eventually take the war to the enemy, they would only be able to accomplish that mission with the help of hundreds of nonflying personnel. Mechanics, armorers, flight surgeons, medics, military police, cooks, and a range of other specialists would make up the bulk of the 94th, and they, too, began joining the unit in Tucson. By the time the 94th moved to Biggs Field on November 1, it had received about two-thirds of the 2,400 personnel required by its Table of Organization and Equipment.[6]

What the 94th didn't have at that point, however, was sufficient aircraft.

The urgent need to deploy heavy bomber groups to Europe—and to replace aircraft lost in action there, in North Africa, and, to a lesser extent, in the Pacific—meant that most units still in training in the United States had to make do with fewer and generally older aircraft. This meant that stateside Flying Fortress units were usually equipped with B-17E models, the variant that had flown the early bombing missions from the United Kingdom in the summer and fall of 1942; the newer and more capable B-17F variants were only issued to the groups as they were preparing for overseas movement. In practical terms, this meant that even two weeks after arriving in Texas the 94th had just one Fortress for each squadron. And while the situation gradually improved, it wasn't until after the group's transfer to Pueblo Army Airfield, Colorado, in early January 1943 that it had acquired enough aircraft to begin flying three- and four-squadron training missions. These included both local-area flights and long-distance trips to bombing ranges in Arizona and California. Fortunately for Ed Purdy, Carroll Harris, and Russ Crisp, the transition from B-24 to B-17 was both easier and more enjoyable than they had expected it to be.

By February the 94th had progressed far enough in its training that USAAF planners deemed the unit ready for deployment to the United Kingdom. The group would travel in two echelons—the ground personnel by ship, and the combat crews by air along what was referred to as the northern ferry route.[7] The former left New York harbor aboard the passenger liner–turned-troopship *Queen Elizabeth* on May 5, and after arrival in Scotland six days later boarded trains for the journey to the 94th's first home in the British Isles, the former Royal Air Force base at Earls Colne in Essex.

For the aircrews, the trip across the Atlantic was somewhat less direct. On March 2 they undertook the first leg of the journey by train—to Smoky Hill Army Air Base in Salina, Kansas. Dozens of factory-fresh B-17F Fortresses awaited the aviators on the cold, windswept field, and among the first orders of business was for the pilot of each crew to select the aircraft he and his men would take to Britain and then into combat. The selection process was far from scientific: The serial numbers of the nine aircraft allocated to each squadron were written down on slips of paper and tossed together in an upturned hat. The squadron commander then held the hat as each pilot in turn pulled out a single slip; the serial number on the paper indicated the aircraft that the pilot and crew were assigned to.

Over the next few days the aviators got to know their new mounts, a process that involved one or two test flights to determine that the bombers were mechanically ready for the long overseas flight and that all of their subsystems worked as required. Since the final stages of the ferry route would cross areas where encounters with the enemy were possible, the breaking-in process included extensive testing of each Fortress's powered gun turrets and individual handheld machine guns. The crews also used the shakedown period to apply a mutually agreed upon nickname to the side of their aircraft's nose. These monikers ran the gamut from prosaic to witty to obscene, and were usually accompanied by a fitting illustration—most of which were painted on the aircraft by local airfield staffers who'd found a lucrative outlet for their artistic talents.

In the case of the Purdy crew, the choice of a name for their brand-new Fortress was based on the serial number emblazoned in yellow on the bomber's olive-drab vertical stabilizer—42-29711. In craps, the dice game widely played by American servicemen of that era, the final three numbers of the B-17's serial signified a "natural" 7 or 11 win on the first roll. Rolling a natural was considered an omen of very good luck—something everyone on the Purdy crew desperately hoped would accompany them throughout their time overseas—so the Fortress was unanimously christened *Natural*.[8] The next order of business, of course, was to have the name and some sort of appropriate artwork applied to the bomber. The crew took up a collection and hired one of Smoky Hill's most sought-after soldier-artists, a young African-American technical sergeant whose name has unfortunately been lost to history.

The man first painted *Natural* on the right side of the B-17's nose. Though done in letters several inches tall, the nickname was dwarfed by the large and colorful artwork the young artist then applied on the same side, just forward of and below the cockpit. Within a two-foot-wide bright yellow circle stooped an African-American man wearing a red-and-white striped shirt, matching socks, black pants, and black shoes. The figure was frozen in the act of rolling a pair of dice, which appeared enlarged at his feet to show that the top face of one bore four black dots and the other three, while the lower side of the first showed five dots and the second, six. We have to wonder, of course, how the young artist felt about the image he was asked to create.[9]

Within two weeks of arriving in Kansas the 94th's air echelon was ready to move on, though that turned out to be more of a problem than anyone had anticipated. The individual squadrons left Smoky Hill over a period of two days, but engine problems soon forced many aircraft—including *Natural*—to land at military airfields and civilian airports along the route. Close inspection of the affected Wright Cyclone power plants showed that the core problem was defective metal in the piston rings. With the long trans-Atlantic flight ahead there was no alternative but to replace all four engines on all of the group's thirty-six Fortresses, a task that was carried out at the USAAF Air Depot in Mobile, Alabama, over three weeks in late March and early April. As aircraft were repaired they were assembled into flights of three and dispatched up the East Coast to Presque Isle Army Airfield, Maine, the jump-off point for the flight to Britain via Labrador, Greenland, Iceland, and Scotland.

Natural and its crew spent four days in America's northernmost state, waiting for additional aircraft to arrive from Alabama. Other than an afternoon visit to a pub in Andover, New Brunswick—the nearest town on the other side of the U.S.-Canadian border—Joe Cornwall and his crewmates spent most of their time at Presque Isle either testing and retesting the B-17's mechanical systems or undergoing refresher training on survival at sea.[10] By April 14 enough 94th Bomb Group Fortresses had arrived in Maine to permit a formation of twelve to begin the first leg of the long flight to Britain. The following morning the crews of the dozen bombers attended a lengthy briefing that covered en route weather, navigation issues, and emergency radio frequencies. The aviators also received a detailed intelligence update on sightings of enemy submarines, surface ships, and aircraft along the route—a sobering reality check that was reinforced by the announcement that, in addition to maximum fuel, each aircraft would carry a full combat load of ammunition for its twelve .50-caliber machine guns.[11]

One after another the Fortresses trundled from the Presque Isle ramp area to the end of the active runway. After a brief, final engine run-up the aircraft took off at one-minute intervals, formed up, and headed northwest on the 650-mile leg to Gander, Newfoundland. As the formation reached its cruise altitude of 18,000 feet the Fortresses were briefly joined by a flight of Hurricane fighters of the Royal Canadian Air Force, their camouflage patterns and large roundels providing a glimpse of the future awaiting the American aviators.

In *Natural*'s rear fuselage the waist gun windows had been closed off with sliding panels and the small heat outlets turned up full, so Joe Cornwall, Frank Santangelo, John Smith, and Larry Templeton were relatively comfortable despite the below-freezing outside temperature. The men settled in for the flight, trying to get comfortable amid the jumble of footlockers, duffel bags, ammunition boxes, and crates of spare parts that took up every inch of space.

For Joe, the long flight provided ample time to digest a letter he'd received just before takeoff from Presque Isle. Forwarded several times, the quick note from Clara Gypin confirmed something Joe had assumed for some time. She had met someone, she wrote, a man named Clarence Rebuck. He was about to be discharged from the Army for medical reasons, so he wouldn't be going off to war. He was kind to her and the children, she said, and while she would always care for Joe, she had decided to marry the man—as much for security, she admitted, as out of any great love. Though the news was painful, Joe admitted to himself that it was the right choice for Clara, and he couldn't fault her for making it.[12]

Some 3,500 miles and four days later *Natural* and her eleven companions touched down in Britain, where they were soon joined by the rest of the 94th Bomb Group. Because the B-26–equipped 322nd Bomb Group, which had been operating out of Earls Colne, in Essex, had not yet vacated the base, the 94th's aircraft were sent elsewhere. The men and aircraft of the 331st and 332nd squadrons gathered at the former RAF field at Bassingbourn, Cambridgeshire, already home to the USAAF's combat-tested 91st Bomb Group. The equally experienced 305th Bomb Group at Thurleigh, Bedfordshire, welcomed the Fortresses and crews of the 333rd and 410th squadrons.

THOUGH THE AIR CREWS OF THE 94TH'S FOUR SQUADRONS UNDOUBTEDLY considered themselves already well trained and highly proficient by the time they arrived in England, the Eighth Air Force's experiences thus far in the air war over the Continent had convinced General Ira C. Eaker— the Eighth's commander—that all incoming personnel needed additional training in high-altitude formation flying, gunnery, and bad-weather operations before being considered combat-ready.[13] Beginning near the end of April the 94th crews at both Bassingbourn and Thurleigh began flying high-altitude training missions almost daily, initially in squadrons and then as a complete group.[14]

The practice flights helped bolster the aviators' navigation, bombing, and air-to-air gunnery skills, but the main focus was on perfecting the group's ability to fly the tight "combat box" formation. Developed and refined during the early USAAF bomber missions over Europe, the formation was intended to both increase the group's defensive firepower and better concentrate its bombs on target. Although the exact configuration and composition varied with the number of aircraft involved, at the time of the 94th's arrival in England the formation's basic grouping was the three-aircraft element. This consisted of one Fortress in the lead, with another off its right wing, slightly behind and slightly higher, and the third off the lead's left wing, slightly behind and slightly lower. Three (and later four) such elements made up a "squadron box," with the elements also arranged in the staggered arrowhead or diamond pattern. The lead element was also the squadron lead, with a high element flying above, to the right and behind it; a low element below, to the left and behind; and a low-low element almost directly astern of and below the lead element. Three (and later four) squadron boxes would constitute a "group box," with each squadron arranged in the same lead, high, low, and low-low pattern. And, eventually, three (or four) group boxes would form a "combat wing," again arranged in the same offset, staggered formation.

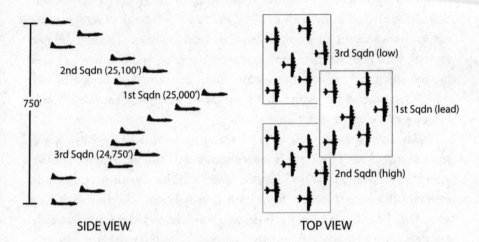

2nd Sqdn (25,100')

1st Sqdn (25,000')

750'

3rd Sqdn (24,750')

SIDE VIEW

3rd Sqdn (low)

1st Sqdn (lead)

2nd Sqdn (high)

TOP VIEW

When flown correctly, no two aircraft in any part of the combat box formation flew at exactly the same altitude or directly ahead of or behind another, opening clear fields of fire for the bombers' gunners and reducing the chances of a midair collision. Although challenging to fly, especially through high-altitude turbulence and concentrations of heavy antiaircraft fire (referred to by the air crews as "flak"), the box was extremely daunting for incoming enemy fighters and allowed a greater percentage of the formation's bombs to land in the same area.[15] From the bomber crews' point of view, however, the formation had one glaring flaw: the low aircraft in the low squadron or low group were the most exposed to flak and to tail attacks by German fighters seeking to avoid the greater concentration of defensive fire thrown out by the higher and farther-forward aircraft. As a result, the "tail-end Charlie" position in the formation was widely referred to as "Coffin Corner" and "Purple Heart Corner," the latter after the medal awarded to those wounded in combat.

During the 94th's sojourn at Bassingbourn and Thurleigh several of the group's key officers and enlisted men had the opportunity to take part in missions flown by the 91st's Fortresses, either as observers or as replacements for ill or injured regular crewmen. These flights undoubtedly helped the participants better understand the nature of the air war they and their unit were about to enter, but not all the lessons were purely theoretical. On May 1, twenty-four-year-old Major Maurice Rosener, one of the 94th's original officers and the commander of the group's 332nd Bomb Squadron, elected to fly with the 91st on a raid against the German submarine base at Saint-Nazaire, on France's Brittany coast. The raid did not go well, with poor weather hampering the bombing and German flak and fighters downing seven of the seventy-eight attacking bombers. Rosener was aboard one of the planes that went down, becoming the 94th Bomb Group's first combat loss.[16]

As much of a shock as Rosener's loss was to the men of the 94th, it was soon overshadowed by a much more momentous announcement. On the afternoon of May 12 "Dinty" Moore summoned his squadron commanders and other senior leaders from both Bassingbourn and Thurleigh to a command briefing, held in his borrowed office in the 91st Group's headquarters. After looking around the room, Moore cleared his throat and announced to the gathered officers that their training was over. The group had been designated combat-ready, he said, and the following morning the unit's men and aircraft would do what they had come so far to do—the 94th was going to war.

Within hours the news of the group's premier mission spread quickly around Bassingbourn, though Joe Cornwall and the majority of the 94th's members would have to wait until the next morning's pre-mission briefing to learn the details about the intended target. The lack of specifics didn't particularly bother Joe, however. As he lay on his cot that night in the Quonset hut he shared with eleven other gunners, unable to sleep and smoking one cigarette after another, he had much larger questions swirling through his mind. He had spent two years training for combat, and now he wondered how he would react when he first saw the enemy up close. Would he keep his nerve and do his duty when the time came, or would he lose heart, leaving his friends to face the consequences? Would he live, or would he die?

OWING TO HIS REQUIRED PRESENCE AT A SENIOR COMMANDERS' MEETING AT Pinetree—the code name given to the Eighth Air Force's VIII Bomber Command headquarters outside London—"Dinty" Moore would not be leading the 94th's first combat mission.[17] He instead tapped the charismatic commander of the 331st Bomb Squadron, Major Ralph H. Saltsman Jr., to fly lead.

Though just twenty-seven years old, "Salty"—as Saltsman was inevitably known—was already a seasoned aviator. A 1940 graduate of the Air Corps Flying School at Kelly Field, Texas, he had gone on to instruct at the school and attended the U.S. Army War College. He had been a key member of Moore's early cadre and was instrumental in getting both his own squadron and the entire group staffed, trained, and deployed. In the process Saltsman had proven himself to be an outstanding pilot, an able administrator, and a man who treated both superiors and subordinates with equal regard. He had also been among the first of the 94th's officers to participate in a combat sortie, flying as an observer with the 91st Bomb Group.

The 94th's first combat mission saw it joining three other recently arrived groups—the 95th, 96th, and 351st—to form the 4th Provisional Bomb Wing, which would send seventy-two Fortresses to hit two Luftwaffe airfields in the suburbs of Saint-Omer, France, a city fourteen miles southwest of the Belgian border.[18] The fields, at Longuenesse and Fort Rouge, were home to elements of the Fw 190–equipped Jagdgeschwader 26, which along with Jagdgeschwader 2 was tasked with the daylight air defense of Northwest Europe.

The operation started well enough on the morning of May 13, with all aircraft taking off on schedule. The linkup with other groups of the 4th Wing also took place without a hitch, and the Fortresses set course for France in clear weather. Things started to fall apart, however, when the formation reached mid-Channel. The lead B-17 of the 96th Bomb Group suffered a major mechanical failure and had to "abort" the mission. That aircraft's abrupt about-face caused the remainder of the 96th and the entire 351st to become disorganized, and to Saltsman's chagrin both groups elected to return to base. Not only did their departure reduce the size and defensive firepower of the 4th Wing formation by almost half, it meant the remaining bombers would not be able to attack the airfield at Fort

Rouge. Saltsman had no choice but to continue the mission, and led the 94th and 95th Bomb Groups on toward Longuenesse. The Fortresses were over the target by 4:37 P.M., and though the two groups' bombing accuracy wasn't all it could have been, the formation encountered no flak or fighters, and all the 94th aircraft returned to Bassingbourn without incident.

While the Longuenesse raid had been relatively straightforward—at least in terms of the 94th's participation—over the following month the group was forced to come to grips with the realities of the air war over Occupied Europe. Between May 14 and June 11 the 94th flew seven additional strikes, hitting targets in Belgium, Germany, and France. In the process the group encountered heavy flak and determined fighter attacks—and also suffered its first losses: one aircraft during the May 17 mission to bomb sub pens in Lorient and three Fortresses on May 21 over Emden. Sadly, the latter operation led to a personal tragedy for the men of *Natural*. Russ Crisp, the crew's flight engineer and top turret gunner, had been tapped as a last-minute replacement for a sick man on another crew, and was killed when the aircraft he was on was shot down over Holland. Crisp's death was a blow to *Natural*'s close-knit crew, and despite the fact that the men had acquitted themselves well thus far—Joe Cornwall had even been awarded an Air Medal for shooting down a German fighter on the May 21 mission—the stress common to all combat aviators was starting to take a toll on their nerves. While an occasional weekend pass to London or more frequent visits to local pubs helped allay the men's anxiety somewhat, they had begun to wonder aloud when it might be their "turn in the barrel."[19]

A change of station from Bassingbourn to the now available Earls Colne gave the 94th Group a brief stand-down from operational flying, but on the first raid from the new base—on May 29, to Rennes, France—the 94th lost three more B-17s. Although the mission flown on June 11 against U-boat facilities in Cuxhaven, Germany, resulted in no losses for the group, "Dinty" Moore and his aviators had to face the hard facts. In its first month of combat operations the 94th had lost seven bombers and seventy-three men: a grim statistic for aviators required to fly twenty-five missions before being rotated back to the United States.

And things were about to go from bad to worse, for at noon on June 12 the 94th was alerted for a mission that would turn out to be the greatest single air battle of the war thus far. It would also test the men of *Natural* almost to the breaking point.

ONE OF THE FIRST MEMBERS OF THE 94TH TO HEAR THE DETAILS OF THE upcoming mission was "Salty" Saltsman, who on the afternoon of June 12 was summoned along with the group's other squadron commanders to a pre-operational briefing. Held at 4th Bomb Wing Headquarters at Elveden Hall—a stately home in Thetford, some thirty miles north of Earls Colne—the gathering included the leaders of the 95th and 96th Bomb Groups and was hosted by the wing commander, Brigadier General Frederick L. Anderson.[20] Also present at the briefing was Brigadier General Nathan Bedford Forrest III—great-grandson of the famous Confederate general of the U.S. Civil War—who had been tapped to lead a new provisional bomb wing. An accomplished pilot who had done much to organize USAAF heavy bombardment training both before and after Pearl Harbor, Forrest would participate in the mission as part of his preparation for wing command.

As outlined to those at the briefing, the next day's mission was to be a "maximum effort," meaning that the groups involved were to get as many of their bombers into the air as possible. The targets would be the naval facilities and port complexes at Bremen and Kiel, Germany, with Forrest leading some 150 Fortresses of the 1st Bomb Wing against the latter. The Kiel attack group, designated the 4th Air Division, would consist of the 94th, 95th, and 96th Bomb Groups. They, in turn, would be split into the 401st and 402nd Combat Wings. The first would consist of the bulk of the 94th and a composite group made up of remaining 94th aircraft and about half of the 96th's Fortresses, and the second would comprise the bulk of the 95th and a composite group of 95th and 96th B-17s. Saltsman would lead both the 94th and the 401st Combat Wing.[21]

While the squadron and group commanders present at Elveden Hall grasped the importance of the mission, they were concerned by two aspects of the plan. First, though Allied fighters would fly wide-ranging sweeps over western Europe on the day of the raid, neither air division would have fighter escorts. Second, and perhaps more troubling, the attacking bombers were to abandon their normal wing combat boxes for two types of new and as yet untried formations. The 401st Combat Wing and the 402nd's composite 95th-96th Group would fly the so-called "javelin-down," in which each group box trailed the lead in descending altitudes. The reason for the change was apparently to increase bombing accuracy, but it was clear to many of those at the briefing that the alteration would reduce the effectiveness of the formation's defensive fire. An even greater puzzlement was Forrest's announcement that the bulk of the 95th Group would fly a formation he had devised, in which the second elements of the lead, high, and low squadrons would fly tightly behind the lead elements. Forrest believed the positioning of the aircraft would increase the formation's defensive fire, though several combat veterans among those at the briefing saw immediately that such a tight grouping would prevent the B-17s in the second elements from employing their guns against frontal attacks. Forrest was apparently unmoved by their opinions, however.[22]

The mission overview presented to Saltsman and the others at Elveden Hall was fleshed out over the following hours by a series of teletype messages sent from VIII Bomber Command to all of the participating units. While the information in such communiqués often changed over the course of the night preceding the mission—usually due to weather issues over the Continent, or updated intelligence on German defenses—Saltsman noted that this particular mission seemed to be generating a greater-than-normal amount of confusion. When the bomb groups involved received the first warning order at noon on June 12—even before the Elveden Hall meeting—the ordnance load for all aircraft was specified as ten 500-pound general-purpose bombs. Ground crews at the three bases were well into the loading process when, in the late afternoon, a teletype message canceled the use of 500-pounders. The already tired ordnance men were unloading all the B-17s that had already been "bombed up" when, at 9:15 P.M., yet another message arrived at the various group bases reinstating the loading of the 500-pound bombs. Then, at 4:30 A.M. on June 13 a further message instructed armorers to change out the tail fuzes on the bombs to be used in the raid.

Bureaucratic indecision was not the only challenge the 94th Bomb Group had to deal with as it prepared for the Kiel mission. Despite having moved from Bassingbourn to Earls Colne just weeks earlier, the unit had been ordered to relocate once again—to the former B-26 medium bomber base at Rougham, just outside Bury St. Edmunds in Suffolk.[23] All of the group's ground personnel were to make the twenty-mile road trip north to the new base once the aircraft had taken off early on June 13, while the 94th's B-17s would depart on the mission from Earls Colne but return to Rougham. The impending move added considerably to the pre-flight confusion, and when the crews reached their aircraft following the morning mission briefing many found that bomb loading hadn't yet been completed, nor had some of the Fortresses been fully fueled. These problems could only have added to the anxiety many of the aviators likely were feeling after being told during the briefing that they could expect some of the heaviest German fighter opposition they'd yet encountered.[24]

Despite the glitches that had plagued the 94th's preparation for the Kiel mission, all fourteen bombers that constituted the group's contribution to the raid were airborne within less than twenty minutes. Soon after forming up, the bombers were joined by the aircraft of the 94th-96th composite group, and the entire formation—now totaling fifty-six aircraft rather than the planned seventy-six—turned to the northwest to pull in behind the 402nd Combat Wing. By 7:30 A.M. the mass of aircraft had crossed the English coast at the Wash—a vast estuary on the northwest edge of East Anglia—and set a course out over the North Sea. At a point about ninety-five miles north of the Dutch coast, Forrest in the lead aircraft turned the formation to the southeast on a heading for Kiel.

The progress of the American bomber formation had not gone unnoticed, of course. By 8:45 A.M. German controllers had started launching interceptors—Bf 109s from an airfield on the island of Heligoland-Düne in the German Bight, and Fw 190s from Jever, just west of Wilhelmshaven. More than one hundred Luftwaffe fighters began hitting the leading 95th Group before the Fortresses reached the west coast of Schleswig-Holstein, and furious head-on attacks quickly showed the folly of Forrest's altered formation. His aircraft was among the first to go down, giving Forrest the dubious distinction of being the first American general killed in action in the European Theater. Within moments, nine more Fortresses from the 95th were spiraling earthward.

After decimating the lead group, the German 109s and 190s—now joined by twin-engine Bf 110s, Messerschmitt Me 210s, and Junkers Ju 88s lobbing 20mm cannon rounds from long range—turned their attention to the 94th. Among the first B-17s to suffer the Germans' wrath was *Natural*. Flying lead in the second element at 27,500 feet, the Fortress was well short of the target when an Fw 190 bored straight in from directly ahead. The German pilot pumped a stream of 20mm rounds into *Natural's* right wing, and one of the explosive rounds detonated against the propeller hub of the inboard right engine, knocking it out and sparking a fire. Shrapnel from the hit ripped through the right side of the cockpit, slightly wounding copilot Carroll Harris and knocking out the B-17's flight-deck oxygen system. Almost immediately both Harris and Ed Purdy lost consciousness; *Natural* dropped abruptly out of formation and began rapidly losing altitude as engineer/top turret gunner Technical Sergeant Richard Marquardt—Russ Crisp's replacement—struggled to put the mask of his portable oxygen bottle over Purdy's face. By the time he succeeded and the pilot regained consciousness the B-17 had lost more than 3,000 feet of altitude and was on its own, just the type of damaged straggler guaranteed to attract enemy fighters looking for an easy kill.

The sudden loss of altitude had caught the men in the rear of the plane by surprise, first tossing both Joe Cornwall and Frank Santangelo upward against the rough ceiling of the bomber's fuselage, then dropping them onto the machine's equally unforgiving floor. Initially convinced *Natural* was beginning a terminal dive, the two men struggled toward the tail where their parachutes were stored. But when they realized that the aircraft was still on an even keel, rather than in the flat spin that usually marked the beginning of a bomber's death spiral, both men pulled themselves back along the floor toward their guns. When Purdy regained consciousness and leveled the aircraft out, both waist gunners knew it wouldn't take long for the enemy fighters to come after the damaged bomber like wolves after an injured deer.

And come the wolves did. Over the next two hours some thirty German fighters took turns savaging *Natural*, knocking out the mechanism that operated the ball turret, killing a second engine, and punching fist-sized holes through the bomber's vertical stabilizer and both wings. Joe and the other gunners did their best to drive the hunters off, scoring hits on several of the fighters and sending two into the clouds trailing smoke. Purdy and the semiconscious Harris took the plane progressively lower, eventually leveling off a mere one hundred feet above the choppy North Sea. This prevented the German fighters from attacking the B-17's now-undefended belly, and made it highly unlikely that an attacker coming in from above would have time to pull out before slamming into the unforgiving ocean. Apparently convinced that the obviously crippled Fortress would eventually crash of its own accord, the German fighters eventually turned for home, leaving *Natural* limping westward just off the Dutch coast on a course for the 94th's new base at Rougham. The flight was uneventful—until the B-17 was almost in sight of the English coastline. Two twin-engine Bf 110s suddenly appeared out of the clouds and, carefully dropping in directly astern of the bomber, began hurling 20mm cannon rounds at the Fortress's tail. A few of the explosive shells found their target, further holing the rudder and horizontal stabilizers, but accurate return fire from tail gunner Larry Templeton eventually drove the marauders away.

Through excellent airmanship and sheer strength of will, Purdy was able to keep *Natural* in the air despite its injuries. His approach into Rougham was hindered by the fact that he couldn't lower the Fortress's flaps, and when he extended the landing gear Joe Cornwall informed him that the left tire was flat. This caused the B-17 to swerve to the left when it touched the runway, but Purdy quickly straightened *Natural* out and it rolled to a halt. As soon as the aircraft stopped moving an ambulance pulled up alongside in response to the red flare Marquardt had fired as the plane had turned onto its final approach. Medics carefully lowered the injured Harris through the lower fuselage hatch just forward of the cockpit, allowed him to climb into the ambulance on his own, and then raced off to the base hospital.

Natural had made it home—unlike twenty-two other Fortresses dispatched to Kiel, nine of them from the 94th—but a quick survey of their damaged aircraft convinced the remaining crew members that she would likely never fly again.[25] Purdy and his men knew just how lucky they had been, but they also realized that as soon as they'd been assigned a replacement aircraft they'd go back on the flight roster. In the meantime, they would explore the countryside around their new home in search of ways to relax.

For Joe and his best friend, twenty-seven-year-old Staff Sergeant Richard S. Davitt—a top turret gunner on another 331st Bomb Squadron Fortress—the quest for relaxation led to a humorous and ironic encounter. After attending the usual postmission debriefing the two men secured permission to go into Bury St. Edmunds, their intention being to seek out a pub that had been recommended to them. The Sword in Hand was on Southgate Street, barely a mile and a half from the airfield. Rather than walk the distance, the tired airmen "borrowed" a bicycle left unattended near the Quonset hut in which both gunners slept, and set off with Joe pedaling and Davitt riding on the handlebars.

As the two airmen entered Bury St. Edmunds a U.S. Army military policeman sitting in a jeep motioned them to a halt.

"You'll have to get off the handlebars and walk," the MP said to Davitt.

Puzzled, the gunner responded, "Why?"

"It's too dangerous," was the response.

The two young men, who earlier that day had participated in the greatest air battle yet fought by Americans in the skies over Europe, looked at the man in disbelief and then dissolved in helpless laughter.[26]

Almost exactly one month later both gunners would find themselves in a far less humorous situation—shot down, on the run from the Gestapo, and being hidden almost in plain sight by a dedicated French family in the city that was the administrative heart of Germany's occupation of France.

Paris.

Chapter 2

KEEPERS OF THE TOMB

I T WAS A SIGHT CERTAIN TO SEAR THE SOULS OF THE MORIN FAMILY, AND OF any other true son or daughter of France.

On the morning of Friday, June 14, 1940—eight days before France's June 22 acceptance of the armistice with Germany—elements of General Fedor von Bock's Army Group B took time off from their pursuit of retreating French units to undertake an impromptu victory march down the Champs-Élysées in the heart of Paris.[1] The capital had been declared an open city four days earlier, so the invaders encountered no resistance, and the formations of triumphant troops—still carrying their rifles and many with stick hand grenades wedged under their belts—did not even bother to goose-step as they marched in review past Bock, the Arc de Triomphe soaring into the summer sky behind them. The infantry soldiers were followed in turn by dozens of horse-drawn artillery pieces, and behind them came squads of bicycle-mounted reconnaissance troops, pedaling along with an almost nonchalant air.

Although it was not the first time the hated Boche had paraded through the French capital—Kaiser Wilhelm I himself had led his Prussians down the Champs-Élysées on March 1, 1871, following the North German Confederation's victory in the Franco-Prussian War—it was a spectacle most of France's people had not expected to witness in the twentieth century. Following their nation's declaration of war against Germany in the wake of the latter's September 1939 invasion of Poland, most of France's citizens had assumed that the new conflict would unfold in much the same way as had World War I: years of back-and-forth combat that, while expensive in blood, would at worst result in a German occupation of Alsace and perhaps parts of Lorraine. Gathered in sidewalk cafés and around tables laden with Sunday dinner during the first months of what came to be known as the "Phoney War," people from the Belgian border to the sunny shores of Provence assured each other that with the grudging help of Britain—that irritating little island that had been both friend and foe over the centuries—the nation of Napoléon and the Sun King would rout the Germans, who would fail in their latest attempt to dismember La Belle France and would ultimately be sent scurrying back over the border like a pack of feral dogs that had been taught a necessary lesson in obedience.

It is understandable, then, why the people of France were collectively dumbfounded by the speed and completeness of the German victory. In just six weeks the Boche[2] had rolled up the vaunted French army like a threadbare rug, bypassing or destroying entire units—most of which seemed unable to organize a coherent defense. The fabled Maginot Line, that chain of supposedly impregnable fortresses built along the Franco-German border after the last war, had done nothing to stop the ravening Teutonic hordes. Certainly, the French agreed, there had been some actions in which the advancing Wehrmacht[3] had initially come out second-best—the armored clash in mid-May at Stonne, for example.[4] Yet in the final reckoning there had been no last-minute salvation; the British, those pasty-faced sales clerks, had abandoned France in her darkest hour, characteristically racing back across the Channel in such a panic that they left behind most of their weapons and equipment. Shameful, the French muttered, but what else could one expect of the English?[5]

Nor were France's own leaders any better, people agreed. On June 10 Prime Minister Paul Reynaud and his government fled Paris for the presumed safety of Tours, and the following day the French capital was declared an open city. The announcement sparked a massive exodus from the metropolis and its environs: some 2 million people—both Parisians and refugees who had flooded Paris in the weeks since the beginning of the German assault—choked the roads leading west and south in an ultimately futile attempt to escape the catastrophe that was about to engulf the City of Light. The sudden appearance of the first German troops on the streets of Paris early on June 14 convinced the majority of Reynaud's nomadic cabinet that further resistance was futile, and on the fifteenth the ministers voted to ask the Nazis for armistice terms.[6] Reynaud had argued that France could carry on the fight from its colonies abroad, and saw the cabinet vote as tantamount to treason. He resigned on the sixteenth, and was promptly replaced as prime minister by the eighty-four-year-old World War I hero Marshal Philippe Pétain. He, in turn, quickly announced his intention to seek peace with Germany, and that intent became reality when France signed the armistice agreement on June 22.[7]

The Pétain government framed the ceremony held in the historic railcar at Compiègne as an "accommodation" necessary for France's survival and touted the establishment of the Zone Libre—an area in the southern half of the country not occupied by German troops and nominally controlled by Pétain's Vichy-based collaborationist regime—as proof that the nation remained at least partially in command of its own fate.[8] Yet the French people, whatever their political beliefs and wherever they lived in their newly divided nation, understood that La Belle France was now a German vassal state. Nor did their subjugation seem likely to end any time soon—in less than a year Nazi Germany had conquered virtually all of Europe, proving itself to be the continent's dominant military power and raising the specter of a "Greater German Reich" that might last for decades, if not centuries. Stunned by their nation's defeat and swift capitulation, and convinced of their conqueror's invincibility and the futility of continued resistance, the vast majority of France's people initially chose to seek whatever semblance of normalcy might now be possible. For some— indeed, more than France would ultimately care to admit—the key to a "normal" life was collaboration with, and even military service on behalf of, the new masters. Many others declared their own personal armistices, neither confronting nor supporting the Germans or their Vichy lapdogs, striving to stay unnoticed and seeking solace and some measure of peace in the traditional refuges of family, church, and community.

But there were also those French men and women—as well as foreigners living in France by choice or chance—who simply could not stand idly by as the Nazis and their accomplices brutalized and exploited the nation. Even before the armistice was signed, individuals and small groups of friends or coworkers throughout the country had begun harassing and impeding the invader in any way they could—tearing down phone lines and street signs, helping stranded French and British soldiers return to

their retreating units, pouring sugar in the gas tanks of temporarily unattended Wehrmacht vehicles, and carrying out dozens of other acts of
defiance both passive and active. These initial actions were unorganized,
largely spontaneous, and rarely amounted to more than an irritating nui-
sance to the Germans, who nonetheless responded by putting captured
perpetrators in front of firing squads.

Not surprisingly, the Nazis' penchant for responding in the most dra-
conian manner to even relatively harmless and ineffective acts of resistance
helped fuel the spread of the very sort of defiance the punishments were intended to deter. The swing toward resistance was exacerbated in the months
following the armistice by the increasingly invasive and repressive nature of
German rule in the Zone Occupée (mirrored, not coincidentally, by Vichy
in the so-called Zone Libre). Random identity checks and arbitrary arrests
quickly became a fact of everyday life, as did the harassment of veterans'
associations, trade unions, political organizations, and social and religious
groups deemed to be "anti-German." The latter obviously included France's
Jews, who by the autumn of 1940 were being subjected to increasing
persecution—their property and financial assets confiscated, their movements and civil rights severely restricted, their physical safety at risk.

The undeniably onerous political restrictions placed on the people of
France over the year following the German conquest were further aggra-
vated by the occupiers' insistence on stripping the vanquished nation of
its valuable resources. Stocks of gasoline, diesel fuel, heating oil, and coal
were appropriated for "official" use, making private cars a rare sight on the
roads and ensuring that the winter of 1940–1941 was especially harsh for
those without easy access to firewood. The Germans also shipped the bulk
of France's agricultural output off to the Fatherland, causing increasingly
strict food rationing in their new vassal state, especially in the cities. Cases
of malnutrition surged, and starvation took an ever-larger toll of the very
young and very old alike. Nor was much solace from hunger or despair to
be found in France's traditional refuge—alcohol in all its myriad forms
was expropriated and sent east. Indeed, the Germans' thirst for French
wine and spirits was so intense that the occupation authorities established
a rationing system—for non-Germans, every other day was a *jour sans*, a
"day without" alcohol. To be caught drinking on other than a *jour avec*—
a "day with"—was a serious offense.[9]

The increasingly difficult political and domestic conditions in Occupied France helped spawn dozens, even scores, of nascent resistance groups in the cities and countryside. Some were established by former soldiers or intelligence officers with the skills required to undertake covert military action against the occupiers. Others consisted of public servants—policemen, firefighters, railway workers, civil servants—whose knowledge of the nation's infrastructure or bureaucracy gave them special insight into the most effective ways to hinder, obstruct, and generally bedevil the Germans and their collaborators. But the majority of those who chose to take part in the progressively more dangerous shadow struggle against the hated Boche were "average" people—farmers, artists, intellectuals, trade unionists, shopkeepers—willing to offer whatever help they could.

And in Paris—the "capital" of the occupation and the headquarters of those whose task it was to eliminate opposition to it—among the most willing to aid the growing resistance were the Morins of Invalides.

HATRED FOR ALL THINGS GERMAN HAD BEEN A DEFINING PART OF GEORGES Julien Morin's character long before Bock's troops marched down the Champs-Élysées on that summer morning in 1940.

A native Parisian, Georges was born August 14, 1898, in the city's 14th arrondissement. The second of four children, he grew up believing that the truly valuable things in life were family, church, and nation. The importance of the former was sadly emphasized when he was still a young teenager—his father's sudden death left Georges and his older brother to help their mother care for their younger brother and sister. Though not destitute, the family led something of a hardscrabble life, with the older boys and their "maman" working at a variety of jobs to pay the rent and keep food on the table. Georges understandably came to see responsibility for one's family as the foundation of a man's life, and regular attendance at the local Roman Catholic parish church imbued him with a firm conviction that the care and concern one showed for relatives should also be bestowed on those in the larger society who were in need of aid or less fortunate than oneself.

While the need to work on his family's behalf meant Georges's formal education ended relatively early, he was an avid reader with an abiding interest in the world around him—traits encouraged by his mother and the older brother whom he idolized. Georges's tastes in books were wide-ranging, and though he appreciated everything from the French literary classics to adventure stories to the wildly divergent views presented by Paris's leading daily newspapers, he most enjoyed reading about his country's long, proud, and often tumultuous history. He was especially fascinated by France's military heroes, and the martial exploits of Turenne, Louis XIV, and Napoléon Bonaparte helped instill within him both an ardent patriotism and an elemental understanding of the human costs of war.[10] The latter insight was not only the result of Georges's extensive reading, however. Growing up, the young man had often heard the story of his own grandfather's death while manning a barricade during the Paris Commune of 1871—a family history that ensured Georges viewed French history through a decidedly egalitarian lens.[11]

Unfortunately, the outbreak of World War I meant that Georges's study of French military history quickly became all too personal. His older brother had been called up for service in the initial mobilization, and his unit was among those that took part in what is now widely considered to be the first important Allied victory of the conflict—the First Battle of the Marne. Fought from September 6 through 10, 1914, the campaign resulted in French and British armies halting the German advance on Paris and then forcing the invaders to retreat some fifty miles. The outcome of the battle was to have a profound effect on the subsequent nature of the war—it was largely responsible for the shift to the static trench warfare that thereafter characterized combat on the Western Front—but the immediate impact on France in human terms was appalling. Most estimates put the number of French troops injured in the lead-up to the battle and during its conduct at just over 200,000, with between 75,000 and 85,000 others being killed outright or later dying of wounds. The Morins, like many other French families, were directly and tragically touched by the battle. Georges's beloved older brother died during the first few days of fighting, and when the news reached the family a few weeks later it devastated his mother and surviving siblings.[12]

But in addition to his tremendous feelings of loss, Georges was gripped by a burning desire for revenge against those who had killed his brother.

It was not an impulse he could act on immediately, however, because as the family's oldest surviving male he felt duty-bound to remain at home to support his mother and younger siblings. He did so until February 1917, at which time—and with his mother's reluctant blessing—Georges enlisted in the infantry.[13] Georges had his first opportunity to exact his revenge against the Boche in May, during the latter stages of the Second Battle of the Aisne. He distinguished himself during fierce hand-to-hand combat but also suffered the first of an eventual three near-fatal encounters with poison gas fired into the French lines by German artillery. Each gassing resulted in a scant few weeks of rear-area convalescence, after which he returned to his unit.

By the fall of 1918 Georges was a seasoned combat veteran who had been awarded both the Médaille militaire and Croix de Guerre for his actions in some of the fiercest battles on the Western Front. He and his comrades would undoubtedly have been cheered by the fact that the Germans' defeat at the Second Battle of the Marne in July and August had led to a widespread Allied advance that promised a swift end to the war, and Georges would likely have been thanking God that he had managed to survive with "only" gas-scarred lungs and a permanent limp caused by the loss of several toes to frostbite. His optimism was sadly premature, however, for on November 9—just two days before the armistice went into effect—a German artillery shell slammed into the top of the sandbag-and-timber bunker sheltering Georges's platoon. The resultant explosion killed most of the men outright and buried the few survivors under several feet of dirt and debris. Georges was eventually pulled alive from the rubble, but he had suffered a grievous head injury and severe damage to his left eye.

While undergoing treatment in an army hospital over the following weeks he must have often pondered the bitter irony of having nearly been killed by a German artillery shell. Eight months earlier, on March 21, his beloved mother had died when a shell fired from a German super-long-range cannon hit the Paris church of Saint-Gervais-et-Saint-Protais. More than eighty people attending a Good Friday service perished and scores of others were injured by the blast, one of many that occurred throughout the city that day. The death of Georges's mother had initially left his sister homeless—his younger brother having entered the army some months before—though she had ultimately been taken in by nuns of Georges's home parish.[14]

With the end of the war the French government sought to shift wounded soldiers from hospitals in the former combat areas to recuperation centers nearer the patients' homes of record. But when Georges was told he would be sent to a facility in Paris he protested that he no longer had a home there—his mother was dead, his still-serving younger brother was taking part in the occupation of Germany, and his sister was being cared for by nuns. Georges seemed destined to spend the balance of his recuperation in whatever facility the army chose for him, until Gaston Bourinet came up with a better idea. A member of Georges's unit and the injured man's best friend, Bourinet suggested that Georges agree to be transferred to the Château-des-Eaux-Claires, a stately home-turned–convalescent center in the Charente region of southwestern France. Bourinet's family lived nearby—in Voeuil et Giget, a village of some five hundred people a few miles south of Angoulême—and he said he would write to them to ask that they visit Georges. Time spent near Gaston's family seemed a pleasant alternative to remaining in the army hospital, so Georges agreed to undergo his recuperation at Château-des-Eaux-Claires.

True to Gaston's prediction, the Bourinets embraced Georges as though he were an adopted son. The family patriarch, Gaston's father Charles, took an immediate liking to the wounded young soldier and visited him frequently during the first difficult weeks of Georges's convalescence. More importantly, as it turned out, the elder Bourinet was often accompanied by his daughter. A vivacious, charming, and confident young woman, Denise Laure Marie Bourinet was just four months younger than Georges, and despite their different backgrounds the two young people quickly developed a deep and abiding affection for one another. By the time Georges was released from Château-des-Eaux-Claires in the spring of 1919 he and Denise had gained her parents' permission to marry, though the ceremony was delayed by a seemingly inexplicable decision on the part of the French military.

Despite the fact that Georges was nearly blind in his left eye, had severe and persistent bronchitis because of poison gas, and walked with a permanent limp, he was still considered to be on active duty. Upon the completion of his convalescence he was therefore ordered to rejoin his unit, which by that time had been sent east for occupation duty. After an emotional send-off by Denise and her family, Georges dutifully rejoined the ranks, but after his arrival in Germany it quickly became apparent that he was physically incapable of remaining in the military and he was sent back to France. Following a thorough medical examination he was rated as 45 percent disabled and honorably discharged, and in early 1920 he and Denise were married. Among those attending the ceremony was Georges's sister, who at the suggestion of Denise's father had left what was by all accounts a hard life with the nuns in Paris and traveled to Charente to become part of the extended Bourinet clan.

Georges had never really known any other profession than soldiering, and he was understandably concerned that his disabilities would prevent him from securing a decent civilian job to supplement his small pension and support himself and his new bride. As it turned out, however, it was his disabilities themselves that won him the position he was to hold for the rest of his life. Before the wedding Georges had applied for employment with l'Office nationale des mutilés et réformés (National Office for the Wounded and Discharged),[15] the governmental agency responsible for validating military veterans' pension claims and providing eligible former service members with the identity cards that gave them access to free medical care and other benefits. As a disabled veteran himself, Georges knew how important ONMR's work was and was overjoyed when in January 1921 he was offered a position as an editor in the organization's Paris headquarters—at the Hôtel des Invalides.

While the job paid a decent wage it was nowhere near enough to allow the young couple to live in the well-to-do 7th arrondissement that was home to Invalides. Georges and Denise instead found a small apartment in Vitry-sur-Seine, a Paris suburb six miles to the southeast. While affordable, the area at that time had only limited public transportation and in order to save money Georges declined to use even that. Instead, he bought a second-hand bicycle and rode to and from work each day. Denise had intended to find what odd jobs she could, but soon after the couple arrived in Paris she became pregnant and Georges insisted that for the good of their unborn child she should remain at home.

The young couple's daughter—and, as it turned out, their only child— was born on Friday, October 21, 1921. From the instant she first drew breath, Yvette Edmée Eugénie Morin was the undisputed center of her parents' universe. From infancy onward she showed a delighted interest in the world around her, and as soon as she could walk she set about exploring as much of it as she could—under close maternal supervision, of course. Her doting father was unable to spend as much time with her as he would have liked, however, because his job—and the daily twelve-mile round-trip bicycle commute it necessitated—meant the dedicated family man had all too few hours at home with his wife and child.

Denise and Yvette's loss was ONMR's gain, for Georges's position as an editor was an ideal use of his talents. His lifelong interest in reading had given him both a broad knowledge of history and politics and helped him hone his already significant skills as a writer. These traits were quickly recognized within the organization, and less than a year after arriving at ONMR Georges had become the agency's chief editor. Much of his work consisted of shaping the writings of senior leaders, for whom he also wrote speeches and policy papers. Georges was also responsible for monitoring the way ONMR was portrayed in the press, which required him to read several newspapers each day and then write concise summaries for his superiors. In addition, Georges's intelligence, maturity, work ethic, and obvious dedication to ONMR's mission of aiding veterans like himself soon resulted in his being trusted with increasingly important administrative duties outside the editorial office.

Despite his routinely heavy workload, Georges enjoyed his job and found it both professionally fulfilling and personally rewarding. Indeed, only two things kept it from being the perfect situation. The first, of course, was that he had too little time with Denise and Yvette, but the second was potentially far more damaging—Georges's twelve-mile bicycle commute was seriously worsening his already precarious health. The ride strained his legs and frostbite-damaged feet, and more importantly, the air pollution and often damp weather that were normal facets of his daily journey to Invalides were beginning to wreak havoc on his gas-weakened lungs. By early 1925 Georges was near physical exhaustion and considering leaving his position with ONMR simply in order to preserve both his family and his health. At that point the organization's director made a suggestion that would not only allow Georges to remain at Invalides, it would also have consequences that would only become apparent when German troops once more walked the streets of Paris.

LIKE MANY PEOPLE WITH WHOM GEORGES WORKED AT ONMR, MONSIEUR Lucien Possoz—the director—was aware of the young veteran's physical handicaps and of his dismay at having so little time with his wife and child. And, again like many of Georges's colleagues, Possoz was loath to see the hardworking and personable chief editor leave Invalides. It was therefore with a great deal of pleasure that the director realized he was in a position to offer Georges a solution.

Though the sprawling Invalides complex was home to a variety of governmental and cultural organizations, the Office of the Architect bore overall responsibility for the care and preservation of all buildings and infrastructure. Engineers constantly monitored the structural integrity of the centuries-old edifices, and made repairs and modifications when necessary. Carpenters, electricians, and plumbers handled the less historic but no less important challenges that arose, while a small army of horticulturists and greenskeepers maintained the ornamental gardens and other vegetation. In addition, a specialized subsection of the Office of the Architect was responsible for the preservation of many of the objets d'art that graced Invalides' eight miles of hallways and fifteen courtyards. A small team of art conservators oversaw the ongoing maintenance of, and repairs to, hundreds of paintings, sculptures, tapestries, and statues—as well as Napoléon's sarcophagus and the other tombs and memorials within the Dôme. And it was within this Fine Arts Office that Monsieur Possoz saw a solution to Georges Morin's two problems.

The majority of the conservation and repair work undertaken on Invalides' art works was performed by outside contractors, who were brought into the complex as needed. Security protocols intended to prevent the theft of what were in many cases priceless objets d'art required that these contractors be signed in and out, and that they be given access only to those specific areas where their particular expertise was required. The staff members of the small Fine Arts Office were too occupied with their professional functions to supervise the daily comings and goings of the contractors, so that duty was given to an individual variously referred to as the "supervisor of fine arts building sites" or the "fine arts concierge." While the position did not come with a salary it did offer a very valuable perk: the incumbent and his or her family were allowed to live rent-free in a small apartment in the southeast corner of the Invalides complex. When Monsieur Possoz learned that the position was about to become vacant, he urged Georges to apply—if given the job, the young veteran's physically taxing twelve-mile round-trip commute would be reduced to less than one hundred yards, and he would see far more of his family during the workday. Moreover, Monsieur Possoz pointed out, Denise Morin could actually undertake most of the duties, meaning that Georges could retain his ONMR position and salary.

The Morins saw Possoz's suggestion as the ideal solution to their difficulties, and Georges applied for the job as soon as the vacancy was officially announced. He and Denise were interviewed by the director of the Fine Arts Office, who knew and liked them both, and who understood that if given the position the young veteran would remain with ONMR and that most of the daily "concierge" tasks would be carried out by his wife. The job was duly awarded to the Morins, and in the summer of 1925 Georges, Denise, Yvette, and Denise's recently widowed sixty-two-year-old father, Charles Bourinet, moved into their new home.

The 680-square-foot, two-bedroom, two-level apartment was part of a long row of connected structures—other apartments, a garage, and small workshops and storage rooms—built over a section of the original seventeenth-century moat and facing the rear of a three-story complex of offices across a narrow, mews-like alley.[16] The Morins' home and the adjoining structures shared a common rear wall that backed up to the sidewalk bordering the west side of the tree-lined boulevard des Invalides. There were no openings piercing the rear wall at street level, but two large dormer windows on the second floor of the Morins' apartment let in light and offered a fine view of the boulevard. On the entry level were a small living room with a window looking out on the narrow alley and, at the rear, a pantry and a compact but functional kitchen. Upstairs were the single bathroom and the bedrooms—Georges and Denise's facing the street and Yvette's the alley—each room with two dormer windows and a double bed. Charles Bourinet slept on the fold-out couch in the living room.

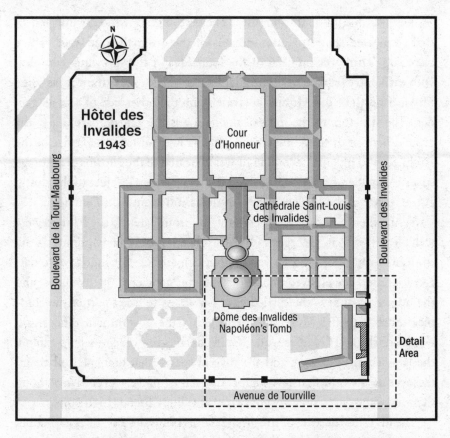

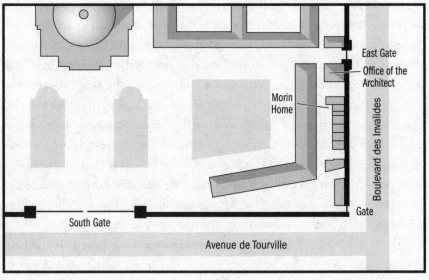

At that time all of Invalides was enclosed by tall, wrought iron fences that connected the remaining sections of the original stone walls. There were large entrances on each of the four sides of the sprawling complex, with each entry flanked by stone guard houses. The east entrance was some fifty feet north of the Morins' apartment, on the other side of a small garden. The structure to the right of the gate was the actual guardhouse; the ground floor of the building on the left side was home to the Office of the Architect and its small second floor was allocated to the Morins as a storage space. A smaller, barred gate pierced the fence about 150 feet to the south, at the corner of the boulevard des Invalides and avenue de Tourville.[17]

While their new home was certainly far from palatial, the Morins were well pleased with it. Georges's ONMR office was only a few minutes' walk from his front door, and he was able to come home for lunch every day. Denise found she enjoyed being the de facto "concierge" of Invalides, and the huge ring of keys she carried gave her access to every part of the complex other than the Musée de l'Armée and the government offices. On weekends she and Georges—and Yvette, as she grew older—would explore the labyrinthine hallways and the myriad spaces that branched off them, discovering a world that few visitors or even employees ever saw. Among their favorite places to visit were two of Invalides' literal "high points."

The first was the attic of the ornate Saint-Louis des Invalides cathedral. Reached via a series of small doors and narrow, vertigo-inducing wooden stairways, the attic rests atop the cathedral's vaulted ceiling and is some ninety feet above floor level. The interior of the attic is dark, dank, and dusty, and the massive arched timbers supporting the cathedral roof look for all the world like an inverted ship's hull. Among the attic's most interesting features, they discovered, is a small circular hole in the stout wooden floor. When the piece of wood covering the hole is removed, a visitor can look directly down at the cathedral's altar. A little research on Denise's part revealed that Louis XIV had ordered the hole installed so that white doves could be passed down through it during services, both to underscore the spiritual nature of the proceedings and to hold the attention of the aging and infirm veterans who were its primary congregants.

The second of the Morins' favorite hidden spots is reached via the first. At the south end of the attic two sets of wooden stairs steep enough to qualify as ladders lead to two small metal doors, both of which open out onto an exterior landing on the cathedral's roof. Immediately in front of the doors is the circular metal cupola that is the exterior covering of the small dome just behind and above the altar. Narrow walkways lead around the cupola to either side, and terminate on a relative flat area that separates the smaller cupola from the much larger and vastly more ornate golden dome directly above Napoléon's tomb. The view of Invalides, and indeed of much of Paris, is spectacular, but not enjoyed without risk. The winds that are funneled between the dome and the smaller cupola are often strong enough to blow a person over, and the walls that surround the open area—while tall enough to prevent visitors from being seen from below—are too short to prevent a fall of almost one hundred feet.[18]

As it happened, the Morins' intimate familiarity with Invalides' hidden places—and their possession of the keys to most of the complex's doors—would ultimately prove vital to the safety of Allied airmen when war came again to La Belle France.

LIFE QUICKLY FELL INTO A COMFORTABLE RHYTHM FOR THE MORINS FOLLOWING their move onto the grounds of Invalides. Georges continued his important work for ONMR—which in 1935 adopted the decidedly more unwieldy name l'Office national des mutilés, combattants, victimes de guerre et pupilles de la nation (National Office for the Maimed, Veterans, Victims of War and Wards of the Nation)[19]—steadily rising in the organization's hierarchy and often traveling to regional offices across France. Denise quickly made herself an indispensable member of the Architect's staff, and was to be seen every day bustling about the complex, groups of workmen in tow and her enormous ring of keys jangling on her belt. When not assisting his daughter in her duties, Charles Bourinet kept an eye on his growing granddaughter. He walked Yvette to school when she was young, and when she no longer needed such an escort Charles often spent time with friends among Invalides' long-term residents.

As the years passed, Yvette grew into an intelligent, self-confident, and engaging young woman. Slender and standing just over five foot four, she was graced with lush, light-brown hair, and striking, emerald-green eyes. While her looks and outgoing personality ensured her social popularity, she was also known as a thoughtful and principled individual with a strong moral compass. These attributes were the product of both her parents' influence and Yvette's deep religious convictions. The Morins were devoutly Roman Catholic, and the church was an integral part of family life.

Although Invalides was within the parish of the nearby Basilica of Sainte-Clotilde, Yvette and her parents and grandfather chose to attend Saint-François-Xavier church, 450 yards straight down the boulevard des Invalides on the place André Tardieu. Their preference stemmed largely from their friendship with, and admiration for, Saint-François-Xavier's charismatic Monsignor Georges Chevrot. A well-known and widely respected priest and a prolific author on religious topics, he had also created a church youth movement to which Yvette had belonged for most of her adolescence. In addition to emphasizing equality and social justice, Chevrot imbued his young charges with a love of their nation's history and the role of the church in that history. Nor was Chevrot's patriotism merely intellectual, for when the clouds of war once again gathered over France he would prove himself more than ready to turn words into action—as would those who revered him.

LIKE MILLIONS OF OTHER EUROPEANS, THE MORINS HAD WATCHED WITH growing anxiety as increasingly aggressive moves by Adolf Hitler—notably the 1936 occupation of the Rhineland and the March 1938 "Anschluss" with Austria—had ratcheted up martial tensions on the continent.[20] British prime minister Neville Chamberlain's attempts to appease Hitler at the September 1938 Munich Conference did nothing to ease those tensions; indeed, allowing the Nazi leader's October annexation of the Czech Sudetenland simply stoked his desire to further expand the "Greater Reich." Hitler did so in mid-March 1939 by sending the Wehrmacht into the rest of Czechoslovakia and declaring a "protectorate" over the regions of Bohemia and Moravia.

While Georges Morin was not surprised by the latter move, which he saw as a typically duplicitous act by the never-to-be-trusted Boche, he was incensed by the fact that France had failed to honor its long-standing treaty of alliance with Czechoslovakia.[21] Indeed, so infuriated was Georges by what he saw as his nation's failure to confront the very real threat presented by a resurgent Germany that—despite Denise's logical and vocal objections—the forty-one-year-old disabled veteran actually explored the possibility of volunteering for the belated military mobilization ordered by Prime Minister Édouard Daladier. A cursory examination by an army physician assigned to Invalides put a quick end to Georges's understandable but quixotic notion.[22]

Although her father had been denied the chance to serve, seventeen-year-old Yvette had more success in her own search for a way to contribute to her nation's preparedness. In the spring of 1939 she started taking Red Cross classes in nursing as part of a program referred to as the "passive defense" initiative. Several afternoons a week and on occasional weekends she joined other young women from the area in a classroom at a local hospital, where instruction centered on basic and advanced first aid. Shadowing the facility's physicians and nurses during their rounds provided Yvette and the others with both a realistic view of what they might be required to deal with should war erupt, and with the occasional opportunity for hands-on experience with real patients.

With the outbreak of war on September 3, 1939, Yvette assumed that her nursing skills would immediately be put to the test. That proved not to be the case, however, since there were no significant air attacks on Paris during the initial eight months of the new conflict—the period that came to be known as the Phoney War. Yvette instead spent time participating in the Saint-François-Xavier church youth group's efforts to provide the families of mobilized servicemen with supplementary meals and other aid, and when needed, the young woman also tended to her increasingly frail grandfather.

The months following the outbreak of war were also busy ones for Georges and Denise. In their dual role as the concierges of Invalides the couple were key players in the French government's plans to protect many of Paris's most famed art treasures in the event the capital came under attack. Larger items such as statues, fountains, and memorials were to be surrounded by protective enclosures, while more portable items would be crated and stored in central locations so they could be quickly evacuated to safer locales. This was an especially complex undertaking at Invalides, with its many collections and thousands of individual objects—indeed, the number of items just in the Musée de l'Armée judged significant enough to warrant evacuation ran to several scores of large crates. The Morins, including Yvette when she was free, spent weeks assisting in the identification, documentation, and crating of objects from within Saint-Louis des Invalides and the Tomb of Napoléon. The emperor's huge and obviously immovable sarcophagus itself disappeared beneath extensive wooden scaffolding, which was then covered with a pyramid of protective sandbags.[23]

The somewhat deliberate pace of the effort to prepare Invalides' treasures for safekeeping elsewhere turned frenetic following the May 1940 German invasion of France and the Low Countries. As the seemingly unstoppable Boche rolled ever closer to Paris in early June, the process of carefully documenting and packing each item gave way to a far faster and less painstaking procedure. Those items that had already been crated were moved into the complex's various courtyards, ready for loading aboard the trucks that would haul them to the presumed safety of western and southern France. Other pieces for which no crates could be quickly found were simply covered with tarps and stacked near the loading areas. But Invalides' priceless art works were not the only items being prepared for quick removal. The various government offices within the complex began boxing up their most important files and burning those that were deemed less essential. Even the pensioners living on the grounds were told they should prepare to be evacuated to a safer location.

All these preparations came to fruition following the Luftwaffe's June 3 bombardment of various targets in the Paris region. While no bombs landed anywhere near Invalides, the director of the hospital ordered the immediate evacuation of the pensioners, and the crates of artworks and items from the Musée de l'Armée were swiftly loaded on the waiting trucks and dispatched. The convoy of buses carrying the human evacuees toward the Pyrenees and the trucks bearing the inanimate items were not alone on the roads, however. The June 10 departure from Paris of Paul Reynaud and his government turned what had been a steady trickle of people leaving the city into a torrent; over the following two days fully two-thirds of the capital's inhabitants abandoned their homes. The routes leading south and west were soon clogged with vehicles and masses of people, and the Germans—seeking to both sow terror among the civilians and prevent retreating French and British forces from reaching the Atlantic and Channel ports—routinely strafed and bombed the packed roadways.[24]

Though the Morins helped dispatch the artwork and pensioners, they themselves chose not to join the mass exodus from their beloved Paris. Georges and Denise saw it as their duty to remain and do what they could to protect Invalides from whatever depredations the Boche might attempt to inflict upon it, and Yvette would not abandon her parents or sickly grandfather. The family thus stayed within the complex, spending the days following the departure of the pensioners and artworks doing what they could to prepare for the Germans' now-inevitable arrival. While Georges was occupied with boxing his agency's records for storage—so the enemy couldn't use them to identify veterans that might oppose the coming occupation—Denise used her enormous ring of keys to begin locking the doors that led to smaller and less obvious hallways and storage areas, the better to keep hidden from prying German eyes those items of value that had not already been shipped elsewhere.[25] By the afternoon of June 13 the lead German elements were rumored to be entering Paris's northern suburbs, and that evening the Morins closed the shutters on the windows of their apartment and settled in to await whatever the dawn would bring.

What the morning of June 14 brought was a vigorous banging on the Morins' front door. When Georges opened the portal he was greeted by the sight of several young and heavily armed German soldiers staring menacingly at him. His initial alarm was calmed, however, when a tall and imposing officer stepped forward and in correct but somewhat accented French introduced himself as Major Hermann Oehmichen, commander of the Wehrmacht's Panzerjäger Abteilung 187.[26] His unit, he explained, was responsible for securing several important facilities along the Left Bank, including Invalides, and he had been told that monsieur and his wife had all the keys to the complex. Would they be so kind as to accompany him as he and his men ensured that everything was in order?

There was only one possible response to the German officer's request, of course, so Georges and Denise spent most of that first morning of the occupation of Paris leading Oehmichen and a group of his subordinates through Invalides. The French couple obviously could not avoid responding to direct questions from the Boche, but they did not volunteer information and managed to restrict the Germans' explorations to the main hallways and public spaces. And though the new "visitors" were aware that Invalides was home to the headquarters of General Henri-Fernand Dentz, commander of the Paris military region, they seemed remarkably uninformed about the several other government agencies housed within the complex. Georges assumed that the speed of the German advance had surprised the attackers as much as it had the defenders, and that the Boche had simply not had time to do the necessary intelligence research. Indeed, the only thing Oehmichen and his troops seemed intensely interested in was the chance to see Napoléon's Tomb—and they were clearly disappointed when they discovered that the emperor's famous sarcophagus was still completely hidden within its pyramid of protective sandbags.

In the days following their initial arrival the Germans began requisitioning buildings throughout Paris—now the administrative hub of the Zone Occupée—for their own use. The city's best hotels, stately homes, and office buildings were appropriated for use by senior military and political leaders, and by the various police and intelligence organizations tasked with rooting out any opposition to the occupation. Invalides was itself tapped to serve as both an administrative center for several second-tier organizations and as a housing area for troops assigned to various support units throughout the city. The Germans announced that they would occupy the western half of the complex, along the boulevard de la Tour-Maubourg, while the eastern half would remain home to various French government offices and the veterans' hospital and accommodations.[27] The first Wehrmacht troops to arrive en masse initially slept in tents erected in several of the courtyards, but after moving into the east-side barracks newly vacated by French garrison soldiers, the newcomers used the elegant enclosures for another purpose—they pulled up the lawns and planted vegetables.

Though the Germans planned to occupy only part of Invalides they quickly moved to secure the entire complex. Wooden sentry boxes were placed at every entrance, and armed soldiers checked the papers of anyone seeking to enter between the time the gates opened at 7 A.M. and when they closed for the night at 7 P.M. Twelve soldiers manned the combination vehicle gate and personnel entrance on the east side of Invalides, just north of the Morins' apartment, though they returned to their west-side barracks each night. Because the Germans had decreed that the Office of the Architect would continue to oversee the maintenance and preservation of the buildings and the objets d'art they contained, Georges and

Denise retained their joint position as "concierges" of Invalides. They also kept possession of the large ring of keys, and were authorized to continue escorting outside workers who came onto the grounds. In order to alert the French couple when workers arrived at the nearby guardhouse, the Germans manning the personnel gate continued to use the existing button that rang a doorbell in the Morins' apartment—the bell's tune, ironically, was the *dit-dit-dit-dah* opening of the first movement of Beethoven's Fifth Symphony in C Minor.[28]

Despite the Germans' decision that the French should retain responsibility for the care and maintenance of Invalides and its treasures, the first large-scale project within the complex after the occupation of Paris was undertaken by the invaders themselves. One morning less than a week after Major Oehmichen's sudden appearance on the Morins' doorstep, troops of Panzerjäger Abteilung 187 drove several large military trucks through the east-side vehicle gate and backed them up in front of the steps leading into the Dôme chapel housing Napoléon's Tomb. Alerted by the noise of the vehicles' arrival, the Morins hurried from their home and arrived outside the chapel in time to see dozens of soldiers bearing hammers, crowbars, and other tools clambering out of the trucks and hurrying up the steps.

Understandably alarmed, Georges and Denise followed the soldiers into the building, where to their relief they realized that the men were not intent on vandalism—they were under orders to remove the sandbags covering Napoléon's ornate sarcophagus. As the French couple watched, soldiers scaled crude wooden ladders laid against the sides of the protective pyramid and began tossing the upper sandbags toward their comrades below. The situation immediately turned comical, however—at least for Georges and Denise—because the damp and brittle sandbags burst open as soon as they left the throwers' hands. Sand soon covered the soldiers and the floor, and a haze of dust clouded the chapel. The effort to uncover the tomb quickly devolved into what Oehmichen himself later described as a "pathetic fiasco," and it was only the arrival of several Paris fire brigade trucks equipped with suction pumps that allowed all of the sand to finally be cleared away.[29]

The reason for the hurried cleanup of Napoléon's Tomb became clear early on the morning of Sunday, June 23, when several Mercedes-Benz G4 open touring cars rolled to a halt before Invalides' south gate.[30] The quartet of German troops acting as an honor guard at the open portal snapped to attention as Adolf Hitler stepped from the lead vehicle and strode purposefully toward the steps leading into the Dôme church, closely followed by an entourage that included four of the Führer's favorite artists—his personal photographer, Heinrich Hoffmann; architects Albert Speer and Hermann Giesler; and sculptor Arno Breker.[31] Hitler had flown into Le Bourget airport just after dawn for a whirlwind tour of the city; Invalides was one of the final stops, and apparently one of the most meaningful for the German dictator. He stood motionless for several minutes in the circular gallery above Napoléon's sarcophagus, his head bowed toward the final resting place of the soldier-emperor with whom he most closely identified. As the group left the rotunda to descend into the crypt before moving on to the Cour d'honneur (Court of Honor), the obviously deeply affected Führer told photographer Hoffmann that the visit to the tomb was "the greatest and finest moment" of his life.[32] Minutes later, as the members of the entourage were about to board their vehicles, Hitler turned to Martin Bormann and said, "I want the Duke of Reichstadt to be brought back to Paris."[33]

With that one comment regarding Napoléon's only legitimate child, Hitler set in motion the chain of events that would result in the Morins' first overt act of resistance.

ALTHOUGH HITLER'S REASON FOR WANTING THE REMAINS OF NAPOLÉON François Charles Joseph Bonaparte moved from their resting place in Vienna to Paris—and specifically to Invalides—are unclear, it is generally assumed to have been intended as a gesture of reconciliation toward the French.[34]

Though styled Duke of Reichstadt at the time of his death at the age of twenty-one, the young man had been Emperor Napoléon II for two weeks in 1815—at the age of four—following his father's defeat at Waterloo and subsequent abdication. When France reinstated the monarchy and put Louis XVIII back on the throne, the child and his mother, the Austrian-born former Empress Marie-Louise, went into exile in Vienna.[35] The boy, thereafter known as Franz, grew up in the court of his maternal grandfather, the Hapsburg emperor Francis I, who bestowed the

Reichstadt title. The lad was groomed for life as a military officer, but only served for a few years before his death from tuberculosis in 1832. The ornate bronze coffin bearing his body was placed in the Imperial Crypt beneath Vienna's Capuchin Church, where it remained undisturbed until December 12, 1940.[36] On that day, in response to Hitler's directive to Bormann six months earlier, the coffin was removed from the crypt and transported to Vienna's main train station. Loaded aboard a boxcar that had been fitted out as an ornate mini-chapel, the casket of L'Aiglon—"the Eaglet," as the young duke was referred to in France—reached Paris's Gare de l'Est station on December 14.

Two events were to be held at Invalides marking the return of the former Napoléon II. The first, which took place that very night, was the actual arrival of the casket, brought from the train station atop a gun carriage towed behind a German half-track and escorted by a Wehrmacht honor guard. During a solemn, torch-lit ceremony at the bottom of the steps leading into the Dôme church, German ambassador Otto Abetz officially turned the remains of L'Aiglon over to Marshal Pétain's representatives, Admiral Jean Darlan and General Auguste Laure, as senior French and German military and political leaders looked on. There was a brief service inside once the casket had been placed on a bier in front of the altar, but the major observance—akin to a funeral mass—was scheduled for the following day. During the latter service, huge wreaths from Pétain and Hitler were to be placed on either side of the casket as both a sign of respect and as a visual representation of Franco-German cooperation. Many smaller wreaths and other types of floral tributes would then be ceremonially arranged around the bier.

In the afternoon before the nighttime ceremony Georges, Denise, and Yvette Morin had been directed to arrange the many wreaths and floral tributes to be used the next day in orderly rows in a small alley off to the side of the Dôme church. The largest of the wreaths was a huge swastika made of black pansies and bearing a ribbon inscribed "From Chancellor Hitler to the Duke of Reichstadt" in French. The obscene wreath—and its proximity to the final resting place of so many of the nation's heroes—infuriated the Morins, though they could do nothing about it with so many German troops in the area preparing for the event. Later, as darkness fell and before the torches were lighted for the ceremony, Denise left the warmth of home and carefully made her way through falling snow to where the Hitler wreath stood. Whether out of repugnance for the Germans or as a gesture on behalf of her deeply patriotic father—who had died just over a month earlier—Denise impulsively grabbed the offensive wreath and carried it home. Minutes later the hated symbol was burning in the fireplace. Later that night, when the ceremony in the church was over and the complex was quiet, Georges pulled the wire frame of the wreath from the hearth and buried it at the foot of a tree in one of the nearby gardens.[37]

Denise's spontaneous act of resistance was incredibly dangerous, of course, for had she been discovered she would undoubtedly have been turned over to the Gestapo, the Germans' dreaded secret police.[38] Georges and Yvette would also likely have been arrested, and all three would almost certainly have faced torture and eventual execution. Denise was not caught in the act, however, and the removal of Hitler's wreath was not discovered until the following morning, when dignitaries began arriving for the church service. Those attending the ceremony included many of the same French and German luminaries who had witnessed the casket's arrival the night before—including Abetz and Darlan—who were joined by such others as the Archbishop of Paris; Lieutenant General Otto von Stülpnagel, the military governor of Occupied France; the disabled French general Augustine Mariaux, director of Invalides; and various distant relatives of Napoléon. As the attendees filed in, German protocol officers realized the Führer's floral tribute was missing, and despite frantic searching found no trace of it (and, thanks to the snow that had fallen overnight, there were no telltale footprints leading back to the Morins' home). The arrangement's absence became something of a diplomatic incident when, at the end of the service, Darlan placed a huge wreath bearing a French tricolor and the words "Maréchal Pétain" next to Napoléon's sarcophagus. Abetz, visibly furious at the absence of Hitler's floral offering, could only stand by, empty-handed.[39]

As helpful as it might have been in preventing the Germans from discovering the Morins' role in the disappearance of Hitler's wreath, the snow that fell on Invalides the night before the church service was not a sign of divine intervention. It was, in fact, yet another unwelcome reminder of how harsh and unforgiving the first winter of the German occupation was for the people of Paris. The fall rains had come early, and had quickly given way to frigid temperatures, ice storms, and snowfall that was both deeper and more frequent than most of the capital's residents had ever experienced. The punishing weather only exacerbated the already severe conditions caused by the Germans' continuing expropriation of Occupied France's agricultural goods and energy sources.

While life was certainly difficult for the Morins during the winter of 1940–1941, it was not as bleak as it might have been, for two reasons. The first, ironically, was the largesse of the Germans themselves.

After the men of Major Oehmichen's Panzerjäger Abteilung 187 had removed the protective sandbag pyramid covering Napoléon's sarcophagus, they had piled the wood planks and beams that had made up its frame in one of the storage areas near the Morins' home. Protective barriers around other immovable objects on the grounds and from nearby neighborhoods were torn down over the course of the spring and fall and added to the growing storage pile, as were the dismantled crates and pallets that had borne the now-returned objets d'art evacuated during the spring. As the weather turned increasingly bitter, the Morins were permitted to use some of the wood for their home fireplace and cook stove—so long, the Germans warned, as they didn't overdo it.

The Boche also contributed to the Morins' well-being in another way, though the donation was unwitting and indirect. The troops billeted within Invalides ate well—so well, in fact, that the refuse bins outside their barracks on the west side of the complex often overflowed with discarded potatoes, carrots, and other vegetables. Denise and Yvette were regular visitors to the bins, where they scavenged every remnant of vegetable they could find. The scraps were not for their own consumption, however.

During the mass civilian exodus through Paris that accompanied the German advance in May and June 1940, many of the refugees from rural areas who sought temporary shelter within Invalides brought poultry and rabbits with them, carried in small wire cages. One morning, just days before the arrival of Panzerjäger Abteilung 187, Denise had found a hugely pregnant female rabbit hiding beneath a shrub in one of the areas in which refugees had been housed. Knowing a providential sign when they saw one, Denise and Georges built a basic hutch inside one of the now vacant garage spaces near their apartment and installed the four-footed mother-to-be. Fed on a combination of grass taken from Invalides' lawns and discarded German vegetables, that first rabbit and her offspring quickly multiplied into a reliable and much-needed food source for Georges, Denise, and Yvette.[40]

But the Morins would not be the only ones to gain sustenance from the rabbits, for the French family would soon be playing host to a series of young, frightened, and very hungry men on the run.

Chapter 3

A BAD DAY AT LE BOURGET

THE JUNE 13, 1943, MISSION TO KIEL HAD BEEN AN UNQUALIFIED disaster for the 94th Bomb Group. Nine B-17s and ninety men had gone down over the German port city or on the return flight to England, bringing the unit's total losses since its combat debut to sixteen aircraft and nearly 160 men dead or missing in action.[1] Some twenty-five additional airmen were wounded on the raid, and eight aircraft were damaged to the point that they needed extensive repairs before going back on operational status.

As Joe Cornwall and his crewmates had anticipated, the beating *Natural* had taken on the Kiel strike led to their being assigned another Fortress. Though slightly older than the machine it replaced, the second aircraft was an essentially identical B-17F and bore the serial number 42-3331.[2] Ed Purdy and his men discussed a variety of possible names and nose art designs for their new mount, but ultimately decided on variations of those that had graced their first bomber. The name emblazoned on the replacement's nose—this time on the left side rather than the right—was the plural *Naturals*.[3] And rather than attempting to reproduce the first Fortress's gaudy image of the kneeling African-American man, the crew instead opted for two white dice, their faces still showing 7 and 11, caught in midroll within an offset black cube applied just aft of and slightly below the aircraft's name.

Though Purdy and his crew had assumed they would take *Naturals* into combat sooner rather than later, bad weather over most of western Europe—coupled with the need to replace its losses in men and aircraft—kept the 94th Bomb Group on the ground for more than a week after the Kiel debacle. The lull might have helped revive the unit's flagging morale, had it not been for a decision made by General Ira Eaker a few days after the Kiel raid. Apparently believing that the heavy losses the 94th had experienced since its arrival in England were the result, at least in part, of inadequate leadership by "Dinty" Moore, on June 20 the Eighth Air Force commander relieved him of duty and assigned him to a staff position at Elveden Hall. Moore's sudden departure was a huge shock to the men of the 94th, who revered him as both a leader and as something of a father figure.[4]

Nor were the aviators at Rougham initially impressed with the man who arrived late on June 21 to replace Moore. Colonel Frederick W. Castle had been a staff officer at Eaker's headquarters, and most of the men in the 94th assumed he was a "desk jockey"—though in reality he was an accomplished pilot who had already flown eight combat missions. Castle's brief from Eaker was to "tighten up" the 94th, to reintroduce "standards for appearance, social and professional conduct, and mission dedication" to a unit whose flying personnel "felt that with combat came the privilege of being a swashbuckling warrior with little regard" for the niceties of military discipline.[5] Though calm and soft-spoken, Castle began the tightening-up process immediately upon his arrival, announcing that all regulations pertaining to uniforms and military courtesy would be strictly observed, and that violations would result in fines or the loss of leave and pass privileges. And to the surprise of many in the 94th, the new commander also announced that he would lead the group's next mission, which would take place the following day.[6]

Castle not only led the 94th in the June 22 raid against the rubber factories in and around Hüls, Germany, he also commanded all but two of the subsequent six missions against targets in the Reich and France. On the July 4 mission to bomb the harbor facilities at La Pallice, Castle flew as an observer in the lead aircraft of "Salty" Saltsman's 331st Bomb Squadron, which had been tapped to lead the group. Saltsman, in turn, chose *Naturals* to lead both the squadron and the group, with himself flying as pilot in command and Ed Purdy as copilot. In recognition of the honor, and as a sign of their admiration and respect for their squadron leader, Purdy and his men unanimously agreed to slightly modify the name of their bomber. Just before takeoff on the morning of July 4, the crew gathered near the nose of the B-17 and, with Saltsman looking on, applauded as a mechanic atop a ladder used a small can of white paint to hastily add the 331st commander's nickname just above and slightly forward of *Naturals*. From that point on the Fortress was known throughout the squadron as *Salty's Naturals*.[6]

Castle's leadership style apparently had a salutary effect on the 94th Bomb Group, for though two aircraft went down on the June 22 mission, none were lost on the six missions that were flown between June 25 and July 10. All of the raids were flown as part of the USAAF's contribution to what Allied military leaders referred to as the Combined Bomber Offensive—the round-the-clock Anglo-American bombardment of enemy targets in Germany and Occupied Europe—that had officially begun on June 10. The stated purpose of the offensive was "the progressive destruction and dislocation of the German military, industrial and economic system, and the undermining of the morale of the German people to the point where their capacity for armed resistance is fatally weakened."[7]

By the middle of July all fifteen of the B-17 groups then operational in the United Kingdom were participating in the offensive, and the Eighth Air Force was steadily increasing both its reach—in terms of distances flown and targets hit—and the accuracy of its bombing.[8] But the Germans were also improving, both with regard to their ability to track incoming raids and in the effectiveness of their defenses. In June alone, the Eighth lost ninety-three heavy bombers—shot down, missing in action, or damaged beyond repair—and nearly one thousand crewmen dead or missing.[9] While the 94th Bomb Group had lost no aircraft since the June 22 raid, several crewmen had been killed and dozens injured on the five subsequent missions, and morale at Rougham, as at most other U.S. bomber bases, was far from good. Evenings spent in the on-base officers and enlisted clubs and off-duty visits to nearby pubs—there were nearly fifty in the Bury St. Edmunds area at the time—were of only marginal help in improving the men's spirits.[10] Not even an afternoon performance on June 29 by American comedian Bob Hope, guitarist Tony Romano, and singer Frances Langford had done much to lift the pall of gloom that hovered over the 94th like a cloud.

Bad weather over the United Kingdom kept the Eighth Air Force's heavy bombers grounded for six days following the July 4 mission to La

Pallice. Conditions improved enough by the tenth to allow the launch of a major attack against three Luftwaffe airfields in France, at Abbeville, Caen, and Le Bourget—the latter a former civilian field outside Paris— with 277 Fortresses from all fifteen operational groups participating.[11] The 94th was part of the 101-aircraft contingent sent against Le Bourget, with *Salty's Naturals* leading the 331st's second element. The raid was strongly opposed by German fighters on the way to the target, which the B-17s were unable to bomb because of heavy cloud cover, and two Fortresses from other groups were shot down. Although several enemy interceptors also went down in flames, the mission was for all intents a failure—Le Bourget remained intact and operational.[12]

Though *Salty's Naturals* returned to Rougham undamaged and with her crew unharmed, the grueling and ultimately futile sortie further reinforced Joe Cornwall's belief that his chances of completing the required twenty-five missions were increasingly slim. While ineffably sad, the thought did not frighten him as much as it had during his first few combat missions. That gut-wrenching, barely controlled terror had given way to something akin to resigned fatalism. Having seen so many bombers spiraling out of control, their wings missing or engines engulfed in flames, and having watched as dead and dying men were pulled from aircraft that had managed to limp home, Joe no longer thought in terms of whether he'd be shot down—he now assumed it was merely a question of when. He only hoped that he would have the courage to face whatever came and, even more importantly, that he would not disappoint or let down his crewmates.[13]

Joe didn't have much longer to ponder his fate, however, for his next combat mission was destined to be his last.

THE FAILURE OF THE JULY 10 RAID AGAINST LE BOURGET, AND THE AIRFIELD'S continuing importance as both a Luftwaffe fighter base and a major air-craft repair facility, guaranteed a return visit by the Eighth Air Force. That second strike was scheduled for July 14—Bastille Day—as part of VIII Bomber Command Mission No. 73. The three-pronged assault would see other groups attacking the Luftwaffe air depot at Villacoublay and the fighter field at Amiens/Glisy, while the 94th, 95th, 96th, and 100th Bomb Groups headed for Paris.

On the afternoon of July 13 Fred Castle called his squadron and element leaders together for a pre-mission briefing. There he announced—to the groans and curses of most everyone in the room—that the 94th would be flying as low group in the wing formation. Castle himself would fly the lead bomber in the lead 332nd Squadron, with Major Kee Harrison—a founding member of the 94th and one of its most capable and popular officers—commanding the 332nd's second element. The 410th's commander, Major Franklin Colby (known as "Pappy" because at forty he was the oldest operational pilot in the Eighth Air Force at that time), would lead the high squadron, and "Salty" Saltsman and the 331st would be low squadron. Saltsman announced that he would fly as copilot in Captain Willis Frank's *Good Time Cholly II*, and then turned to Ed Purdy and tapped him as leader of the 331st's second element. The assignment was a clear indication of Saltsman's trust in Purdy and his crew, but it also meant that *Salty's Naturals* and the two other Fortresses in the second element would be the three lowest bombers in the entire wing formation—solidly in "Purple Heart Corner."

After giving a few further details of the mission, Castle beckoned to an officer who had been quietly observing the meeting from the back of the room. As the man walked forward, the others immediately noted a few curious things about him. For a start, though he wore captain's bars on his immaculately tailored uniform, his graying air indicated that he was decidedly older than most men of his rank. And while his branch insignia and the Eighth Air Force patch on his shoulder confirmed his USAAF status, the absence of wings on his left breast clearly indicated that he was not a pilot, bombardier, navigator, or gunner.[14] And, finally, several of those present recognized the man's several campaign ribbons as dating to World War I.

When the man joined Castle at the front of the room, the group commander introduced him as Captain Jeff Dickson, the photographic officer from 4th Wing headquarters at Elveden Hall. In a slow but cultured Mississippi drawl, the forty-seven-year-old Dickson explained that he had been directed by the wing commander, Brigadier General Frederick L. Anderson, to shoot motion-picture footage of raids launched against targets in Occupied Europe. He had already flown several combat missions with other units, and would join the 94th the following day for the attack on Le Bourget. The flight would be bittersweet for him, he confided to his listeners, because after U.S. Army service as an enlisted photographer during World War I he had stayed on in France. He'd spent twenty years in Paris, first as the owner of an English-language news service and later as a promoter of sports events. He'd done pretty well for himself in the French capital, he said, and he still considered it home.[15]

As the meeting broke up, Saltsman took Dickson aside and asked him which aircraft he wanted to fly in the following day. Smiling slowly, the photographer replied, "Which is least likely to turn back?" Without missing a beat, the squadron commander responded, "Purdy's." Dickson said that sounded fine to him, and asked Saltsman to introduce him to the bomber's crew. Minutes later, Dickson was seated at a makeshift picnic table outside the enlisted men's club, sharing a beer with the ten men of *Salty's Naturals*. He told them that for takeoff and landing he would sit on the floor in Chuck Sprague's radio room, but for most of the mission he would be in the nose or moving throughout the aircraft—using one of the walk-around oxygen bottles—and would be shooting footage with a handheld 16mm movie camera. He would try not to get in anyone's way, he said, but if he did, they should feel free to just shove him aside—but not too hard, or he'd have to pay for the broken camera. His easy humor and relaxed manner immediately put the others at ease, and when the "official" discussion was over Dickson sat with Joe Cornwall and a couple of the other enlisted men in the warmth of an English summer afternoon, drinking beer and talking of home and of Dickson's life in Paris. Later, after dinner, Dickson joined Purdy and *Salty's Naturals'* three other officers for more conversation and a nightcap.[16]

It proved to be a short night for all concerned, however.

JUST AFTER TWO O'CLOCK ON THE MORNING OF JULY 14, A LONE FIGURE walked down the narrow gravel pathway leading to the hastily constructed Nissen huts that were home to the officers and men of the 331st Bomb Squadron. Though dawn would bring the warmth of summer, at that hour it was cool and misty. Wearing a fleece-lined flying jacket to ward off the chill, the man carried a nearly empty enamel mug of coffee in one gloved hand, a red-lensed flashlight in the other, and a wooden clipboard wedged securely beneath one arm.

Threading his way carefully between the bicycles haphazardly arrayed near the door of the first hut, he drained the mug and shoved it into one of the jacket's two large exterior pockets. After pausing briefly to take in the smell of the night air—a combination of loamy earthiness from nearby farm fields and the faint but unmistakable tang of high-octane aviation gasoline—the man ran the flashlight's subdued beam down the list of names on the clipboard. Satisfied, he opened the hut's door, pushed aside the suspended hunk of old drapery that served as both blackout curtain and draft preventer, then snapped on the lights and started bellowing in his best drill-field voice.

"Rise and shine gentlemen. Breakfast at zero-two-thirty, briefing at zero-three-thirty!" He repeated his message twice more, then, his task done, he strode back out the door and moved on down the path to rouse other crewmen.

Jolted from sleep, the twelve occupants of the hut—the enlisted men of *Salty's Naturals* and *Good Time Cholly II*, the bomber in which Saltsman was to fly the mission—each greeted the new day with a quiet groan, or a shallow cough or a softly muttered string of inventive profanities. Tossing back their rough wool blankets, the men rolled out of their narrow beds and gasped as their feet hit the hut's cold wooden floor. Tendrils of smoke soon curled into the air from the first cigarettes of the day as the men slipped lightweight coveralls over their heavy cotton underwear, shoved their now sock-encased feet into fleece-lined boots, and donned leather flying jackets, the back of each one adorned with the name of the man's aircraft and hand-painted bomb symbols indicating the number of times its owner had faced death in the hostile skies above German-occupied Europe. Dressed but not yet fully awake, the men shuffled out the door and headed for the chow hall, Joe Cornwall walking with his friends Dick Davitt—*Good Time Cholly II*'s flight engineer and top turret gunner—and Staff Sergeant Harry Eastman, *Cholly*'s thirty-four-year-old left waist gunner, whom Cornwall and Davitt affectionately called "Old Man Harry" both because of his age and his premature baldness.[17] The three men spent much of their free time together, and jokingly referred to themselves as the "Gunner Trio."

After a breakfast of powdered eggs, Spam, toast, and copious amounts of coffee, the three friends walked to the briefing hall. All of the 94th's twenty operational Fortresses had been scheduled for the day's mission, so the large space was packed with two hundred crewmen—officers on folding chairs toward the front, enlisted men on long wooden benches in the back. Some of the aviators were animated and talking loudly; others sat quietly, gazing toward the covered map boards at the front of the room; and still others sat hunched, looking downward with unfocused eyes. At exactly 3:30 A.M. a senior NCO shouted "Attention!" as Castle strode in, followed by his squadron commanders, the group intelligence and weather officers, and, bringing up the rear, Jeff Dickson. After the group reached the small raised dais at the front of the room Castle turned to face his men, barked "As you were!" and took his own seat as the gathered aviators sat down, lit cigarettes, and waited to hear the details of what most hoped would be a "milk run"—an easy mission from which men and aircraft would most likely return unscathed.

As soon as the group intelligence officer pulled back the drapes masking the largest map board it was clear to all in the room that VIII Bomber Command Mission No. 73 would be no milk run. Three lengths of black string—one each for the group's lead, high, and low squadrons—started at Rougham and stretched southward, skirting London to the east and then turning slightly west to hit the English Channel near the Isle of Wight. The strings then turned southeast, crossed the Channel, and reached the French coast at a spot halfway between Dieppe and Le Havre in Normandy. At Évreux the black lines turned sharply to the northeast, tracing a straight course to a point some twenty-four miles northwest of central Paris. There the lines changed direction again, directly toward Le Bourget, eight miles northeast of the capital. Up to that point the strings had indicated the formation's "ingress route," but from the target on they marked the "egress" route. After plunging straight southeastward of Paris, at Evry the black lines turned northwest, crossed the French coast south of Le Havre, and at the Isle of Wight turned back toward Rougham, basically reversing the first leg of the outbound journey.

The briefing room had fallen eerily quiet as the gathered airmen took in the information depicted by the long black strings, and most of those present understood the reasons for the apparently circuitous route. Not only would it allow the formation to avoid the heavy German flak belts that fronted the English Channel from upper Normandy to southern Holland, it would mean that the escorting RAF Spitfires—most of which were based in southern England—could stay on the ground until the last minute, conserving their fuel and thus being able to stay with the bombers longer after joining up.

But most of the men in the briefing room also immediately saw the drawbacks of the planned route. Though perhaps not so well protected by antiaircraft batteries as upper Normandy and the Pas de Calais, lower Normandy was by no means defenseless. The region between the Channel coast and Paris was home to several German fighter fields—all of which were defended by significant numbers of flak guns—and the Luftwaffe could always be counted on to fiercely engage any incoming threat. Moreover, the greater Paris region was among the most heavily defended areas in German-occupied Europe, with layered antiaircraft defenses backed up by still more fighter fields. And while the route would indeed allow the escorting Spitfires to remain with the formation longer than they might otherwise be able to, the nimble British fighters would still have to turn back long before the bombers reached Le Bourget. Finally, more than a few of the men in the room were puzzled and not a little dismayed by the fact that the mission route was not all that different from the one followed on the unsuccessful July 10 raid. Once German radar detected the formation's general heading, they worried, wouldn't Luftwaffe ground controllers be able to guess the formation's destination and deploy fighters accordingly?[18]

Castle gave the airmen a few additional moments to take in the information displayed on the large map, then stepped forward, cleared his throat, and gave the gathered aircrews a broad overview of the mission's purpose and execution. Le Bourget and the other airfields targeted by the 4th Wing were vital to the Luftwaffe's ability to operate and maintain fighter aircraft over France and the Low Countries, he said, and destroying or severely damaging the installations would allow the USAAF and RAF to further ramp up the Combined Bomber Offensive. That, in turn, would hasten the day when Allied forces could land in France and begin the long and undoubtedly hard process of freeing all of Europe from the Nazi yoke. His remarks concluded, Castle released all the enlisted gunners from the remainder of the briefing. The group's operations, intelligence, and weather officers then spent the following hour providing the pilots, navigators, and bombardiers with the details each would need for the mission.

Being excused from the briefing did not mean that Joe Cornwall and his fellow gunners could relax until takeoff time. Outside the briefing hall the men split into two groups, with the top turret, ball turret, and tail gunners boarding trucks that would take them directly to the hardstands where their aircraft were being fueled and loaded with the sixteen 300-pound general-purpose bombs each Fortress would later drop on Le Bourget. The turret and tail guns normally remained in place between missions, and the gunners manning those positions used the preflight time to load the weapons and check the mechanical operation of the turrets.

Joe and the other "flexible gunners," on the other hand, boarded a second truck that took them to the squadron armory, where each man signed out the .50-caliber M2 machine gun he would use to defend his aircraft. The gunners for each Fortress also signed out the three weapons that would be installed in the bomber's nose and manned by the bombardier and navigator. Though all of the flexible guns had been cleaned by their operators after the previous mission, Joe and his colleagues nevertheless dismantled and closely inspected each weapon, not trusting the gun's operation—and their lives—to whomever had previously signed it out. Once satisfied, Joe and the others loaded the weapons aboard a truck, then climbed in themselves for the ride to the hardstand area, where each weapon was installed in its proper location.

At about 5:15 A.M. a crowded jeep rolled to a stop near the nose of *Salty's Naturals* and off hopped Ed Purdy, the crew's other three officers, and Jeff Dickson. As the ground crew did their final mechanical checks and the ordnance specialists winched the last few bombs into the Fortress's open bay, Purdy called his men together near the B-17's nose. The pilot reviewed the broad outlines of the mission, ensured that none of the men had discovered any new mechanical issues, then wished them all good luck. After tugging bright-blue, electrically heated flying suits over their coveralls and then donning fleece-lined flying pants and jackets, each man pulled a bright yellow "Mae West" life jacket over his head. Next came a heavy stitched-canvas parachute harness—the chutes themselves were stored in strategic positions throughout the aircraft—followed by gloves and fleece-lined leather flying helmets fitted with radio earphones for the gunners and Jeff Dickson, while the crew's officers retained their stylishly "crushed" dress caps.[19]

Once suitably attired, the men of *Salty's Naturals* boarded their aircraft. The "front office" crew—Ed Purdy, copilot Carroll Harris, navigator Charlie Lichtenberger, bombardier Ed Jones, and flight engineer/top turret gunner Rick Marquardt—pulled themselves upward through the hatch on the left side of the bomber's nose, just forward of and below the cockpit. Radio operator Chuck Sprague, photographer Jeff Dickson, ball turret gunner John Smith, and waist gunners Joe Cornwall and Frank Santangelo had an easier entry, clambering into the aft fuselage through the crew door just forward of the horizontal stabilizer on the right side of the Fortress. Tail gunner Larry Templeton, the only crew member with a personal entrance, boarded through a small, hinged hatch directly aft of the right-side crew door, beneath the broad expanse of the right stabilizer. Upon reaching his position, every man save Smith—who would have to wait until after takeoff to enter the ball turret—plugged the cords for his headphones and flying suit and the long, ribbed hose of his oxygen mask into nearby outlets.

After a quick communications check, and having assured himself that his oxygen would flow when needed, each man removed his mask and settled down to await takeoff. In Joe Cornwall's case, this meant reclining in his favorite spot: sitting atop the slightly raised firing step beneath his left waist gun position, his back against the large wooden box holding the belted ammunition for his machine gun and his legs stretched toward the rear of the fuselage. Directly across from him, in almost the identical position, was the lanky Santangelo, while Smith sat further forward, just to one side of the closed bulkhead door separating the gunners' area from Sprague's radio room. The three men sipped hot coffee from thermoses, each deep in his own thoughts, the warmth of their as-yet-unnecessary heavy flying gear making them drowsy.

Their languor was soon dissipated, however. As takeoff time neared, Purdy and Harris brought *Salty's Naturals* to life, her four Wright Cyclone engines awakening one after the other, each coughing a cloud of acrid, blue-white exhaust smoke that drifted across the field to mingle with the fog created by seventy-six other thundering power plants. The noise rose to an even more deafening crescendo as one by one the 94th's heavily laden B-17s moved slowly off their hardstands in the aircraft dispersal areas and joined the queue of bombers rolling ponderously along the perimeter track encircling the airfield's three intersecting runways.

Castle led the parade of Fortresses, rolling onto the active runway less than a minute ahead of the scheduled takeoff time. At exactly 6 A.M. a green flare shot into the air from the roof of Rougham's control tower, and the group commander smoothly advanced the B-17's four throttles and accelerated down the long strip of concrete. Even before his aircraft lifted off, the next machine in line had begun its own takeoff roll. Within twenty minutes all nineteen bombers that constituted the 94th Bomb Group's contribution to the raid—one aircraft aborted due to a mechanical problem—were in the air and assembling into the stepped, three-squadron formation.

Over the next forty-five minutes the 94th joined up with the three other groups bound for Le Bourget, and by the time the eighty-four B-17s passed over the Isle of Wight and turned east over the Channel they had formed into two combat wings of two groups each, with the wings in the usual staggered box formation. The high squadron of the high group of the high wing was at 25,575 feet, while *Salty's Naturals* and the other two Fortresses in the second element of Saltsman's low-low squadron were cruising at just over 21,000 feet.[20] As soon as the formation crossed the English coast Joe Cornwall and the other gunners sought and received permission to test-fire their guns, and streams of tracer rounds briefly arced across the sunlight sky in all directions. Minutes later, dozens of RAF Spitfire fighters dropped into escort position above and around the eighty-four Fortresses. The arrival of the "Little Friends" was always a welcome event, for though the bomber crewmen knew their formation was formidable they also realized all too well that it was far from invulnerable. They also knew that fuel limitations meant the Spits would not be around for long. And as soon as they left, the predators would arrive in force.

EVEN BEFORE THE RAF FIGHTERS HAD JOINED THE AMERICAN BOMBERS, German air-defense controllers had been tracking the course of the incoming raiders and alerting interceptor squadrons across central France.

Among the first Luftwaffe units dispatched against the Fortress formations was Major Egon Mayer's Jagdgeschwader 2. The fighter wing's pilots had been sitting in their fueled and fully armed aircraft since just before 7 A.M., and at 7:26 were ordered to launch.[21] Within minutes some ninety Fw 190 and Bf 109 fighters were lifting off from the fields at Beaumont-le-Roger and Évreux, with Mayer leading twelve Fw 190s of his headquarters flight. The majority of the interceptors were vectored toward what the fighter controller called "a very large formation" of *Viermots* that had crossed the French coast at Fécamp and was headed southwest, in the direction of Évreux. Mayer estimated that he and his men would be in position to hit the bombers just after they crossed the River Seine about halfway between Le Havre and Rouen, and hoped that the formations were being escorted by Spitfires, rather than the longer-legged American P-47 Thunderbolts.

Mayer was in luck, for the RAF fighters began hitting their fuel limits minutes after the 4th Bomb Wing formation crossed the Seine near Ville-quier. As the Spits began turning back toward the Channel, German controllers vectored interceptors from other units after them, hoping to both bag a few of the nimble British fighters and to prevent them from interfering in any way with the assault Mayer and his men were about to launch. In preparation for that attack, the JG 2 airmen had climbed to 28,000 feet and maneuvered into a position that would allow them to hit the bombers head-on at a point about fifteen miles northwest of Évreux. The bright July sun would be behind and off to the right of the incoming German fighters, and the glare would give them a few extra precious moments of cover before they were sighted and engaged by the Fortress gunners.

The first inkling the men of the 94th Bomb Group had of the impending attack was at 7:40 when Castle, in the lead Fortress, called out a sighting of unidentified fighters crossing ahead of the bomber stream from southwest to northeast at a slightly higher altitude and about three miles distant. He cautioned that they might be "friendlies" that had been escorting some other Allied formation and were now heading back to England, and ordered the group's gunners not to engage them until they had been positively identified as hostile. That confirmation came all too quickly, for no sooner had Castle ended his brief message than the JG 2 aircraft—mostly Fw 190s—turned directly toward the bomber stream and bored in. Some of the fighters engaged the high and lead groups, while others concentrated on the 94th. The first gaggle of attackers scythed through the low group's formation from twelve o'clock high—directly in front of and above the bombers—in tight, three-aircraft "*ketten*," each pilot aiming at the cockpit and nose area of his chosen victim in a three-to-four-second firing run before turning sharply to one side or rolling inverted and passing beneath his target.[22] Once clear of the formation's return fire, the German fighter pilots reversed course, pulled parallel to the bombers and raced ahead for two or three miles, then turned back for another run.

Aboard *Salty's Naturals* the first to call out the incoming fighters was Charlie Lichtenberger. The navigator's shouted warning of "Here they come!" was immediately followed by bursts of fire from the Fortress's nose and top turret guns, and as the German fighters flashed past off the bomber's left side Joe Cornwall and tail gunner Larry Templeton both scored hits.[23] There was no time to savor the moment however, for Rick Marquardt in the top turret called out that a second trio of Fw 190s was boring in toward Saltsman's lead aircraft; all aboard *Salty's Naturals* knew instinctively that their bomber—almost directly behind and slightly below *Good Time Cholly II*—would be squarely in the enemy's gunsights as the fighters screamed through the 331st's formation.

At the moment, however, the Fw 190s were *Cholly's* problem. Several men aboard the squadron lead aircraft had called out the incoming fighters, and as the first attacker closed in, Dick Davitt engaged the German machine with his twin .50-caliber top turret guns. The two streams of thumb-sized rounds converged on the fighter with immediate and spectacular effect: the Fw exploded while still one hundred yards ahead of the formation, and pilot Willis Frank had to quickly raise *Cholly's* left wing to avoid the three large chunks of tumbling, burning debris that were all that remained of the fighter.[24] Frank's quick thinking saved his aircraft—for the moment—but it also doomed *Salty's Naturals*.

Everyone in that Fortress's front end—Purdy and Harris in the cockpit, Marquardt in the top turret, and Jones, Lichtenberger, and photographer Dickson in the nose—almost certainly saw the German fighter disintegrate and likely knew they were helpless to prevent the disaster that was about to engulf them. But all Sprague in the radio room and the gunners in the rear of the B-17 heard was a strangled shout of "Oh my God!" over the intercom just seconds before the Fw's blazing fuselage slammed into the Fortress's left wing. The wreckage and the bomber collided at a closing speed of some 450 miles an hour, and the impact sheared off twenty-five feet of the B-17's wing beyond the No. 1 (outboard) engine.

Two equally catastrophic events occurred within one or two seconds after the collision. The first was the instantaneous detonation of the 100-octane aviation gasoline spewing from the severed lines that moments before had connected the Fortress's main tanks with the nine smaller tanks in the now-vanished outboard wing section. The searing heat immediately and fatally compromised what was left of the wing's internal structure, and a long, roiling tongue of flame and dark black smoke arced back toward the bomber's tail. The second and nearly simultaneous event was the al-most total loss of lift on the B-17's left side, which caused *Salty's Naturals* to snap roll violently to the left, enter a spin, and immediately shed several hundred feet of altitude.

While Ed Purdy must have known that his aircraft was doomed, the young aviator apparently did all he could to pull *Salty's Naturals* out of its death spiral. In flight school, Purdy had learned that under normal circumstances a pilot attempting to recover from a spin should reduce en-gine power to idle to prevent the airflow of the propellers from striking the aircraft's horizontal stabilizer and thereby forcing the nose upward, prolonging the spin. But the loss of the B-17's outboard wing section and resulting radically asymmetrical lift meant that Purdy's only chance to re-cover from the spin was to add full power for as long as possible on the two left engines, shove the right aileron down hard, and put the bomber's rudder as far to the right as it would go. He appears to have successfully performed each action, for after falling about 4,500 feet *Salty's Naturals* leveled out just long enough for two men to jump from the bomber before it once more snap-rolled, and with flames trailing from its mangled wing, headed for the ground.[25]

One of the jumpers was Joe Cornwall.

JOE WAS LOOKING DIRECTLY OUT HIS WAIST WINDOW—TRACKING A TWIN-engine Bf 110 that was pacing the 94th formation, just out of range—when the Fw 190 collided with *Salty's Naturals*. The impact threw Joe and Frank Santangelo to the fuselage floor and away from their guns, the sudden movement disconnecting their interphone cords and oxygen hoses. Neither man had time to move before the bomber's snap-roll lifted them and hurled them against the ceiling, where the intense centrifugal force caused by the aircraft's gyrations kept them momentarily pinned in place. Seconds later, as Ed Purdy's efforts in the cockpit began to have an effect, the gunners again crashed to the hard floor, with Frank landing atop Joe's legs. Though to that point the experience was much like what had happened to the waist gunners on the Kiel raid, both men intuitively understood that *Salty's Naturals* would not be returning to Rougham this time. Not waiting for the bailout bell, the airmen struggled to reach the parachute packs stowed in small metal racks just aft of their respective waist windows.[26] The short journey was complicated by the bomber's continuing convolutions, by the hundreds of expended .50-caliber machine-gun cartridges flying around the fuselage interior like a swarm of very angry brass bees, and by the first stages of anoxia resulting from oxygen deprivation.

Upon finally reaching the stowage rack, each gunner snapped the two large metal hooks on the back of the chest-pack parachute into the D-rings on the front of his harness. After a quick check to ensure that the chutes were firmly attached and not damaged, Joe and Frank crawled to the crew entry door on the right side of the rear fuselage.[27] Frank pulled the emergency release lever that sent the door spinning away, then dived head-first after it. Joe paused for a moment and, assuming that everyone who was capable of leaving the ship had, hurled himself into space.[28]

Like all USAAF aircrew, Joe had undergone parachute training before attaining flight status. The instruction had been rudimentary, consisting mainly of how to correctly wear the harness, how to attach the chest-pack chute, and how to influence the speed and direction of descent by pulling on the suspension lines that connected the chest pack to the inflated canopy. What the training hadn't included was an actual jump—so when Joe abandoned *Salty's Naturals* he encountered an entirely new range of sensations. The first was the panic-inducing feeling of tumbling uncontrollably through the air, thousands of feet above the ground, green earth and blue sky changing places every few seconds.

As disorienting and frightening as the roughly 160-feet-per-second free fall was, however, Joe judged that he was still above 10,000 feet and delayed opening his chute for a few moments so that he could more quickly get down into breathable air.[29] Some thirty seconds after leaving the bomber he brought his elbows tightly into his sides, forced his knees and ankles together to bring his feet directly below him, and, once upright, used his right hand to pull the bright aluminum ripcord handle protruding from the chute pack. That action brought on yet another new sensation: the deployment of the pack's small drogue chute was followed immediately by the opening of the main canopy, jerking Joe to a virtual standstill. The sudden deceleration wrenched his back, sending sharp jolts of searing pain through both shoulders, and the lower straps of the harness bit painfully into his groin. The g-forces and the pain in his upper body momentarily made it difficult for him to raise his arms to grasp the suspension lines. Once he had control of the chute he looked beneath him, where he saw Santangelo's fully deployed canopy. Off to one side and a few thousand feet below he saw *Salty's Naturals* slowing spinning toward the ground, a long plume of greasy black and gray smoke marking its final passage through the morning sky. Suddenly, a parachute blossomed from the dying bomber's tail section, and with a surge of relief Joe realized that Larry Templeton had made it out.

The tail gunner's escape and been a close-run thing, however. When Joe and Frank jumped, Larry was slumped forward and to one side in his cramped tail gun position, unconscious. The B-17's collision with the Fw 190 and subsequent spin had thrown him violently sideways, knocking his oxygen mask out of position and inflicting a significant cut over his eye. As he struggled to get back into position he caught a brief glimpse of flames streaming back from the aircraft's left wing, then passed out from anoxia. When Larry came to, the plane was again in a spin and had lost considerable altitude. He hurriedly unhooked his seatbelt, slipped backward off his bicycle-style seat, and crawled the few feet to the small escape hatch under the right stabilizer. He pulled his parachute from its stowage rack and, knowing the ground must be perilously close, attached only one of the chest pack's two buckles to his harness before jettisoning the hatch's small door and tumbling out. As soon as he cleared the aircraft he pulled the ripcord, and before his chute blossomed fully he caught a glimpse of someone swinging beneath an open canopy far above him.[30] Larry assumed that the other members of the crew must have bailed out well before he had, and were likely already on the ground. Unfortunately, he was sadly mistaken.

For reasons that will remain forever unknown, seven of the eight men in the forward section of *Salty's Naturals* never made it out of the doomed bomber. It's entirely possible that the three in the B-17's nose—Ed Jones, Charlie Lichtenberger, and Jeff Dickson—and top turret gunner Rick Marquardt were either seriously injured or killed outright by debris from the demolished German fighter, or were prevented by centrifugal force from reaching their designated escape hatches. Purdy and Harris would have had their hands full trying to hold the B-17 steady so that others could bail out, and may themselves have been unable to move from their seats once *Salty's Naturals* reentered a spin. For ball turret gunner John Smith, just getting out of his cramped fighting position and up into the aircraft's fuselage would have been a Herculean task. If there were still electrical power to operate the turret, Smith would have rotated the ball so that its guns pointed straight down and the entry hatch was inside the aircraft. But if the B-17's electrical systems had failed—a more than likely possibility given the extensive damage *Salty's Naturals* had suffered—the gunner would have had to hand-crank the turret into the proper position in order to escape. Smith's efforts may have been greatly hampered, of course, by injuries, disorientation, or anoxia. In the end, all we know for certain is that he never took to his parachute.[31]

And in one of those cruel ironies that are so widespread in wartime, the one man in the B-17's forward fuselage who did manage to escape fell victim to an all-too-common hazard. While it is unclear how radio operator Chuck Sprague actually exited the Fortress—his normal route was through the bomb bay, but the doors were never opened—it is certain that he pulled his ripcord before he was fully clear of the aircraft. When the spring-loaded drogue chute popped out it briefly hung up on something—a gun mount perhaps, or a jagged piece of damaged fuselage— that hampered the proper deployment of the suspension lines. They, in turn, wrapped around the canopy, fouling it and preventing its inflation.

With no secondary parachute to save him, Sprague fell thousands of feet to his death, the useless folds of silk flapping above him.[32]

As abrupt and horrific as the demise of *Salty's Naturals* had been, the continuing attacks by German fighters meant that the men in the 94th Group's other Fortresses didn't have long to ponder the fate of the dying bomber's crew. Within minutes after the Fw collided with Purdy's aircraft a second B-17—flown by Kee Harrison—was in deep trouble.[33] And the Luftwaffe pilot most intent on the Fortress's destruction was Germany's leading bomber-killer—Egon Mayer.

On his second head-on pass through the 94th Group's formation, Mayer had focused his attention on the lead squadron. He'd snapped off a few rounds at Castle's aircraft, but then shifted to the leader of the second element. Seeing that the Fw was coming directly at him, Harrison had pushed the B-17's nose down and the 20mm rounds that Mayer had intended for the cockpit instead slammed into the upper fuselage just in front of and to one side of the top turret. Though the gunner was miraculously unhurt, the fusillade sparked an intense fire directly behind Harrison's seat. The copilot, Second Lieutenant David Turner, immediately extinguished the flames, but dense smoke filled the entire front end of the B-17. Unable to see the instrument panel, Harrison moved the bomber away from the formation to avoid a collision.[34]

Seeing the Fortress's predicament, Mayer brought his fighter around on the bomber's tail and began pumping rounds into the vertical stabilizer, shredding the rudder. The German pilot then shifted his fire, knocking out two of the aircraft's four engines and blowing huge, ragged holes in the trailing edge of the right wing. The Fortress began losing altitude, and Mayer and several of his colleagues followed it down, taking turns raking it with cannon and machine-gun fire.[35] In the bomber's cockpit Harrison was doing what he could to throw off the Germans' aim, rolling the aircraft from side to side and using what was left of the rudder to jink right and left. As the B-17 neared 5,000 feet Harrison decided it was time to get his crew out. He rang the alarm bell, and the navigator and bombardier—lieutenants Robert Conroy and Roscoe Greene—quickly left the Fortress, opening their chutes immediately. The pilot himself was preparing to leave his seat when Turner, the copilot, told him that the top turret gunner couldn't bail out because his parachute had been destroyed in the fire following the initial attack. Not wanting to leave the man to die in a pilotless airplane, Harrison decided to crash-land the bomber and over the intercom told the remaining crewmen to brace for impact.

THE GERMAN ASSAULT ON KEE HARRISON'S AIRCRAFT WAS CLEARLY VISIBLE from the cockpit of *Good Time Cholly II,* and Ralph Saltsman was trying to keep an eye on the rapidly descending Fortress when *Cholly* itself became the focus of the Luftwaffe's attention.

A *ketten* of Fw 190s came barreling straight at the 331st's lead ship, their 20mm cannon rounds arcing toward *Cholly*'s cockpit, Saltsman later recalled, like "a series of hot rivets."[36] The explosive shells pounded into the bomber's dorsal fin and horizontal stabilizer, blowing holes in the B-17's metal skin and the fabric covering the control surfaces and, more importantly, severing the control lines that stretched from the cockpit to the tail. Saltsman and Willis Frank immediately lost lateral control, and *Cholly* began drifting out of formation and losing altitude. Frank, in his capacity as aircraft commander, decided that the Fortress could not be saved. Keying his intercom, he told the crew to "hit the silk boys, she's a dead duck!"[37]

The navigator and bombardier, lieutenants John Wholley and Thurman Burnett, had donned their chute packs as the first German rounds had chewed into the B-17's aft fuselage, and as soon as they heard Frank's bail-out command they both turned toward the nose escape hatch, just a few feet behind them in the short tunnel leading to the flight deck. Wholley went first, and as he crawled his boot accidentally pulled the ripcord on Burnett's chute, which immediately popped out, filling the aft part of the nose compartment. Lying belly down in the tunnel, Wholley was unable to completely jettison the escape hatch door, so he simply pushed his way past it and fell headfirst away from the aircraft.

Burnett was attempting to bundle his chute in his arms when Dick Davitt dropped into the tunnel from the flight deck end. The top turret gunner helped the bombardier gather the few remaining loose folds of the nylon canopy, then, with a wry smile, politely motioned for the officer to go out first through the escape hatch. Burnett grinned in return, then dropped out into space. Davitt sat hunched over in the narrow tunnel for a moment, waiting for Saltsman and Frank, until a sudden lurch of the aircraft smacked his head against a metal bulkhead, knocking him out. He regained consciousness several minutes later, swinging gently beneath his canopy in breathable air and having absolutely no idea how he'd managed to open his chute.[38]

Davitt's departure—and that of most of *Cholly*'s crew—turned out to be a bit premature, however. Moments after Frank's intercom announcement, Saltsman had countermanded the bail-out order—without realizing that most everyone aboard the aircraft had already disconnected their headsets in preparation for leaving the bomber.

Though *Cholly*'s increasingly serious control issues had left it some 2,000 feet below and several hundred yards to one side of the formation, all four engines were still running normally and "Salty" believed the aircraft might actually make it to the target. He and Frank were in the process of trying to counter the lateral control problem by readjusting the power settings on the bomber's four Wright Cyclones when a German fighter zoomed up from below and raked the B-17's belly from nose to tail with cannon and machine-gun fire. Incendiary rounds slammed into the oxygen bottles anchored to the fuselage walls on either side of the now-unmanned top turret, and bright orange flames immediately flashed through the cockpit. Now convinced the B-17 couldn't be saved, Saltsman took to the intercom to order the crew to abandon the aircraft. In the waist, Harry Eastman— who had chosen to stay at his gun until the last possible moment—clicked his chute pack into place and went out the already open aft crew hatch. He was the third member of the Gunner Trio to hit the silk within less than ten minutes.

In *Cholly*'s cockpit, Willis Frank had been attempting to attach his chute to his harness when he, too, accidentally pulled the ripcord and his chute deployed in the cramped area near the nose hatch. With no alternative, the young aviator gathered the open chute in his arms and held it tightly as he went out the hatch. Once clear of the bomber he simply opened his arms and let gravity and air pressure do the rest. Saltsman had followed Frank down from the cockpit and was poised near the hatch when *Cholly* suddenly lurched downward. "Salty" was thrown backward, and had just started to pull himself back into position when another violent movement tossed him headfirst out the hatch and away from the now fiercely burning Fortress. He delayed opening his chute until he thought he was below 10,000 feet, then yanked the ripcord. He had just enough time to see his canopy inflate properly—and to count seven other open parachutes in the sky around him—before anoxia began to overcome him. As Saltsman passed out, it occurred to him that he'd misjudged his altitude.[39]

AFTER *GOOD TIME CHOLLY II* STARTED LOSING ALTITUDE, THE THREE Fortresses remaining out of the original five low-squadron machines carried on with the mission, with First Lieutenant Floyd Watts as the new element leader. All of the men aboard the trio of bombers now inhabiting "Purple Heart Corner" must have been understandably shaken by the rapid loss of *Salty's Naturals* and *Cholly* and the apparent demise of Kee Harrison's Fortress, and were certainly hoping that the worst of the German fighter attacks were over. Such was not the case, however.

Some ten minutes after Watts took over as element leader a gaggle of Fw 190s came roaring in from dead ahead, with the lead fighter firing as it came. The No. 3 engine on Watts's Fortress was knocked out, forcing the B-17 to slowly drop out of position. A second attack killed the bomber's two waist gunners, destroyed the intercom system, and punctured the oil tanks for the two left engines, which quickly seized up and stopped. The bomber could not possibly stay in the air with only one operable Wright Cyclone, so Watts salvoed the aircraft's bombs, then hit the bailout bell and held the B-17 as steady as he could while his crew abandoned the ship.[40] The pilot himself waited to leave until the aircraft had descended below 10,000 feet and opened his parachute at what he later estimated to be 8,000 feet. Once he had control of the canopy he quickly spotted his Fortress, which to his horror was by then a flaming torch arcing straight toward the center of a seemingly peaceful French town.[41]

THOUGH THE 94TH BOMB GROUP ULTIMATELY MANAGED TO SUCCESSFULLY bomb Le Bourget, Egon Mayer and the pilots of JG 2 had ensured that July 14 was indeed a very bad Bastille Day for the Americans. In less than twenty minutes four B-17s had been brought down, and forty-one men would not be returning to Rougham. Of those, ten aviators were dead and fourteen were destined to spend the remainder of the war in German prisoner-of-war camps.[42]

For the remaining seventeen crew members, the following days, weeks, and months would be spent on the run, desperately trying to evade capture by the Germans and ultimately return to England. While all of the evaders would have the help of the French Resistance, only a handful would encounter the Morins of Invalides. And of those fortunate few, only one would find a love that would transcend time.

Chapter 4

MEN ON THE RUN

T HOUGH GLAD TO HAVE ESCAPED *SALTY'S NATURALS* AND HEARTENED by the sudden appearance of Larry Templeton's parachute from the tail of the doomed bomber, Joe Cornwall knew that his own continued survival was by no means assured. The sun-dappled fields, woodlands, and small villages spread out in all directions beneath him looked both idyllic and benign, but Joe knew that German troops were already organizing sweeps across the countryside in search of American aviators who may have survived the downing of their aircraft. He understood full well that capture by the enemy would at best result in spending years in a prisoner-of-war camp, and at worst could mean a bullet to the back of the head and burial in an unmarked grave.

Nor were the Germans the only danger. The men of the Eighth Air Force had been briefed on the many fissures that ran through French society, and were well aware that many in France not only tolerated the German occupation, they actively supported it. The American aviators had been warned of the existence of several French fascist paramilitary organizations—most notably the Milice française—that were often even more brutal in their treatment of resistance fighters and captured Allied personnel than were the Germans. U.S. aircrew members were instructed that, if possible, they should covertly observe French civilians and their homes for some time before approaching them, the better to determine whether the people posed a threat. Even if the aviators were welcomed and given food, they were told, they shouldn't entirely let their guard down—French civilians could be executed for helping Allied personnel, so even individuals who hated the Germans and their collaborationist lack-eys might opt to betray downed aviators simply to protect themselves and their families.

While the escape and evasion briefings Joe and his colleagues received emphasized extreme caution when dealing with civilians in German-occupied Europe, the aviators were also assured that there were well-organized escape lines operating across the Continent. The organizations might consist of several dozen people, they were told, but were built around loosely affiliated cells of six or eight individuals who knew and trusted each other. The cell members would know very little about the larger organi-zation, to prevent them from betraying the group under torture, and the American airmen were warned explicitly that asking too many questions about an escape line's members, organization, or operations could lead to the aviator being seen as a German spy. Such a determination, Joe and the others were told, could lead to summary execution.

Making contact with an escape line's members—called "helpers" by the Allies—was more likely if the downed aviator headed east, away from the fortified and heavily patrolled coast, intelligence officials said. If shot down over northern or central France, aircrews were told, they should try to make their way toward one of the major cities—especially Paris—both because they would blend in far better than they might in a small town, and because the escape lines were more active in the larger metropolitan areas.

Members of Eighth Air Force combat crews were also provided with a variety of items meant to improve the odds of making a successful "home run" should their aircraft go down in enemy territory. In addition to a standard personal first aid kit, these included several passport-sized pho-tos of the aviator in civilian clothes—intended for use in forged identity papers provided by the escape line—an easily concealable map of northern France printed on silk, a small compass, matches, Benzedrine tablets to combat exhaustion, and one or two bars of chocolate. Also included was a small zippered purse containing French currency—in Joe's case, 2,000 francs—to be used for bribes or to purchase necessary items.

All of the advice about how to become a successful "evader" was swirl-ing in Joe's head as he floated ever closer to the soil of German-occupied

France, but he knew that his most immediate concern was getting on the ground without breaking a leg. After a quick scan of the surrounding sky—neither Santangelo's chute nor Templeton's was still visible— he focused his attention on the fast-approaching earth, pulled his heels and knees together, and slightly bent his knees. Seconds later he slammed down in the middle of a grain field, about a half mile southeast from where the scattered wreckage of *Salty's Naturals* burned furiously.[1] White-hot needles of pain shot up Joe's spine and across his shoulders, but he stood up immediately, and after gathering his chute in his arms he ran toward a nearby wood line. Once under cover of the trees he knelt and buried his harness, life jacket, and parachute in a shallow hole he scraped out with his hands, and he was just standing up when the bombs in the hulk of the blazing Fortress began "cooking off." The explosions could be heard for miles in every direction, and Joe knew he had to get moving before the detonations attracted German troops.

Thinking the enemy would likely scour the woods and villages in the vicinity of the crash site, Joe decided to put the small river he'd seen from the air between him and the final resting place of *Salty's Naturals*—and of the men he was fairly certain had gone down with it. A quick glance at his wristwatch told him it was just a few minutes after eight, and he was momentarily surprised. His Bastille Day had begun six hours earlier and 250 miles to the northwest in the relative safety of rural Sussex, and had already been filled with myriad sights, sensations, and emotions with which he hadn't even begun to grapple. There would be time later to deal with all that, he told himself, because the most important thing now was to move, as fast and as far as possible.

After taking a quick look at his escape map, Joe decided on a northeast bearing toward the Iton River.[2] He had just started walking when a middle-aged French woman appeared ahead, obviously as surprised to see him as he was to see her. The woman peered at Joe for a moment, taking in the fleece-lined pants and jacket he was still wearing, then cautiously motioned him forward. She spoke for a moment in quick French, the only word of which Joe understood was "Americain." He nodded his head enthusiastically, repeating the word while at the same time pulling from his jacket pocket the small box of escape aids and the zippered purse. The woman seemed to take these as proof of his nationality, and as she turned to walk back the way she'd come she gestured for Joe to follow her.

A few minutes' walk brought the pair to what was apparently the woman's home, set back in a clearing, and after standing quietly for a moment to ensure that no one was nearby, she gestured for Joe to follow her inside. She pantomimed eating, and when Joe smiled and nodded the woman set a large slice of rough dark bread and a mug of milk on the long table that dominated the room. After finishing the impromptu meal, the airman gestured his thanks and, when it became clear the woman could offer no further help, he walked to the door. Pointing to a small barn on the other side of the yard, Joe rested his head on his hands as if sleeping. The woman nodded her assent, and within a few moments Joe was stretched out on the barn's hay-covered floor. He hadn't really intended to sleep, only while away the time until dark, but the morning's exertions ensured that drowsiness soon overtook him. As he drifted off, he could hear the sound of German fighters circling the funeral pyre of *Salty's Naturals*.[3]

JOE CORNWALL WAS NOT, OF COURSE, THE ONLY MEMBER OF THE 94TH Bomb Group on the run that morning. As he slept, more than a dozen other of the unit's aviators were doing everything possible to avoid capture by the Germans—though not all would succeed. The closest, in terms of physical proximity to the place Joe landed, was his crewmate Larry Templeton.

The diminutive tail gunner had pulled his ripcord as soon as he'd cleared the aft escape hatch on *Salty's Naturals*, and his chute had barely opened fully when he heard the B-17 slam into the ground. Templeton touched down just seconds later, about 150 feet from the aircraft's blazing wreckage. Unhurt except for the gash above his eye, he scooped up his chute and ran toward a stand of trees some two hundred yards away on a steep hillside. No German aircraft had yet arrived over the crash site, but as he ran the gunner noticed another parachute at what he later estimated to be 3,000 feet, and a B-17 flying level at low altitude with several German fighters taking turns attacking it from behind.[4]

After entering the woods Templeton kept moving until he crested the hill, and soon after starting down the other side he heard a series of explosions that he assumed were the bombs still aboard *Salty's Naturals.* At the bottom of the hill the tail gunner stopped long enough to remove his harness and throw it and the parachute into a ditch. He quickly moved on, and about five minutes later tossed his leather helmet and Mae West behind a log.

Templeton determined that he had moved far enough from the crash site that he could chance going back up the hill, believing he was less likely to be discovered than on the flat ground. The climb back up the hillside was more tiring than he had expected, however, and about halfway to the top he decided to stop and rest. He wiggled his way into a clump of foliage and settled in and, after eating some of the chocolate from his escape kit, he dozed off.

SLEEP WAS AT THAT MOMENT THE LAST THING ON KEE HARRISON'S MIND—IT was his aircraft that Templeton had seen at low level and being pursued by a gaggle of Fw 190s.

Having made the decision to crash-land the Fortress, Harrison lowered the aircraft's landing gear as a sign to the German fighters that he was giving up the fight and that they should stop their attacks. He passed the word that his gunners should also cease fire, unaware that the intercom had been knocked out soon after he'd told the crew about his plan to land the bomber. As a result, the tail and waist gunners continued to throw rounds at the attackers and they, in turn, continued to pound the B-17 with cannon and machine-gun fire. Harrison realized that he needed to get the plane on the ground as soon as possible if he and his crew were to have a chance of surviving, so he retracted the airplane's gear, picked out what looked like a suitably flat and unobstructed field, and took the ship down for a belly landing. Within minutes the Fortress was bumping along through a wheat field, its props bent backward at odd angles and the now vacant ball turret crushed upward into the fuselage. The B-17 had come to earth just under a mile to the southwest of the hamlet of Bérengeville-la-Campagne, just off the 94th Group's flight path and about three and a half miles northwest of where the remains of *Salty's Naturals* still blazed.[5]

As soon as Harrison's aircraft slid to a halt, all those still aboard scattered into the surrounding countryside. The pilot stayed with the bomber only long enough to push the buttons in the cockpit that were supposed to initiate the aircraft's destruction, then removed his parachute harness and life vest and clambered out through the cockpit window—quite a feat of agility, considering Harrison's fire-plug physique.[6] Once on the ground outside the Fortress, he ran into a nearby stand of trees and burrowed into a thicket. He lay there for five hours as German troops moved through the woods around him, obviously searching for downed aviators. And though Harrison wasn't aware of it, the failure of the bomber's self-destruct mechanism had made it possible for another German to take a personal interest in the crash-landed B-17—Egon Mayer had driven out from Beaumont-le-Roger to personally inspect the aircraft, which he had claimed as his fourteenth *Viermot*.[7]

Once Harrison was sure the German searchers had moved on, he slowly left his hiding place and moved some two miles across several cultivated fields to another small wood. He had just settled in under a tangle of brush when he saw a group of French civilians running in the direction of his downed aircraft. After taking a deep breath to steady himself, he carefully straightened up so they could see him. The people noticed him but kept moving, so he returned to his hide. Not long afterward a teenaged boy arrived, located Harrison, and gave the American some food and civilian clothing. The stocky pilot quickly changed out of his flying outfit, and he and the boy settled down to wait for dark.

"Salty" Saltsman's misjudgment about his altitude after leaving *Good Time Cholly II* had caused him to pass out from anoxia soon after his canopy opened—and he only regained consciousness when he landed with a "terrific jolt" in a large patch of flowers in the middle of a field surrounded by woods. Slightly disoriented, it took him a moment to realize that his now collapsed parachute was streamed out behind him, rustling in the breeze. Knowing the canopy's movement might well attract unwanted attention, he unbuckled his harness, gathered his chute in a bundle, and then lay atop it while he dug a hole using the blade of his small penknife. After pushing the chute and life jacket into the hole he covered them with dirt, then crawled to an adjacent wheat field he hoped would offer better concealment.[8]

After settling himself in a furrow surrounded by tall wheat, Saltsman realized that he had a small shell fragment embedded in one arm, and that in the cockpit fire he had suffered minor but irritating burns on his forehead and around his eyes. He pulled a tube of milk paste from his first aid kit and applied the creamy substance to his burns, then wrapped his silk aviator's scarf around the affected area. The pilot then swallowed a Benzedrine tablet to keep himself from falling asleep in the warmth of the morning sun.

Knowing that it was a French holiday, Saltsman was surprised about an hour later to see two teenaged boys on a spray wagon, moving slowly through the field. Once they neared his position he whistled to attract their attention, but they motioned him to stay down and moved off. Thirty minutes later one of the boys came crawling through the wheat to where Saltsman lay, and with hand signals indicated that there were many Germans in the area and that someone would come back when it was safe.

The boy himself returned an hour later, and motioned Saltsman to follow him. They crawled about two hundred yards to a small wood, not far from a farmhouse near the village of Houlbec-Cocherel. There Saltsman was delighted to find *Cholly*'s radio operator, Technical Sergeant Robert Mabie, who had landed near the house, which belonged to the boy's family, the Girardels.[9] The two Americans were given bread and some wine, and directed to hide in a tangled thicket until further assistance arrived later in the day. Despite their best intentions to stay awake and alert, the exhausted aviators soon drifted off to sleep. About four thirty in the afternoon members of the Girardel family returned with bread, milk, and raw eggs, and Saltsman and Mabie crawled out of the thicket to the base of a large tree to enjoy the impromptu meal.

Later in the evening the sound of movement on a nearby road caused the Girardels to hurriedly disperse in all directions. The Americans moved farther into the woods, and about ten minutes later they were suddenly surrounded by German troops. As they were being searched the officer in charge smiled at them and said, "For you, gentlemen, the war is over."

Saltsman and Mabie were put aboard a truck that already contained Willis Frank and *Cholly*'s tail gunner, Warren Jones. The aviators were taken to the Luftwaffe airfield at Évreux, where Saltsman's injuries were treated and he was told that four other members of his crew had also been captured. After spending the night in a civilian prison in the city, on the morning of July 15 Saltsman, Mabie, Frank, and Jones boarded another truck, this one ultimately bound for a Luftwaffe-run POW camp for Allied aviators. As Saltsman settled in for the ride into captivity, he was at least able to take heart from one thing: two members of *Cholly*'s crew were apparently still free.

Those men were Dick Davitt and Harry Eastman.

THE TWO GUNNERS HAD LEFT *GOOD TIME CHOLLY II* WITHIN A FEW MINUTES of each other, though Davitt was unaware he'd done so until he came to, suspended beneath a canopy he had no memory of deploying. His head pounding from a combination of anoxia and the thump that had knocked him out, he looked quickly around and noticed two other open parachutes above him and off to what he assumed was the east. Davitt also noticed that his own chute had a half-dozen dinner plate–sized holes in it—German cannon rounds the likely cause, he thought—and he was descending faster than normal.[10]

As a result, the top-turret gunner landed hard, rolling over several times in a grain field. When he came to a stop, it felt as if he'd broken several ribs, one of his knees was painful, and he had badly sprained an ankle. As he was taking stock of his situation he noticed a greasy plume of black smoke rising into the morning sky about three quarters of a mile away, obviously emanating from a crashed airplane, though he couldn't see it clearly enough to determine whether it was *Cholly*, another Fortress, or a downed German fighter.

Davitt knew he had to get rid of his chute, but the residual effects of his concussion and the pain from his other injuries sapped his motivation. He slowly and painfully gathered the folds of nylon into his arms, then flattened the bundle out and rolled onto it as carefully as he could. He lay on the makeshift mattress for two hours, slipping in and out of exhausted sleep until he eventually felt strong enough to move. Like most engineer-gunners, he always carried a few tools with him on missions in case he needed to make in-flight repairs. In Davitt's case the implements were a small screwdriver and a pair of needle-nose pliers, and he now used them to scrape out the shallow hole in which he buried his Mae West, harness, and chute. He then crawled further into the field, where he lay for several hours.

In the early afternoon the noise of movement on a nearby path caught Davitt's attention. He risked a look, and seeing that it was a young French-man whistled to attract his attention. The man asked if Davitt were Amer-ican, and when the airman replied in the affirmative the Frenchman told him to wait there, and that he would return as soon as he could. When he came back an hour or two later he was accompanied by a second, younger man, who in good English asked to see Davitt's escape kit and queried him about his family and his background—both ways of vetting that he was really an American. The two men then left, and Davitt spent the night in the field.

Just after dawn on the morning of July 15 a young girl brought the injured aviator a bottle of hot coffee and some bread, and motioned for him to remain still. Davitt stayed in the field for the rest of the day, and soon after dark four men appeared and helped the limping airman to move into a more concealed location in a nearby wood. They gave Davitt more food and said they would return for him in the morning. True to their word, the quartet reappeared soon after dawn on the sixteenth, and the English-speaker proffered a note to Davitt that turned out to be from Harry Eastman. The hastily written missive said that Eastman was well, and that Davitt should trust the men bearing the note. They then helped Davitt into a car, and he was driven away to meet his crewmate and fellow member of the Gunner Trio.

The friends' reunion, at the home of the Quérolle family, was an un-derstandably happy one.[11] Eastman related that he had delayed pulling his ripcord until he reached breathable air, and that he'd seen six open parachutes in the sky above him. He told Davitt that he had watched as an Fw 190 circled one of the jumpers a few times, but the German fighter had taken no hostile action and eventually just flew off. East-man had landed in a field about fifty yards from a road, he said, and after dumping his equipment he'd started walking. Within a few minutes a man coming down the road on a bicycle had motioned the American into a nearby wood line, apparently because there were German troops coming along the road. But when Eastman hurried into the trees he'd encountered four men who frantically waved him back the way he'd come. Assuming that enemy troops were approaching from two directions, Eastman had run to the center of a second wheat field and scrambled into a ditch that was overhung by a thorn-studded hedge. He'd stayed in his hiding place through the night, he said, and twice civilians had brought him food, both times using sign language to remind him not to stir. On the morning of the fifteenth, a young French priest—the same English-speaker who had quizzed Davitt—had come and led him to a large patch of trees, Eastman said, and showed him a well-concealed hide within some tangled brush. The clergyman had explained that an injured flyer named Davitt had been found only a short distance away, and asked if Eastman wanted the man brought to him. That's when the gunner had written the note, though it took until just that morning to arrange the logistics.

While the two gunners were catching up, a female physician from Évreux examined Davitt, finding that his ribs were bruised rather than broken. He'd badly twisted his knee and his ankle was indeed sprained, so the doctor gave him a handful of aspirin and told him to stay off his feet as much as possible for a few days. That turned out to be easily accomplished, for the priest said he and his friends would need some time to set up the Americans' onward travel. The two airmen then spent the following three days in a different, thicker stretch of woods, being well cared for by the French and—in keeping with the escape and evasion lectures they'd received back in England—pointedly not asking the helpers their names or that of their organization.

The priest, the doctor, and a second man who had referred to himself as "Merlin" were, in fact, members of the Normandy branch of a Paris-based resistance network, or *réseau*, known as Turma-Vengeance.[12] In addition to gathering intelligence on German activities in the region and facilitating the covert aerial delivery from England of arms, ammunition, and agents, the network also helped Allied aviators evade capture. As part of the latter task, members of the group created false identity documents for the evaders, provided civilian clothes, and organized their travel to Paris and, eventually, from there out of France. It was these preparations that kept Davitt and Eastman in the woods for three days. On July 19, with the groundwork apparently completed, the two aviators were driven to a house in Les Baux-Saint-Croix, a southwestern suburb of Évreux, where to their surprise they found David Turner awaiting them.

The young pilot told the gunners about Kee Harrison's decision to crash-land their damaged B-17 in a field, and said he didn't know what had become of the other crew members because everyone had scattered in different directions as soon as the Fortress had ground to a halt.[13] Other than receiving some directions and a civilian coat from a friendly farmer, Turner had been on his own until the morning of the sixteenth, he said, and had put about four miles between himself and the downed bomber when he saw an older woman walking along a road through a small village and decided to take a chance. The woman was somewhat startled, but when Turner had pulled his pilot's wings from the pocket of his civilian coat she'd smiled and motioned for him to follow. She'd led the young aviator to her daughter's home in the adjacent village of Verdun-la-Vacherie. The younger woman had introduced herself as Henriette, and Turner had stayed with her until that morning, when a car had brought him to the Les Baux-Saint-Croix house, which belonged to Hubert and Reneé Renaudin.[14]

Davitt, Eastman, and Turner remained at the house until the morning of Thursday, July 22, when they were given fresh civilian clothes, forged identity cards, and work documents. The three airmen were then driven to the Évreux-Embranchement train station by the Renaudins, who bought third-class tickets to Paris for themselves and the young Americans. As the group sat in the station, nervously eyeing the German military police soldiers walking back and forth near the departure gates, Davitt and Eastman simultaneously stiffened as if they'd seen a ghost. Coming through the station's main entrance was a man both aviators had thought they'd watched die just days earlier.

It was Joe Cornwall, and the third member of the Gunner Trio was doing his best not to laugh out loud at the stunned expression on his friends' faces.

JOE HAD AWAKENED FROM HIS UNINTENDED NAP IN THE WOMAN'S BARN ON July 14 to find that the sun had gone down. He'd been eager to put more distance between himself and the *Salty's Naturals* crash site, so he left the barn and headed eastward, toward Paris. He'd been walking for about a half hour when he saw a small farmhouse set back in some trees. Joe had knocked on the door without taking the time to observe the building first, but he was in luck. The residents had given him civilian trousers, a shirt, and a light jacket. They would not let him stay, however, so he'd walked on for another three and a half hours, finally stopping at about 1:30 A.M. on July 15 at another farmhouse that had lights burning. After questioning him closely in broken English the owners had taken him in, and in exchange he'd given them his escape purse and the francs it contained.

Joe had spent the night in the house, and the next morning his hosts had contacted someone in Turma-Vengeance. Late that afternoon two men had shown up in a battered truck. They'd taken the airman to a farmhouse in the hamlet of Le Hamel, just northwest of Sassey, where he was left in the care of Elie Rebours, his wife, and their several children. Though happy to have connected with a resistance group, Joe had been more than a little anxious about his hiding place, for the Rebourses' home was just a mile north of the sprawling Luftwaffe fighter base at Évreux-Fauville.[15] Indeed, the American's anxiety seemed justified when, the day after his arrival at Le Hamel, two trucks bearing German troops had suddenly driven up to the Rebourses' home. The officer in charge of what was obviously a search party had closely questioned Elie Rebours about whether he had seen any Allied airmen. Not only did the farmer convince the officer that the family members had not encountered any aviators—and certainly would not harbor them if they had—Rebours had sent the soldiers off on a wild goose chase.

Joe had spent six days in Le Hamel, and daily visits to the farm by an English-speaking woman everyone simply called "Madame" helped the American and his hosts to communicate on a deeper level than sign language alone allowed.[16] The Rebourses had taken very good care of Joe, and in return—when no Germans were in the area—he had joined Elie and his young sons in the fields. He'd enjoyed pitching in—even though too much physical effort brought back the burning pains in his back and shoulders—both because he liked the family and because their small, neat farm reminded him in many ways of his grandmother Mollie Campbell's place in eastern Washington. And while Joe and the Rebourses were working, so were the Turma-Vengeance helpers.

The resistance members had carefully crafted false identity papers and a work certificate for the American aviator, though they'd run into a temporary snag when the photos of Joe in civilian clothes taken in England turned out to be too large to use on either document. New photos had been shot—in the home of the mayor of nearby Sassey—and early on the evening of July 20 a Turma-Vengeance member whom Joe had not previously met had arrived at the Rebourses' home on a tandem bicycle.[17] Tied to the rear fender was a small, suitably worn suitcase bearing a pair of scuffed shoes and two changes of equally worn clothing. In halting English the man had explained the items had been somewhat difficult to obtain, given that American aviators tended to be taller, heavier, and have larger feet than the average Frenchman. After Joe had changed into one set of clothes, topped by the light jacket he'd been given on the night of the fifteenth, the man had asked for the aviator's watch and cigarette lighter. Seeing Joe's puzzlement, the courier had explained that both items were obviously of American manufacture—something a keen-eyed policeman or Gestapo operative would immediately notice.

After saying a surprisingly emotional goodbye to the Rebours family, Joe had hopped on the bicycle's rear seat and he and the courier had pedaled to the man's home in Évreux. The following thirty-six hours had passed with agonizing slowness for Joe, because for security reasons he was not informed where he would next be going, or when. Finally, early on the morning of the twenty-second, his host had told him to gather his few belongings and they both had set off again on the tandem bicycle. It was only when they arrived at the train station and the courier handed him a third-class ticket to Paris that Joe had realized he was bound for the French capital. Just inside the station's main entrance the man had pointed out the Renaudins and whispered that they would guide Joe from that point on. After a quick handshake and a muttered "bonne chance," the man had turned and hurried away.

Joe had been focused on the French couple the courier had pointed out to him and had not initially paid attention to the three young and rather anxious-looking men sitting near them. But as he'd gotten closer he'd recognized Davitt, Eastman, and Turner—all of whom he'd assumed had made it back to Rougham after the Le Bourget raid. The sudden realization that he was no longer on his own, that he was about to be reunited with his two best friends, had brought the radiant smile to his face. And when the other members of the Gunner Trio had seen Joe, their first impulse had been to jump up and slap him on the back. They hadn't, of course, because any demonstration of surprise or welcome—especially if accompanied by an outburst of raucous English—would have alerted the nearby German soldiers and doomed the Americans and their French escorts. Instead, the airmen had limited themselves to winks and smiles.

An hour later, as the Renaudins and their charges settled into their seats aboard the train bound for Paris's Gare Saint-Lazare, Joe realized his outlook was the most positive it had been since the moment he'd taken to his parachute eight days earlier. He'd survived the death of *Salty's Naturals*, and had so far managed to avoid capture by the Milice or the Germans. Although he knew many things could still go very wrong, he had been impressed by the skill and professionalism of the French helpers he'd met so far, and the fact that he'd be traveling with Davitt and Eastman—at least for the time being—buoyed his spirits more than he would have expected.

And, Joe admitted to himself, there was another reason for the lift in his spirits. Jeff Dickson's description of life in prewar Paris had piqued his interest. While Joe knew the City of Light must certainly have darkened considerably under German occupation, he was excited by the idea of actually seeing the French capital for himself, even if only for a few days. He couldn't take in the sights like a peacetime tourist, of course, but with luck maybe he'd be able to get around a bit, see a few things, and store up a couple memories of a place he'd likely never visit again.

As his train rumbled southeastward through rolling farmland dotted with small towns, Joe could not have imagined just how life-changing his time in Paris would turn out to be.

Though Joe Cornwall didn't know it, his crewmate Larry Templeton had also found shelter with members of Turma-Vengeance and was already in the French capital.

Following his escape from *Salty's Naturals*, the tail gunner ended up spending the rest of July 14, that night, and most of the following day hidden in a clump of foliage, sleeping and occasionally eating chocolate from his escape box. At sunset on the fifteenth he decided it was time to move, so he set off toward the southeast. A few miles of walking brought him to a farmhouse, which he watched for more than an hour from a convenient hiding place. Templeton eventually decided to try his luck, and as he walked toward the building a young man came around it from the other side and stopped, obviously startled, when he saw the aviator. Templeton motioned for a drink of water, and the Frenchman said, "English?" Templeton responded that he was American, and the man motioned him into the house, where Templeton was offered a chair and given a glass of rough red wine.

After about ten minutes in the house, the man motioned the gunner outside and pointed toward a road about a quarter mile away, miming that Templeton should follow the road to the east. After thanking his host, the aviator set off in the indicated direction. As he rounded a curve about an hour later he realized that the figure coming toward him on a bicycle was a German soldier, his rifle slung over his back and his helmet dangling by its buckled chin strap from a handlebar. Templeton was still dressed in his olive-drab, one-piece flying overalls and still had blood on his face from the gash on his forehead, and was certain he was about to be captured. But the fading evening light apparently helped hide his appearance, for the German rode past without a second glance.

Templeton kept walking through the night, and soon after dawn on the sixteenth he left the road and followed a narrow lane toward the lights of a small house. Still cautious, he watched the building for an hour. Then, deciding it was safe, he knocked on the door and waited a few anxious moments until a man the gunner judged to be in his midthirties slowly opened it and peered out. Templeton pointed to himself and said "American" several times, and was invited in. The man, his wife, and their four children were in the middle of breakfast, and they asked the aviator to join them. After the meal the man indicated that he was about to leave for work, and that Templeton should stay and sleep until he came back that evening. Understandably tired from his cross-country jaunt, Templeton agreed. That evening, after having joined the family for supper, the airman got up to leave but the man again asked him to stay, this time adding that he would help him to evade capture by the Germans.

Templeton ended up staying with the family until Sunday the eighteenth. That morning, several young Frenchmen appeared on bicycles, one of which was provided to Templeton. The group rode about fifteen miles to another house, where they spent the night. On the morning of the nineteenth Templeton and two of the Frenchmen cycled to a nearby railway station, where Second Lieutenant Roscoe Greene—the bombardier who had bailed out of Kee Harrison's aircraft before its crash-landing—joined the group. The Americans had not previously been told their destination, and it was with a mixture of anxiety and excitement that they boarded the train for Paris with their escorts. Templeton later paraphrased his ambivalent feelings at the moment of departure as, essentially, "Sure, the city's crawling with Krauts, but it's Paris!"

THE AVIATORS BEING SHEPHERDED BY TURMA-VENGEANCE IN THE AFTERMATH of the Bastille Day raid were not the only 94th Bomb Group crewmen who would spend time in Paris, for other networks were also providing transportation to the French capital.

Although three of the four Rougham-based B-17s lost on that fateful July 14 went down within a relatively small 140-square-mile "box" in the east-central section of northern France's Eure department, the military importance of the greater Normandy region to both the Germans and the Allies ensured that several French Resistance networks were represented in the area. In addition to Turma-Vengeance, the most active *réseaux* in terms of aiding Allied aviators brought down in Europe were the Bourgogne (Burgundy) and Comète (Comet) lines. All three organizations normally funneled evaders through Paris, and which of the networks provided assistance to a particular airman was essentially a matter of luck. If the aviator were fortunate enough to encounter friendly civilians—rather than Germans, the Milice, or collaborators—he would be passed on to the *réseau* with which the civilians or their trusted confidants were affiliated.

For Kee Harrison's navigator, Second Lieutenant Robert Conroy, and Technical Sergeant John Buice of Floyd Watts's crew, for example, that first encounter led to different cells of the Comète line, and both were moved to Paris before onward movement to England. But for six of the sixteen men of the 94th Group who survived the July 14 downing of their aircraft and managed to evade capture, it was the Bourgogne network that was to provide the "home run" to the United Kingdom via the French capital. Harrison and two members of his crew, Technical Sergeant Charles McNemar and Staff Sergeant Jefferson Polk, were collected by members of the *réseau,* as were Technical Sergeant Samuel Potvin and Staff Sergeant John Carpenter of Watts's crew. Watts himself was also sheltered by Bourgogne members, but not until after they'd satisfied themselves the aviator wasn't a German spy.

AS WATTS FLOATED TO EARTH ON JULY 14, THE FARTHEST THING FROM HIS mind was whether he would be able to contact a resistance cell. Instead, the young pilot was focused on the flaming hulk of his Fortress as it arced like a deadly comet into the city of Louvres. He watched in horror as the bomber slammed into what looked like an industrial area and exploded, the detonation quickly followed by the emergence of a greasy black pillar of smoke that looked for all the world like a massive funeral pyre.[18]

Watts landed in a wheat field not far from the town, and immediately dumped his harness and Mae West. Some French farm workers provided him with food and civilian clothes, and after spending the night in a haystack he inadvertently walked in the wrong direction—and right into Louvres. He passed his bomber's crash site, which was surrounded by German troops and several dozen curious civilians, and finally decided to enter a shop and ask for assistance. The premises he chose turned out to be a bicycle store, and when he spoke to the clerk in English the man motioned to him to sit down and wait. The Frenchman hurried off, and minutes later returned with a young woman who introduced herself as Jacqueline.[19] Her English was quite good, and she assured Watts that she knew people who would help him. What the young woman didn't share with the young American was the name of her *réseau*—it was Bourgogne—and the fact that the organization was about to put him to a test.

Just after dark, Watts was taken to an abandoned rock quarry outside the city and told he would have to stay for at least ten days in a dank, wet cave that had once served as a storage area for tools. The French helpers watched the aviator closely as he took in the amenities—a rough cot, a small oil lantern, and a bucket to be used as a latrine—and when Watts did not protest his companions smiled, slapped him heartily on the back and left. After a somewhat uncomfortable night, Watts was surprised when the helpers returned the following morning and took him to the home of the bicycle shop clerk, a man named Bartholomeux. Though the house was small the accommodations were far more agreeable than they had been at the quarry, and Watts realized that by telling him he would have to remain in the cave for an extended period the helpers had been trying to determine if he were a genuine evader. A German agent pretending to be a downed Allied airman would not have wanted to be isolated and out of communication with his handlers for so long, whereas a genuine evader would accept the conditions as a necessary hardship on the journey out of Occupied France.

Having passed the test, Watts was moved further down the evasion line. He would spend three weeks sheltering with another helper before being reunited with radio operator Sam Potvin and ball turret gunner John Carpenter. All eight members of Watts's crew who'd survived the destruction of their B-17 would eventually make the long journey back to England via Paris.[20]

THE TRIP INTO THE FRENCH CAPITAL WAS AN OBVIOUSLY PERILOUS JOURNEY for all of the 94th Bomb Group airmen, no matter which escape line was managing their travel.

There were really only three ways for an evader and his helpers to reach Paris from the countryside—by boat, on the River Seine; by road; or by rail. Given the political and military importance of the greater Paris metropolitan area to the Germans, all three were closely monitored. The first two were especially difficult, however.

Traffic on the Seine was largely confined to vessels carrying either military equipment or other strategically important cargoes, so small patrol boats manned by German troops were active day and night. The few non-military vessels still plying the river with commercial freight were certain to be stopped at some point, with the Germans checking the credentials of everyone on board, going through cargo manifests, and often carrying out thorough searches of the vessel's accommodation spaces and holds. Moreover, those areas along the river where boats and barges loaded and unloaded—both within Paris and outside the city—were subject to random inspection by troops and civilian police. Though the crews of the commercial craft were more than willing to smuggle certain goods, mainly food and coal, virtually all drew the line at covertly moving people. It was an easy decision to make, for if caught with illicit goods the usual punishment was a fine and confiscation of the contraband. If apprehended attempting to transport a résistant or downed Allied aviator, on the other hand, the very least a boatman could expect was severe interrogation followed by a one-way ticket to a concentration camp.

Helpers attempting to move an evader to Paris by road also faced significant challenges, not the least of which was that by the summer of 1943 gasoline shortages had reduced civilian traffic on French roadways to a trickle. While doctors, some farmers, local police, and other people deemed "essential" by the Germans were allocated a certain amount of fuel, most civilians who owned vehicles and could still afford to maintain them had long since converted their cars, trucks, or delivery vans to run on gases generated by burning wood or coal. The scarcity of civilian traffic, coupled with the fact that the roadways leading to the French capital were studded with both fixed and mobile checkpoints, essentially guaranteed that nonmilitary vehicles would be stopped at least once and their occupants' identity documents closely examined. The slightest suspicion on the part of the soldier or gendarme that something was amiss would usually result in a thorough search of the vehicle, and often in the detention of the driver and any passengers.

The third method of transporting evaders to Paris, and from the capital to other locations, certainly also had its drawbacks. The railway stations in most larger cities were continuously patrolled by either German troops, the Milice, or civilian police, and arriving and departing passengers were subject to spot checks and random searches. Gestapo agents, as well as members of the Wehrmacht military police, also carried out document checks aboard the trains themselves. Moreover, German military personnel used the civilian rail system to move around the country, and while many trains had carriages reserved especially for the occupiers' use, it was common for civilians to find themselves in the same compartment with uniformed Germans. Conversations between victor and vanquished were understandably rare, of course, but they did occur. Because far more Germans spoke French than did Allied aviators—especially American airmen—there was always the risk that an evader might be tripped up simply because he was unable to respond to a German's query. To forestall just such a potentially disastrous occurrence, airmen were instructed that in the event a German or unknown French person attempted to speak with them, the correct response was to feign deafness. Somewhat ironically, the fact that French railways were becoming an increasingly frequent target of Allied air attacks meant that a journey usually lasting two hours might stretch to six or eight if the train had to be diverted around a bombed station or rail yard, prolonging the time an evader had to maintain both his silence and his composure. And, of course, there was also the chance that the train carrying the airman and his helpers could itself become the focus of an Allied attack.

Despite these drawbacks, those escape lines that used Paris as a central collection point for Allied evaders preferred to move the airmen and their helpers by rail, rather than take a chance on the River Seine or the roads. Most French civilians who needed to travel had no choice but to do it by rail, and German-imposed curfews and blackout regulations meant that passenger trains normally ran only during the daylight hours. That, in turn, meant that carriages traveling to and from Paris were usually quite full—especially in the early morning and late afternoon. Evaders were thus better able to blend in with other passengers en route, and the vast numbers of people crowding the capital's main stations made it that much harder for the Germans and the police to closely examine peoples' identity and travel documents. In addition, there was an active resistance movement within the SNCF—the state-run railway company.[21] Rail workers could thus often be counted upon to provide the various escape networks with such useful information as which trains were the focus of special police interest on a given day, the best ways to surreptitiously enter and leave particular stations, or even the names of soldiers or police who could be bribed or blackmailed into looking the other way.

Although the various *réseaux* did all they could to ensure the security of evaders and their helpers during their rail journeys, the airmen themselves were also held responsible for their own safety and that of their escorts. At some point before traveling to the station the aviators would be briefed—either vocally or via hand signals, depending on the participants' language skills—on what they should and shouldn't do during the trip. In addition to feigning deafness should someone question them or attempt to engage them in casual conversation, the evaders were told not to sleep during the trip so they wouldn't awake suddenly and inadvertently speak English.

They were instructed to stay in the same carriage as their escort, but cautioned to sit separately. That would allow them to follow the helper's lead in the event they had to leave the train earlier than planned, but would also reduce the chance that the arrest of one would also compromise the other. Upon arrival at their destination, the airmen were told, their escort would pass them off to someone else. For security reasons the escort would not normally know the identity of the new contact, so the evader would be told to calmly leave the train and walk to a certain part of the station. There the airmen was to look for someone displaying a specific attribute—wearing a particular color dress, for example, or holding a certain book—and when that person left the station, the evader was to follow at a distance.

The last part of the pretravel briefing would likely have been the most chilling for the individual evaders. Though delivered in various ways, the meaning was always essentially the same: The escorts on the train and the guides in the stations would do what they could to ensure the airman's journey went according to plan, but there was always the possibility that bad luck, carelessness, or betrayal might lead to disaster. If the escort were compromised before reaching the destination the evader should remain aloof and not attempt to intervene. And likewise, the airman was told, if he were to be taken by the police or soldiers, either on the train or at a station, he would be entirely on his own.

THE TRAIN BEARING JOE CORNWALL AND HIS COMPANIONS ENTERED THE GRIMY outskirts of Paris just before noon on July 22, and as it slowly made its way toward the Gare Saint-Lazare Joe peered out the window with a mix of excitement and anxiety. The trip from Évreux had gone well, and only once had the gunner needed to pretend deafness—in response to the conversational overtures of an elderly and rather odiferous French woman. He was looking forward to getting out of the crowded, close atmosphere of the third-class carriage and into the city, but he realized that he, Davitt, Eastman, and Turner were about to embark on what was likely the most dangerous part of their journey thus far.

In a hurried, whispered conversation before leaving Évreux, Hubert Renaudin had told the Americans that upon arrival in Paris he and his wife would leave the carriage after the majority of the other passengers had disembarked. Joe and the three other aviators were to follow individually, and when they saw Reneé Renaudin stop at a kiosk inside the station's main hall they were to wait until the couple had left, then gather within a few feet of the kiosk. Someone—Hubert only knew that it would be a tall, slender man wearing a dark hat—would approach the kiosk and make a show of lighting a pipe. The three gunners were to follow the man at a distance, and he would guide them on the next leg of their journey.

All went according to plan when the train rolled into Gare Saint-Lazare. The Renaudins walked slowly to the first kiosk inside the main station, stopped briefly, then faded into the crowd. The Americans ambled to the kiosk with as much nonchalance as they could muster, though Joe was startled by the number of German military personnel milling about. There hadn't been any soldiers in the third-class carriage from Évreux, and the sheer number and proximity of uniformed troops in the station made Joe slightly queasy. He recovered quickly, though, when he realized that the majority of the Boche on duty—Joe had picked up the word from Hubert—were simply waiting for trains or on hand to meet someone.

Joe had just tapped the last French cigarette out of a pack Elie Rebours had given him and was about to light it with a wooden match when, true to Hubert Renaudin's briefing, a tall man casually walked up. He said something in French and gestured with his pipe, obviously asking for a light. When Joe handed him the lit match the man subtly tilted his head toward the station's main entrance, and when he walked casually away the trio of aviators followed, careful to keep their distance from him and each other.

Joe had not been in a major city since his last weekend pass in London several weeks earlier, and as he emerged from the station into dazzling summer sunlight he was almost overwhelmed by the sights, sounds, and smells that bombarded his senses. While the streets were relatively devoid of cars and trucks, scores of what appeared to be bicycle-powered rickshaws zipped by, most carrying people who seemed far better dressed than Joe would have expected. While the crowded streets pulsed with life, Joe thought he could detect an undercurrent of, not anger perhaps, but unease, or something akin to sullen resignation. Indeed, the only smiles he saw were on the faces of the uniformed Germans who dotted the moving masses of people like drops of dark paint on an otherwise bright and colorful canvas.

So engrossed was Joe in absorbing the hustle and bustle around him that he momentarily lost sight of the tall man with the pipe. His rising panic subsided quickly when he saw the lanky guide, striding purposefully across the large street in front of the station and about to round a corner. Davitt, Eastman, and Turner were a few paces behind, almost like Fortresses in a V-formation behind the lead ship, Joe thought, and as he hurried to catch up he had to remind himself to be on his guard. He was not on vacation, and this city, no matter how fascinating, was filled with enemies.

Having caught up with his three companions, and with the tall man loping about thirty feet ahead, Joe settled into what the Army called "route step"—an easy, unhurried pace that allowed him to cover ground relatively quickly but without exhausting himself or aggravating the nagging pain in his back and shoulders. By the angle of the sun he judged that they were moving almost directly south, and after a brisk five-minute walk the Americans and their guide passed a large and ornate church that reminded Joe of pictures he'd seen of the Acropolis in Athens. A few minutes more and the narrow, building-lined street the guide had been following opened out into a large, open plaza, in the center of which was a tall, needle-like column. Joe slowed to admire the structure, but then a structure rising into the sky off to the right attracted his attention. With a jolt, Joe realized he was seeing the upper part of the Eiffel Tower, and a broad smile broke out across his face. Damn, he thought to himself, I really am in Paris.[22]

He didn't realize it yet, but Joe would soon catch sight of another famous Parisian landmark—one that would have a far more profound effect on him than even Mr. Eiffel's majestic creation.

HELPERS, GUESTS, AND LOVERS

THE TALL, SLENDER MAN LEADING JOE CORNWALL AND THE THREE other evaders through the streets of Paris that sunny July 22 had gone by many names in the years since his nation's surrender to the Germans. His false papers had at various times identified him as Dubois, a wine merchant; Mazier, a bookseller; and Pichot, a minor functionary in an obscure branch of the Paris city government. The other members of the Turma-Vengeance network with whom he worked called the quiet forty-one-year-old by the nom de guerre "Petrel," and only a handful of people in the French capital knew his true identity. He was André Auguste Schoegel, and despite having a German family name—his forebears originally hailed from Alsace—he was a passionate and dedicated résistant.[1]

An army reservist whose unit was disbanded soon after the fall of France, Schoegel had resumed his work as a building contractor upon returning to his home in Nantes. In September 1940 he was recruited into a resistance group known as Jade-Fitzroy, and for the following year he gathered intelligence on German installations and troop movements. In September 1941 Gestapo agents tried to arrest Schoegel at his home. He escaped, but his wife, Suzanne, was seized and ultimately deported to Ravensbrück concentration camp in Germany.[2] Schoegel went to Vichy seeking to avoid further attention from the Gestapo, but soon after arriving in the "unoccupied zone" he was arrested on the grounds that he was a danger to the state. Following his release in May 1942 he moved to Paris, and in early 1943 he was recruited into Turma-Vengeance. His primary task was to travel throughout northern France to collect weapons and equipment dropped by the Allies and smuggle the items back to the capital. Early on, however, he also started escorting downed aviators to Paris, and also meeting incoming evaders and their guides at various train stations in the capital. Schoegel hid the airmen at his own modest home in the southern suburb of Orly or lodged them elsewhere in Paris with members of Turma-Vengeance. And among those members were the Morins of Invalides.

LIKE MANY PEOPLE IN FRANCE, GEORGES, DENISE, AND YVETTE MORIN HAD spent the first year of the occupation simply trying to deal with the increasingly harsh realities of life. Thanks to the ever-growing number of rabbits filling the hutches in the workshops and garages a few steps from their apartment, their food situation wasn't quite as dire as it was for most people. But that was the only bright spot, for like everyone else in Paris—and indeed, most people in France—the Morins had to contend with shortages of virtually every basic commodity. The Germans' widespread expropriation of French coal and heating oil stocks made the already harsh winter of 1940–1941 all the more brutal—a tragic reality underlined for the Morins when the infant child of one of Yvette's friends froze to death.[3]

The coming of spring eased the effects of the coal and heating oil shortages, but did nothing to alleviate the increasingly onerous weight of the Boche presence in the City of Light. By June 1941 there were some forty thousand German military personnel in the capital and its environs, and it was impossible to ignore them. Giant swastika banners hung from many of the city's most famous buildings, and parades by military bands frequently shut down pedestrian traffic on major thoroughfares. Armed soldiers stood guard outside the dozens of hotels and office buildings the Germans had requisitioned as headquarters for various military and civilian agencies, and the tall, multibranched signs that in cryptic German gave directions to those locations seemed to dominate every street corner. Cafés, restaurants, and theaters all over the city had been reserved exclusively for use by German service members, and movie houses ran only those French- and

German-language films that had been deemed "appropriate" by the first German military governor of France, General Otto von Stülpnagel.

Perhaps most infuriating for many Parisians were the hordes of German military "tourists" that inundated the city's famous landmarks. Their presence was the work of Jeder Einmal in Paris (Everyone in Paris Once), an arm of Germany's official tourist office tasked with ensuring that as many German service members as possible were able to tour the City of Light. Headquartered in the Palais Bourbon, the organization managed the rotational visits to Paris by members of all the German armed services, and provided helpful guides to the capital's many attractions. Composed both of personnel stationed in the capital and troops brought in from other regions, the masses of uniformed men (and occasional women) swarmed the same sites—the Eiffel Tower, Montmartre, the Île de la Cité, the museums, and the rest—that had long attracted less aggressive visitors. Invalides seemed to be particularly popular, the Morins noticed, though it was unclear whether the uniformed "tourists" came out of genuine interest in the complex's history or because they wanted their pictures taken where their Führer had stood. Whatever the reason, so many hobnailed boots were treading the delicate stone of the rotunda overlooking Napoléon's Tomb that the architect of Invalides ordered wooden planking laid over the floor to protect it.

As irritated as the people of Paris were by the sheer numbers of Germans in the capital, it was the occupiers' far less benign activities that prompted many Parisians to abandon their attempts to live "normal" lives and instead engage in active resistance. For some it was the increasingly harsh restrictions placed on French Jews, for others it was the frequent roundups of communists, trade unionists, and outspoken intellectuals and clergymen. For the Morins, the decision to take action came in the late summer of 1941, when France was swept by rumors that the Germans were about to start dragooning young Frenchmen and women for mandatory work in Germany. Though a compulsory work program would not become official until the fall of 1942, the mere idea that French civilians would be used as slave labor in German factories and mines convinced many people to go underground. Among those "refractors" attempting to elude involuntary labor service was a twenty-one-year-old named René-Guy Salomon.

The young man was the son of Gustave Salomon, a disabled World War I veteran Georges Morin knew through his work. When the elder Salomon approached the Morins about hiding René-Guy they readily agreed, and the young man spent several weeks tucked away in various locations around Invalides, including the Morins' apartment. By the time he moved on in the fall of 1941, Georges, Denise, and Yvette had shown themselves willing to risk arrest and imprisonment in order to thwart the intentions of the Germans and their collaborators.[4] And the man to whom they'd proven their patriotism, Gustave Salomon, was in a unique position to help them actively resist the Germans in a much broader and more useful way.

Though the Morins hadn't known it when they agreed to shelter René-Guy, the elder Salomon was a key member of the Turma-Vengeance network. He had joined the organization not long after its founding in late 1940 by three physicians—Victor Dupont, Raymond Chanel, and François Wetterwald.[5] By November 1941, the forty-four-year-old Salomon was the network's chief recruiter in Paris, working under the nom de guerre "Antheaume." Impressed by the Morins—and no doubt thinking of how useful Invalides could be to the Resistance—Salomon invited all three members of the family to formally join Turma-Vengeance. They accepted without hesitation, and from then on were referred to within the network by their noms de guerre—Georges as "Napoléon"; Denise, for obvious reasons, as "Madame Lapin" (Mrs. Rabbit); and Yvette as "Mickey," a name she chose for herself because it sounded American.[6]

Having proven their willingness to shelter people on the run, the Morins' initial task within the network was to do just that—but on a larger scale. During the winter of 1941–1942 they offered refuge to an ever-changing cast of refractors and other young men who were being sought by the Germans for various reasons. At any one time there might be two or three discreet and not-very-talkative "cousins from out of town" visiting the Morins, who normally put the guests up in the attic of the architect's office. In bad weather the visitors would pass the time reading or playing cards there or in the Morins' home, and on warmer days they would lounge in the large ornamental garden a few yards from the apartment or on the broad lawns in front of the entrance to the Dôme church. This was not as risky as it might seem, given that Invalides remained a popular attraction for the hard-pressed people of Paris. On most days the grounds teemed with individuals and families seeking to escape the drabness of their own homes, or to spend time with friends, or to simply recharge themselves emotionally by taking in the grandeur and beauty of the church and its surroundings.

While entry to the western part of the Invalides complex—which housed German military offices and barracks—was tightly controlled around the clock, the arrival and departure of the Morins' "cousins" was facilitated by the laxness of the German sentries posted at the northern, eastern, and southern entrances to Invalides during daylight hours. The sheer number of people flowing into and out of the eastern side of the complex—military "tourists" as well as French civilian visitors and workmen—made it difficult to do more than a cursory check of identity cards. Nor were the sentries able to record the names of everyone entering or leaving the grounds. This laxity, coupled with the special passes the Germans had provided to the Morins to facilitate their official duties, made it relatively easy for the family to move themselves and their "relatives" into and out of the complex during the day. It was more difficult at night, though the Morins also had official documents that allowed them to be out after curfew under certain circumstances.

The visiting "cousins" had to be fed, and the most frequent cuisine served to them, of course, was rabbit. That staple was supplemented by whatever edible scraps could be scrounged from the Germans' trash bins, and by items such as the green tops of carrots for which Denise often had to stand in line for hours. Every few weeks she would go farther afield, traveling by rail out to the suburbs—often as far as Chartres—in search of potatoes and other vegetables. Because bringing foodstuffs into the city was prohibited by the Germans and the discovery of contraband could result in severe punishment for the carrier, Denise had to be extremely inventive in how she transported whatever provisions she had been able to obtain. Her favorite method for bulkier items such as potatoes was to carry them in a large fabric carryall worn strapped to her midsection beneath a larger-than-necessary dress topped with a long, worn coat. She counted on the fact that elderly French women were less likely to be spot-searched during the document checks carried out in the railway stations, and occasionally used a cane to appear older and frailer than she actually was.

During the day the responsibility for keeping an eye on the "cousins" most often fell on the elder Morins. In the months following the Germans' arrival in Paris the veteran-service bureaucracy at Invalides had been all but dismantled, leaving Georges free to aid his wife both in the "concierge" role and in caring for the "relatives." While Yvette helped with both tasks when she could, her days were largely devoted to the job she had gotten in the fall of 1941 in order to bolster the family's finances. She had been hired as a secretary at the Crédit National, the quasi-governmental investment bank located just a few blocks from Invalides on rue Saint-Dominique.[7]

By the summer of 1942 the Morins' role in Turma-Vengeance had begun to expand beyond the sheltering of refractors. Their apartment, for example, became a regular venue for meetings between senior members of their network and the leaders of such other Paris-based resistance organizations as Défense de la France and Ceux de la Libération. Both of those organizations produced underground newspapers, and Invalides quickly became a storage and distribution site for the publications. Other documents distributed with help from the Morins included German General Staff identification cards stolen by a young network member from the Wehrmacht's cartography and map-making office at 35 rue des Invalides. Already bearing the necessary authentication stamps but devoid of names or photographs, the cards were distributed to résistants whose ability to speak German would allow them to impersonate military personnel.

The Morins also stored far more lethal items for the network. These initially consisted of shotguns, hunting rifles, and the occasional target pistol that members of Turma-Vengeance and other networks chose not to turn in as required by German regulations. Later, as André Schoegel and other couriers began bringing air-dropped weapons into Paris from the countryside, the armory stored in various out-of-the-way places around Invalides grew to include military rifles, handguns, Sten submachine guns, Bren machine guns, hand grenades, and plastic explosives and the time pencils used to detonate them.

While the sprawling Invalides complex was the ideal place to store such weapons until they could be put to use against the Germans, the mere presence of war materiel within the precincts for which the Morins were in large part responsible significantly increased the family's risks. The residence of one or two bogus "cousins" might possibly be explained away as ignorance of some obscure German decree, but the discovery of a cache of weapons obviously provided by Britain would result in brutal interrogation and almost certain death. Yvette and her parents were well aware of the danger and accepted the possibility that a traitor within the organization, or a policeman's random curiosity, or even their own carelessness, could bring disaster down upon them at any moment. In an example of sangfroid rare in one so young, Yvette took to wearing a bracelet her grandfather had given her for her first communion. It was engraved with her name and birthdate, and she thought it would help people identify her body should the Germans arrest and then execute her.[8]

THOUGH THE OFFICIAL ESTABLISHMENT OF THE SERVICE DU TRAVAIL obligatore—the German-enforced work program—in the summer of 1942 ensured that large numbers of refractors still sought shelter with France's various resistance organizations, by the following year the nature—and nationality—of the people being hidden in Paris by Turma-Vengeance and the other networks had changed significantly. The underlying reason was the Allies' round-the-clock Combined Bomber Offensive, which was sending ever-larger formations of aircraft ever deeper into Occupied Europe.

One less-than-desirable result of the widening aerial campaign, of course, was the increasing numbers of Allied airmen forced to abandon their crippled machines by parachute or crash-land them in German-held territory. While British and Commonwealth aviators had been regular—if unwilling—visitors since 1939, by early 1943 Americans were making up a larger percentage of the downed airmen being aided by the evasion networks. With the help of people like André Schoegel, increasing numbers of "Yanks" were finding refuge in and around Paris as they awaited onward movement back to Allied territory.

The first Americans to be sheltered by the Morins—albeit briefly—arrived on June 28. Like the majority of the USAAF aviators who would pass through Invalides, sergeants Lester Brown Jr. and John H. Houghton were B-17 crewmen.[9] They were the radio operator and ball turret gunner, respectively, of a Fortress belonging to the 384th Bomb Group, based at Grafton-Underwood in Northamptonshire. Their aircraft was shot down on June 26 during a raid on the airfield at Villacoublay. While three of the bomber's crewmen were captured by the Germans soon after landing, seven others were located by helpers and six of those were sent on to Paris after being given civilian clothes and a hurriedly produced set of identity papers.[10] Brown and Houghton were escorted to the capital by rail on the late afternoon of June 28, arriving at the Gare d'Austerlitz. There they were met by a man they later described as "an ex-major in the French army," who led them down into the Métro. While Gare d'Austerlitz was at most a thirty-five-minute walk from Invalides, the airmen's escort had apparently decided that the hour-long subway journey—which involved some thirteen stops and a transfer among four lines—was safer than making the journey by foot.

The trio arrived at Invalides' east entrance gate just after its 7 P.M. closure, and the German guards had retired for the evening. After waiting across the street for a few minutes to make sure all was quiet, the Frenchman led his two charges across the narrow boulevard des Invalides. The man then pushed the button that rang the *dit-dit-dit-dah* bell inside the Morins' apartment, and moments later Georges opened the smaller door set within the left section of the massive gate. The two Frenchmen shook hands, and the escort hurried off as Georges ushered the Americans in and led them around the corner and into the apartment.

After Brown and Houghton had settled themselves onto a small couch, Denise served them bread, cheese, and wine. As the Americans ate, they gathered from Georges's mixture of hand gestures and few words of English that someone else would be joining them. An hour later the aviators were startled by a sudden knock on the door and Denise admitted two men, one about thirty and the other in his sixties.

In good English the visitors quizzed Brown and Houghton about where they were from originally and how long they'd each been in the military. The older man then asked to see the gunners' dog tags, and handed them back after jotting down the information stamped into the disks. He then wanted to know if the airmen had any more pictures of themselves in civilian clothes. They didn't—the photos had been used for their first set of false papers—but the man said that wasn't a problem, they would take more later.

Having wished Brown and Houghton a good night's rest, the two men said they would return in the morning, then hurried out into the night. A few minutes later Denise led the Americans upstairs to Yvette's room— the family had been told they were likely to have "guests" that evening, so in order to free up space the young woman was spending the night at the home of the Morins' family physician, Dr. Mercier, and his wife, Germaine.[11] The airmen made themselves as comfortable as possible, one on Yvette's bed and the other on a thin, down-filled mattress laid on the floor. Despite their anxiety about what the morning might bring, they were both soon asleep.

Georges awakened the airmen just after 6 A.M. and indicated they would be leaving soon. After a simple breakfast Brown and Houghton said a quick goodbye to Denise, then followed their host out the door and down the narrow alley to one of the workshops. There, Georges handed each of the men a pair of mud-stained overalls and a hoe. At precisely 7 A.M. the German guards opened the eastern gate, and as Brown and Houghton sauntered out the troops ignored them, as Georges had known they would. After all, he'd reasoned, the guards were there to monitor the visitors entering the compound, not to keep track of gardeners leaving to attend to trees and shrubs along the outside walls. Once through the gate, the two Americans turned south on the boulevard des Invalides and walked until the tall man from the night before appeared alongside. After neatly leaning their hoes against a nearby tree, Brown and Houghton followed their guide to the next stop on their journey to freedom.[12]

Despite the brevity of the Americans' stay at Invalides, Georges and Denise Morin had shown themselves entirely capable of hosting evaders whose language they did not speak. And when the next U.S. aviators arrived, Yvette Morin's own very limited English skills would prove no impediment to the blossoming of a deep and committed relationship—and to a proposal.

THE HUGE PLAZA TO WHICH ANDRÉ SCHOEGEL LED JOE CORNWALL AND HIS companions on the afternoon of July 22 was the place de la Concorde.[13] The largest open square in Paris, on that Wednesday it was also among the busiest places in the capital. Though few vehicles moved on the nearby streets, individuals and groups of people traversed the vast open space, some striding or riding bicycles purposefully to jobs or appointments, others simply strolling in the summer sun. The sheer number of people made the esplanade the perfect place for a clandestine rendezvous, and after leading the four American airmen to the huge fountain at the southern end of the plaza Schoegel motioned them to gather around him. As they did so, a stout and rather formidable-looking middle-aged woman walked up to the group. She and Schoegel exchanged a few terse sentences in French, then the woman motioned for Joe and Harry Eastman to follow her. As she led them away, Joe caught a quick glimpse of Turner and Davitt trailing the tall, slender man off into the crowd.[14]

The reason for splitting up the four airmen is now lost to history, but was likely the result of a decision within the Turma-Vengeance network that all their American "eggs" shouldn't be placed in the same basket. Sheltering the airmen in at least two places would prevent all of them being captured in a single German raid, while at the same time reducing the burden placed on those chosen to house and feed the Americans. Whatever the motive, the result was that André Schoegel led Dave Turner and Dick Davitt off to the suburb of Orly, where they would stay with him in his modest home at 2 rue Jenner.[15]

Joe and Harry Eastman had little time to consider the reasons for their friends' sudden departure, for the formidable French woman was striding briskly away. As the two airmen hurried to stay close to her, they realized she was leading them toward a wide bridge over the River Seine. Before reaching the span, however, the woman turned to the right and started down a sloping, tree-shaded walkway paralleling the water. Joe and his fellow gunner followed, bicyclists whizzing by them on either side. The walkway quickly leveled out, and continued along a slight bend in the river toward another ornate bridge—the Pont Alexandre III—with pairs of tall columns flanking either end. Looking to his left, Joe could see barges tied up to wide stone wharves lining both sides of the waterway, and he noticed armed German troops monitoring the loading and unloading of cargo.

When their French guide reached the bridge she paused slightly, then turned and started across the span. The wide sidewalks on either side of the roadway were nearly as busy as the place de la Concorde, and for a few moments it was all Joe and Harry could do to keep the surprisingly fleet Frenchwoman in sight. When they reached the far side of the span the crowds thinned a bit, and a broad green esplanade opened out before the two aviators as they hurried to keep pace with the guide. Their eyes were drawn to what looked like a vast palace at the end of the long, park-like tract, and to the monumental golden dome rising above it. It was their first glimpse of Invalides.

The closer the guide and her charges got to the north end of the palatial building, the easier it was for Joe and Harry to see the red-and-white-striped sentry boxes on either side of the massive, wrought iron entrance gates. In front of each box stood a German soldier with a rifle over one shoulder, and as it became apparent that the Frenchwoman intended to walk directly through the gate the two American aviators realized they had no choice but to follow her. To suddenly stop and abruptly change direction would likely only draw the Germans' attention and, besides, they knew no one in Paris and had nowhere to go. Seeing that the guide and other people were going through the gates with barely a glance from the sentries, Joe and Harry shot a quick look at each other and with only a subtle nod between them agreed to brazen it out. Trying to look as casual as they could, the two men strode nonchalantly toward the gate, both sighing quietly with relief after passing the soldiers without being challenged.

Ahead of them, their guide was walking toward a huge portal in the front of the massive building, which Joe decided looked more like a centuries-old hotel or hospital than a palace. Once through the arched stone entryway, the Americans followed their guide across the vast Cour d'honneur, enclosed on all four sides by two-storied buildings with sharply peaked roofs. At the far end of the courtyard, which Joe assumed was a military drill field or parade ground, the Frenchwoman angled to the left, striding through one of a series of archways into the dim and cool recesses of a long corridor made of dressed stone. The aviators followed, and less than a minute later walked out into what appeared to be a broad, sunlit alley—the Cour de Metz. To the left was a four-story stone building, and to the right the long eastern façade of the Cathédrale Saint-Louis. Towering above the large, rectangular building that made up the far end of the cathedral—the Dôme church—was the soaring golden edifice Joe and Harry had seen from the other side of the river.

At the end of the Cour de Metz the Frenchwoman walked a few steps out into the Cour du Dôme, the broad, open space between the gated southern entrance to Invalides and the steps leading up to the Dôme church. Visitors—many wearing German uniforms—thronged the area, and for a moment Joe thought the Frenchwoman intended to lead Harry and him out the gate, which had its own set of rifle-toting guards. But after looking carefully about for a few seconds, the woman turned to the left and set off down a wide gravel path separating a long, two-story building from the compact, well-manicured Jardin d'Hôpital (Hospital Garden).[16] Joe noticed a second, smaller guarded gate directly ahead, but before reaching it the woman turned right down a narrow alley. When the two airmen followed her, they found her knocking on the door to a small, two-level apartment set into a line of structures that included a small garage and what looked like workshops. As Joe and Harry walked up, the door was opened by a slight, middle-aged man with a small, well-trimmed mustache. After a brief, hushed conversation with the man, the Frenchwoman turned, winked at the Americans, then walked away without a backward glance.

Joe and Harry, somewhat bewildered by their guide's abrupt departure, turned back to the man standing in the doorway. He smiled, tapped himself on the chest, and said, "Georges." Then, with an almost theatrical sweep of his arm, he invited them into his modest home.

IN THE EIGHT DAYS SINCE HE'D LEAPED FROM THE DOOMED *SALTY'S NATURALS*, Joe Cornwall had been on a near-constant emotional roller-coaster. Though undoubtedly thankful to have survived the Fortress's sudden destruction, he was still coming to grips with the fact that most of his crewmates—men with whom he'd lived and trained for months, and who in many ways were closer to him than his own family—were almost certainly dead. Moreover, from the moment he'd thumped painfully to earth Joe had been a hunted man, on the run in a strange country with the threat of capture constantly looming over him. Unable to speak more than a few words of French— and those with a decidedly American accent—he'd had no choice but to entrust himself to a series of complete strangers.

That was proving to be a difficult adjustment for Joe. The vagaries of his early life had molded him into a self-reliant and self-confident man, one used to making his own decisions and accepting responsibility for his actions. Yet, not surprisingly, he also craved order and consistency, an inclination that had tempered his maverick spirit and allowed him to adjust remarkably well to military service. But the realities of life on the run in German-occupied France challenged each of Joe's defining personality traits. He'd not only had to relinquish control over his life to people he'd never met and whose intentions were not always clear, but the helpers' need for secrecy ensured that he was not informed of any change in his location until the last possible moment. It was a disquieting situation, to say the least.

Now, as the Americans settled themselves on the small couch in the Morins' narrow living room, Joe made a quick assessment of the man who had apparently assumed responsibility for him and Harry. Georges appeared to be in his late forties, with silver strands running through his otherwise coal-black hair, and one of his eyes looked as though it might be false. Though slight of stature, the Frenchman exuded an aura of calm competence that Joe found reassuring. Georges obviously did not speak much English, but he had gone to the trouble of writing out a few sentences using a small French-English dictionary and now read them in a clear and steady voice. He and his family were honored to welcome the American guests to the Hôtel des Invalides and to their home, he said, and would do what they could to make the aviators' stay a pleasant one. At that point Georges handed Joe a piece of paper bearing several lines laboriously handwritten in English, saying that these were the rules the American guests must follow for everyone's safety. As the airmen were scanning the document Denise walked in from the kitchen, introduced herself, then handed each of the gunners a small, steaming plate of vegetables and a meat Joe immediately recognized as rabbit.

After the meal Denise led the Americans upstairs to the small front bedroom, which she indicated belonged to her adult daughter, Yvette, who was at work. The aviators gathered that the room was theirs for the length of their stay, and a quick coin toss won Harry the bed and relegated Joe to the thin mattress on the floor. On one wall a framed picture of

Georges and Denise attracted Joe's attention. Obviously taken outside in front of the Dôme church, the image depicted husband and wife in formal attire, he in pleated pants with a white shirt, vest, and tie, and she in a conservative black dress. But it was the person standing between Georges and Denise that caught Joe's eye. Obviously the daughter whose room the Americans now occupied, she was slender and the same height as her mother—about five feet four, Joe estimated. Her dark hair was swept up, and she was wearing what appeared to be an embroidered, knee-length white dress and matching shoes. She stood with her hands behind her back, looking directly at the photographer, her head cocked slightly to one side and the beginnings of a smile just lifting one corner of her mouth. Though the photo depicted her as a teenager, probably at the time of her confirmation or some other religious event, she was beautiful in a natural and unpretentious way. Joe found himself wondering what she looked like now, and hoping he'd have the chance to find out.

His opportunity would come, just not as soon as he would have liked.

THE MORINS HAD BEEN TOLD IN ADVANCE THAT THEY WOULD BE SHELTERING more than one person and, as when Brown and Houghton arrived weeks before, Yvette had arranged to stay with Dr. Mercier and his wife at their home on avenue Daniel Lesueur, which was less than a half mile south of Invalides.[17] She therefore didn't go back to her parents after work at the Crédit National on Thursday or Friday, June 22 or 23. When she did return home, on the afternoon of Saturday the twenty-fourth, she was accompanied by Germaine Mercier.

Though no written account survives of the first meeting between Joe Cornwall and Yvette Morin, all indications are that their initial encounter was a revelation for both of them. Looking at Yvette, Joe would have seen a somewhat older and more sophisticated echo of the girl in the photo. Slender, petite, and lovely, with a winsome smile and vivid green eyes, Yvette would undoubtedly have captivated Joe from the moment he met her. And she was almost certainly equally as enthralled by him. Despite the emotional and physical rigors of his week on the run, Joe remained an impressive figure. Just under six feet tall, lean and sinewy, with dark, wavy

At twenty-five, Joe Cornwall enlisted in what was then known as the U.S. Army Air Corps. After basic training at McChord Field, Washington, he traveled to Colorado's Lowry Field for training as an aircraft armorer. He is seen here, second from the left in the front row, upon his graduation from the course on November 28, 1941. Still ahead was training as an aerial gunner.

The crew to which Joe Cornwall was assigned at the Salt Lake AAB Combat Crew Replacement Pool was led by then First Lieutenant Edward Arum Purdy. The twenty-six-year-old Colorado native was both an excellent pilot and a born leader; both attributes would prove extremely important when he and his crew took to the dangerous skies over German-occupied Europe.

The men of *Natural* pose for the standard crew photo soon after arriving in England. Back row, left to right: John Smith (ball turret), Charles Sprague (radio operator), Russell Crisp (flight engineer/top turret), Joe Cornwall (left waist), Frank Santangelo (right waist), and Larry Templeton (tail). Front row, from left: Edward Jones (bombardier), Carroll Harris (copilot), Ed Purdy (pilot), and Charles Lichtenberger (navigator).

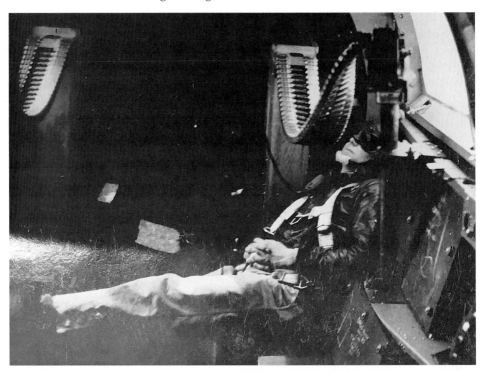

Joe Cornwall relaxes in his favorite spot on the return from an early training mission over England. Note that despite the nature of the flight, both waist guns are connected to full belts of .50-caliber ammunition—an encounter with enemy aircraft was possible over much of the United Kingdom at any time in the spring and summer of 1943.

No in-flight photos of *Natural* exist, but the B-17F would have been identical in layout and markings to these two Fortresses of the 94th Bomb Group's 332nd Bomb Squadron. The large black "A" in a white square on the horizontal stabilizer and right wing tip was the 94th's unit identification marking. Squadron code letters were later added to both sides of each aircraft's fuselage, fore and aft of the waist gun windows, though *Natural* had not received them before the Purdy crew was given the replacement Fortress that became *Naturals*.

During the June 13 raid on Kiel several 20mm cannon rounds hit *Natural*'s right wing, knocking out the inboard right engine and sparking a fire. Shrapnel from the hit ripped through the right side of the cockpit, slightly wounding copilot Carroll Harris. That the aircraft made it to Rougham was a testament to Ed Purdy's piloting skills, and the young aviator was awarded the first of two Distinguished Flying Crosses for this action. Though overlaid by oil spewed by the damaged engine, the aircraft's nose art is clearly visible.

Located just outside Bury St. Edmunds in Suffolk, Rougham airfield became the 94th Bomb Group's permanent home following the Kiel mission. The renovated control tower—now a museum and memorial to the American aviators who flew from the field during World War II—is one of the wartime base's few remaining structures. *(Photo by Stephen Harding)*

The B-17 assigned to the Purdy crew as a replacement for the severely damaged *Natural* was a slightly older but an essentially identical Fortress bearing the serial number 42-3331. The name initially emblazoned on the aircraft's nose—this time on the left side rather than the right—was the plural "*Naturals.*"

Though just twenty-seven years old, 331st Bomb Squadron commander Ralph H. Saltsman had proven himself to be an outstanding pilot, an able administrator, and a man who treated both superiors and subordinates with equal regard. His decision to fly with the Purdy crew on the July 4 mission to La Pallice prompted the men of *Naturals* to modify the aircraft's name in his honor, and from then on the Fortress was known as *Salty's Naturals*.

A World War I veteran and highly successful entrepreneur in Paris between the wars, Jefferson Davis Dickson left his comfortable life behind in order to "do his part" in the fight against the Axis. Seen here just after returning to service, he went on to become the photographic officer at 4th Wing headquarters and was tasked to shoot motion-picture footage of raids launched against targets in Occupied Europe. It was in that capacity that he joined the 94th Bomb Group for the Bastille Day raid on Le Bourget.

Jeff Dickson chose to fly with Ed Purdy's crew after being told the men of *Salty's Naturals* were the "least likely to turn back" during the mission. In this unfortunately poor image, Dickson (far right) and Purdy (far left) are joined by two other officers for a group photo on the evening of July 13.

Three of the four 94th Bomb Group Fortresses lost on July 14 were shot down before the unit bombed Le Bourget. Here, Luftwaffe ace Egon Mayer stands atop one of his victims that day, the severely damaged B-17 that Kee Harrison was able to successfully crash-land in an open field. Images of Mayer and his trophy were used extensively in German propaganda magazines for several months afterward.

Having bombed Le Bourget, the remnants of the 94th Bomb Group begin the long flight back to Rougham. By this point the three remaining 331st Bomb Squadron Fortresses have joined the lead squadron, though minutes after this photo was taken Floyd Watts's aircraft was hit and crashed into a section of rail line leading into the train station at Louvres.

General der Infanterie Kurt von Briesen (on horse, center) takes the salute of the 30th Infantry Division during a triumphal parade through Paris the day following the Germans' June 1940 occupation of the capital. French résistants would manage to move hundreds of Allied evaders through the city despite the presence of thousands of enemy troops.

During his whirlwind tour of Paris Adolf Hitler was photographed in or near many of the capital's best-known landmarks—including the Eiffel Tower—but it was his brief visit to Invalides that apparently meant the most to him. He stood for several minutes in the circular gallery above Napoléon's sarcophagus, his head bowed toward the final resting place of the soldier-emperor with whom he most closely identified. As the entourage left the rotunda, the obviously deeply affected Führer told photographer Heinrich Hoffman that his time at the tomb was "the greatest and finest moment" of his life. The visit also indirectly led to the Morins' first overt act of resistance. *(Bundesarchiv)*

Denise, Yvette, and Georges Morin pose for a formal portrait in front of the building housing Napoléon's Tomb at the Hôtel des Invalides. A partially disabled World War I veteran, Georges went to work as an editor for l'Office nationale des mutilés et réformés in 1921, and Denise ultimately became Invalides' "supervisor of fine arts building sites." Their daughter grew up knowing every nook and cranny of the vast campus. *(Photo courtesy Yvette Morin-Claerebout)*

The attic of the ornate Saint-Louis des Invalides cathedral was one of the Morins' favorite "hidden" places. Reached via a series of small doors and narrow, vertigo-inducing wooden stairways, the attic rests atop the cathedral's vaulted ceiling. The interior of the attic is dark, and the massive arched timbers supporting the cathedral roof look like an inverted ship's hull. The ladder-like staircase at the far end of the space leads to the two small doors that open out onto an exterior landing on the cathedral's roof. *(Photo by Stephen Harding)*

The view from atop the cathedral's roof is spectacular. People sitting or standing in the area between the vast golden dome above Napoléon's Tomb (at left) and the smaller metal cupola above the cathedral's altar cannot be seen from the ground. The vistas are not enjoyed without risk, however, for the winds whistling across the roof are often strong enough to blow a person over, and the walls that surround the open area are too short to prevent a fall of almost one hundred feet. *(Photo by Stephen Harding)*

One of the smaller cupolas atop the Dôme church serves as a platform for a group photo taken by Denise and featuring, from left to right, Georges, Harry Eastman, Yvette, Joe, and Germaine Mercier. In the background rise the twin spires of the Basilique de Sainte-Clotilde. *(Photo courtesy Yvette Morin-Claerebout)*

Having changed places with Georges, Denise joins her daughter and the others for another photo. While posing for such images was something of a calculated risk, the danger was mitigated by the fact that any German who saw the Morins and their guests would likely have assumed that those atop the structure must have had authorization. *(Photo courtesy Yvette Morin-Claerebout)*

Though of poor quality, this image clearly depicts the closeness Joe and Yvette shared. They are perched atop the east side of the Dôme church, and just visible to the right of Yvette's left elbow is the small eastern gate near the Morins' home. The apartment was just on the other side of the large building to the right of Yvette. *(Photo courtesy Yvette Morin-Claerebout)*

Joe and Yvette only have eyes for each other as they sit for a group photo with Tony Trusty (in dark jacket) and Roy Scott. The men were the mid-upper gunner and pilot, respectively, of an RAF Handley Page Halifax II bomber shot down on August 13, 1943, while on a nighttime special-operations mission over France. *(Photo courtesy Yvette Morin-Claerebout)*

On his second or third visit to the top of the Dôme church, Tony Trusty used a small penknife to scratch a brief message into the outer skin of the circular metal cupola above the altar of Saint-Louis des Invalides. Time and the elements have weathered the inscription somewhat, but most of it remains. *(Photo by Stephen Harding)*

Other than carrying a different fuselage code and serial number, this Lysander IIIa of No. 161 (Special Duties) Squadron is identical to the aircraft that picked up Joe Cornwall early on October 19, 1943. Passengers carried into and out of Occupied France entered and left the cramped rear cockpit via the narrow metal ladder welded to the left side of the fuselage. Though the unit's Lysanders were originally painted black overall, Hugh Verity believed that scheme made the aircraft more visible from above at night, and he ordered the upper surfaces of all the machines painted in a dark green and pale gray camouflage pattern that he thought would better allow them to blend in with the terrain over which they flew. Part of that revised color scheme is visible in this photo as a light-colored patch just forward of the aircraft's vertical stabilizer. *(Photo courtesy Chris McCairns)*

In this unfortunately poor image, Flying Officer James McAllister McBride stands in front of another of 161 Squadron's Lysanders about two months after he flew Joe Cornwall out of France. Six hours after this photo was taken, McBride died during an attempt to land at RAF Tangmere upon his return from a pickup mission in France. The aircraft in which he died was the same one that had carried Cornwall to freedom. *(Photo courtesy Chris McCairns)*

Georges, Denise, and Yvette appear calm and relaxed in photos taken for use with false identity documents the family prepared in case they needed to escape Paris. Sadly, all three were arrested by the Gestapo before they were able to flee the city. The images were attached to the family file later compiled by the MIS-X office in Paris and are now held in the U.S. National Archives.

After his evaluation in Atlantic City, New Jersey, Joe was ordered to USAAF Redistribution Center No. 3 in Santa Monica, California, for fifteen days of rest and recuperation. The facility comprised three oceanfront resorts—the Del Mar Beach Club, the Edgewater Beach Club, and the Grand Hotel—and the emphasis for the majority of the assigned service members was on rest and recreation.

Joe looks composed but decidedly detached in a formal portrait shot not long before his October 1, 1945, separation from the USAAF at San Bernardino Army Airfield in Southern California. He received $4,370.29 in final pay, and days later was on his way to Alaska.

After several months working as a hunting guide in southeast Alaska, Joe became the engineer on the Fish and Wildlife Service patrol vessel *Auklet*. Joe served aboard the forty-eight-foot, tugboat-like vessel for the next four years before ultimately rejoining what had by then become the U.S. Air Force. *(Alaska Fisheries Science Center/NOAA)*

During a 1967 event held, appropriately, in Invalides' Cour d'honneur, Yvette Morin-Claerebout wears the insignia of a Chevalier of the Ordre nationale de la Légion d'honneur just awarded to her. Her daughter Denise stands to her right, while to her left her mother Denise chats with the U.S. air attaché at the American embassy. Yvette and her mother both received the U.S. Medal of Freedom, as did Georges, posthumously. *(Photo courtesy Yvette Morin-Claerebout)*

Two plaques honoring Georges Morin grace the halls of Invalides. This, the first one, was installed in the Metz corridor just after the war, and the second was unveiled nearby during a ceremony on April 26, 2001. Speaking to Yvette Morin-Claerebout on the latter occasion, then French prime minister Lionel Jospin said, "To you, Madam, allow me to express in my own name, but also of that of all the French, my profound respect for your father and for your whole family. Through this homage paid to the great résistant that was Georges Morin, the government celebrates the courage of all those who fought for France and marks the recognition of the homeland towards them." *(Photo by Stephen Harding)*

hair and bright blue eyes, he had the rugged good looks of a movie-poster cowboy.

That the initial physical attraction between Joe and Yvette grew into something much deeper was the result, at least in part, of one of the written rules Georges had given Joe and Harry upon their arrival. In addition to admonitions about remaining as quiet as possible while in the apartment, and about remembering to draw the bedroom curtains before turning on a light after dark, the rules understandably stated that the "guests" could not go outside unless escorted by one of the family members. Though it might at first glance seem both foolish and dangerous to permit evaders to leave the relative safety of their helpers' homes under any circumstances, most evasion networks saw carefully arranged and well-chaperoned excursions "outside" as a way to prevent the onset of a potentially catastrophic condition: evader boredom.

For young, healthy men accustomed to the high-flying and adrenalin-fueled life of a combat aviator, being cooped up in a small apartment—no matter how safe or hospitable—could very quickly start to seem like a jail sentence. The evaders' inability to converse with their hosts, and in most cases the total absence of English-language reading materials, meant that airmen were reduced to playing interminable rounds of solitaire (if being sheltered alone) or potentially loud and contentious games of poker with fellow evaders. Such a regimen would quickly pale, prompting the young men to sneak out on their own in a search for entertainment—often of the physical kind. Though wearing civilian clothes and carrying forged identity documents, unless the thrill-seeking aviators spoke French they were almost certain to be quickly unmasked. Whether caught in a spot search or turned in by a prostitute or barman seeking to curry favor with the Germans, the result rarely varied. The evaders ended up in a POW camp, but the helpers they likely betrayed during interrogation always faced more tragic consequences.

Few helpers were in a better position to address the boredom problem than were the Morins. While sheltering refractors early on, the family had learned that the year-round flow of people into and out of the tourist areas of the Invalides complex allowed the "cousins from out of town" to spend a fair amount of time outside in good weather. As long as they were careful they could wander the grounds, or sit on a garden bench reading, or simply soak up the sun. With the help of Denise and her big ring of keys, the "guests" could even explore places that most visitors never got to see—including the roof of the Dôme church. More than one hundred feet above ground level, the semicircular terrace at the base of the dome offers a panoramic view of Paris, and if the "guests" stayed away from the edge of the roof they could not be seen from below.

Georges, Denise, and Yvette intended to allow Allied airmen the same opportunities to leave their hiding places, though the family understood that the non-French-speaking aviators would require a chaperone whenever they went outside—hence the rule. Unfortunately for Joe Cornwall and Harry Eastman, the elder Morins had been too busy during the first days of the aviators' stay to accompany them outside. The July 24 arrival of Yvette and Germaine Mercier solved that particular problem, however, for with a few words from the French-English dictionary and some universal hand gestures the women offered to return the next day, Sunday, and escort the Americans on a brief stroll outside.

Yvette and Germaine were as good as their word, returning to Invalides the next afternoon. The airmen were delighted at the prospect of leaving the Morins' small apartment, and Joe was especially pleased that as the quartet walked out into the sunshine Yvette very naturally looped her arm through his. Since Germaine had also taken Harry's arm, Joe assumed the gesture was simply a security tool—two couples strolling arm in arm, each in companionable silence, would be less conspicuous than four people walking together but not touching or speaking. It would also make it easier for the women to respond more naturally if someone addressed either American in French, Joe thought, though he may have hoped that Yvette's gesture might have a deeper meaning.

That initial outing apparently went quite well, because over the following week Yvette and Germaine returned every afternoon to chaperone the two American aviators on outside excursions. On at least two occasions the couples ventured beyond Invalides together, one day walking north back toward the Seine and on another going south to visit the Morins' church, Saint-François-Xavier. And on at least one other day Harry and Germaine ventured outside the complex on their own, both understanding that Harry's baldness was an especially effective disguise. His lack of hair made him appear even older than his thirty-four years, and with the thirty-something Germaine on his arm Harry looked for all the world like a middle-aged French husband and nothing like an Allied aviator on the run.[18] The two Americans and their escorts were never stopped by the German guards either leaving or reentering Invalides, largely because of the soldiers' laxness but also because the couples made sure that each time they went through the gates they did so as part of a large group of visitors.

Having the opportunity to leave Invalides and walk the nearby streets undoubtedly boosted the spirits of Joe and Harry, but it was their jaunt to a very different destination that would truly exhilarate the American airmen. That sense of exhilaration would be tempered, however, by the news that their time at Invalides was coming to an end.

ON JULY 29, EXACTLY A WEEK AFTER JOE AND HARRY FIRST WALKED IN the Morins' door, Georges took the Americans aside and told them— again with the aid of his pocket dictionary—that the next leg of their on- ward journey had been arranged and they would be leaving the following morning. While both men had certainly been expecting to move on, Joe was deeply saddened by the news. In the few days he'd spent at Invalides he'd become very fond of the Morins, and more than fond of Yvette. She reciprocated his feelings, and in their short time together they'd found themselves able to intuitively understand one another despite only know- ing a few words of each other's language. To their own surprise, they'd each found the kindred spirit that had thus far been missing in their lives. Georges and Denise were aware of the deep emotional bond between their daughter and Joe, and though they liked the young American airman they urged Yvette to be realistic about the future. Joe was duty-bound to try to return to England and get back into the war, they told her, while her duty was to stay and focus her energies on the continuing fight against the hated Boche.

Though heartsick at the thought they were about to be parted so soon after finding each other, Joe and Yvette sought to make the best of the sit- uation. They spoke of the coming separation as a temporary situation—the war would be over soon, they assured each other, and when it ended they swore they'd find a way to be together. It was, of course, a promise that couples have been making for as long as war has existed, and in their hearts Joe and Yvette likely knew all too well that their chances of ever seeing one another again were exceedingly slim.

In part as a way to cheer up both their daughter and the young American who was so obviously downhearted at the thought of leaving, Georges and Yvette suggested that they, Yvette, Joe, Harry, and Germaine spend that evening in one of the most exclusive places in Paris—the narrow terrace atop the Dôme church. It would be a particularly memorable way for the Americans to pass what was probably their last night in the City of Light, for they would be treated to a panorama that very few people ever get to see.

After the German guards closed the eastern gate at 7 P.M. and retired to their barracks on the other side of Invalides, Denise led the group to a small wooden door set into an alcove at the south end of the Cour d'honneur. Using one of the keys on her large ring, she unlocked the portal and ushered the others through before quickly entering herself and pulling the door closed behind her. Georges, now in the lead, started up a steep, narrow, twisting staircase that took the party past several landings, each of which had passages leading off in other directions. After a climb that left Joe and Harry puffing, the group came to another tight landing, at the far end of which was a short flight of stairs leading to a small door. After passing through it the group entered what immediately felt to Joe like a much larger and more open space, and when Georges and Yvette snapped on the small flashlights they'd been carrying the two Americans realized they were in the long, heavily timbered attic above the Cathédrale Saint-Louis.

Georges set off again, and after moving several hundred feet along a broad, wooden catwalk the group reached two narrow sets of stairs, both far steeper than those that had come before. Georges led the way up one and Denise the other, and when they reached the top they each swung open a narrow metal door. The resultant twin shafts of light clearly indicated that the destination was at hand, but nothing could have prepared Joe for the sight that met his eyes as he walked out onto a small stone landing. Directly to his front was a large, dull-colored, metal-clad cupola, flanked on both sides by smaller, turret-like stone edifices that looked almost like small minarets. And looming up behind the central cupola was the massive, gold-topped dome that soared above the final resting place of Napoléon Bonaparte.

Georges and Denise led the others around the lower central cupola on a frighteningly narrow stone walkway. Chancing a quick look over the low wall to his left, Joe estimated they were a good one hundred feet above the ground, and despite his considerable time as an aviator he found himself leaning closer to the cupola. A few more steps brought him out onto the actual roof of the Dôme church, its surface made up of massive, rectangular blocks of stone laid in intricate, interlocking patterns. A central gutter separated the stones that supported the base of the dome from those that sloped upward toward the low walls lining the edge of the roof. The elder Morins motioned the others to follow the gutter around toward the southeast corner of the church roof, the point farthest from the German-occupied areas in the northwest corner of Invalides. Once everyone had assembled, Yvette reached into the pocket of her summer frock and withdrew a small camera. As Germaine Mercier translated, Yvette explained that if this was going to be their last evening together, they should have photos by which to remember it. She knew Joe and Harry would not be able to carry copies of the photos with them, she said, but she promised to find a way to forward them.

It's unclear how many images were taken in the golden sunlight of that early summer evening, but the four that survive depict a group of smiling friends in various poses. Georges was obviously the designated photographer, for he only appears in one of the pictures. Each of the images shows the participants sitting or standing closely together, with their arms linked or their hands on each other's shoulders. In one of the photos they are sitting on a section of upward-sloping stone blocks—looking almost like sports fans seated on a particularly sturdy set of bleachers. In the remaining three images Joe and the others are atop the short stone cupola directly above the right side of the entrance to the church, and the twin spires of the Basilica of Sainte-Clotilde rise behind them in the middle distance.

These last shots were something of a calculated risk, of course, for while standing or sitting atop the cupola the group could have been visible to anyone outside the complex who might have been looking in their direction from the south or southeast. Yet the danger was mitigated by several factors. Most important, the German gate guards who would have been the most likely to have noticed the tableau atop the church had already retired to their barracks area. And even had a wandering German seen the Morins and their guests, he would probably have assumed that no un-authorized persons would have been able to reach the area, so anyone up there must have authorization. The same logic would probably have held true for people outside the complex. If they actually noticed the group—which the time of day and the angle of the soon-to-be-setting sun would likely have made difficult—the assumption that the Germans must be aware of whatever was happening within a complex they presumably controlled would have dampened the curiosity of most passersby.

Following the impromptu photo session the Morins and their guests relaxed in their rooftop aerie, taking in the sights and talking of the journey upon which the two airmen were about to embark. When Denise talked about how difficult it would be for the men to walk over the Pyrenees into Spain, Joe laughingly responded, "Mama, that's not possible! I can't walk, I'm a flier."[19]

When the sun finally went down a little after nine thirty, the group trooped carefully back down to ground level. By that point it was too far past curfew for Yvette and Germaine to attempt to make it back to the latter's home, so the women made themselves comfortable in the attic space above the architect's office while Joe and Harry retired to Yvette's room. The following morning Germaine joined the Morins and the airmen for a simple breakfast, which for Joe and Yvette was an undoubtedly sad and somber meal. The melancholy atmosphere turned tearful with the noon arrival of a woman who was introduced to the Americans as "Marie." She was, in fact, thirty-three-year-old Gabrielle Wiame, a Belgian-born member of the Bourgogne network, and she had come to shepherd Joe and Harry to the next waypoint on their journey.

The airmen's imminent departure prompted a round of farewell hugs and handshakes, and though Joe and Yvette had sworn that they would be together some day, the very real possibility that they would never see each other again brought both of them to tears. After a long, final embrace that only ended when Georges, Denise, and Harry gently pulled the couple apart, Joe reluctantly followed Harry and "Marie" out the door of the Morins' apartment. Just before the Frenchwoman and her two charges disappeared around the corner toward Invalides' eastern gate, Joe turned briefly back toward Yvette, who was standing in the apartment doorway, now sobbing inconsolably. Then, with a sad, final smile, he was gone.

AFTER WALKING AS NONCHALANTLY AS POSSIBLE PAST THE GERMAN TROOPS on duty at the eastern gate, Joe and Harry followed "Marie" at a careful distance as she strode purposefully south for several hundred yards on the boulevard des Invalides. She ultimately turned left down a street lined with what Joe later described as "impressive" multistory apartment buildings, and over the next hour led the Americans generally toward the southeast.[20] Her destination was the home of a friend and fellow Bourgogne member, sixty-year-old Mme. Madeleine Anna Melot, on the rue Larrey in Paris's 5th arrondissement. Roughly two miles from Invalides, the apartment was on the top floor of an old and impressive building a fifteen-minute walk from the Gare d'Austerlitz, the main station for trains serving Bordeaux, Toulouse, and other destinations close to the border with neutral Spain. The recent widow of a French army officer, Mme. Melot—with the help of her housekeeper and the apartment building's female concierge—had turned her large and rather ornate home into a message center and meeting place for résistants. She also occasionally sheltered evaders, and at the time "Marie" arrived with Joe and Harry in tow the dignified older woman was hosting Pilot Officer George Dickson of the Royal New Zealand Air Force (RNZAF). And, much to the Americans' delight, also on hand was the third member of the Gunner Trio, Dick Davitt.[21]

After staying at André Schoegel's apartment in Orly for several days after David Turner had been moved to the home of a female pediatrician who was sheltering Kee Harrison, Davitt had also changed locations. He was now staying with two women, Maud Couvé and Alice Brouard, on rue de Madrid, near the Gare Saint-Lazare, north of the river. Their two-bedroom apartment was more than a little crowded, Davitt said, because Maud's two young children and Alice's fifteen-year-old daughter were also living there.[22] Indeed, Davitt's presence at Mme. Melot's home was essentially just a "day out," and he was as surprised to see Joe and Harry as they were to see him. Given Davitt's description of the tight quarters at the Rue de Madrid apartment, all three airmen were more than a little confused when, after a light lunch with their hostess and "Marie," the latter announced that Joe and Harry were also to be sheltered with Maud and Alice until "some details" of their onward journey were settled.[23]

The reason why Joe and Harry could not just stay at Mme. Melot's spacious apartment is now lost to history, though the most likely explanation is that the elderly Frenchwoman had already been tapped to host other—and perhaps more senior—airmen. Yet soon after "Marie" and the three Americans arrived at the rue de Madrid apartment later that afternoon it became clear that while Maud and Alice could possibly accommodate one evader in addition to Davitt, they simply couldn't take two. Probably hoping that he would be able to return to the Morins at Invalides, Joe insisted that Harry should stay with Maud and Alice with Davitt. When Harry agreed—likely because he understood his friend's motivations—"Marie" concurred, and minutes later she left the apartment with Joe following at a discreet distance.

The young aviator's hopes of returning immediately to Invalides were quickly dashed, for "Marie" instead took him to a different safe house, the apartment of forty-two-year-old Mme. Dora May Rospape on rue du 29 Juillet, in the city's 1st arrondissement.[24] While Joe left no account of his stay with the British-born helper, we may assume that her fluency in English and extensive library of American and British novels would have helped the airman pass the time. But we can also be certain that Joe was haunted by the fact that Yvette was so close—by now he was familiar enough with that part of Paris to know that Invalides was less than a mile to the southwest of Mme. Rospape's home, on the other side of the river—yet he could not go to Yvette. He had been told in no uncertain terms that a sudden increase in German antiresistance activity in the area made it far too dangerous to leave the apartment, and that any attempt to do so could cast suspicion on him. Knowing full well what happened to those of whom the Resistance grew suspicious, Joe had no choice but to keep his ardor in check and hope that fate would give him one more chance to see the woman he loved.

Whether it was fate or just good luck, that chance came relatively quickly. Joe had been with Dora Rospape for eight days when the sudden arrival of a Turma-Vengeance courier signaled an imminent change in the aviator's situation. In good English the man explained that the network's leaders had decided to shift Joe to a different safe house, though no reason was given for the move. After a quick farewell hug from his hostess Joe followed the courier out the door and down the stairs to the building's foyer. Before walking out onto the street the résistant reminded Joe to follow him at a discreet distance, and said that if he—the courier—were stopped by soldiers or police Joe should keep going and eventually make his way back to Mme. Rospape's apartment.

Though his guide had not specified their destination, Joe was immediately heartened by the fact that upon leaving the apartment building the man turned right and began walking south on rue du 29 Juillet. The street ended at the rue de Rivoli, on the other side of which was the sprawling Tuileries Garden on the north bank of the Seine. Joe reasoned that if they crossed the river, there was at least a chance they were headed for Invalides. His hunch was soon proved right, for his guide led him west along the Seine, then over the Pont de la Concorde. Once across the span the men turned right on the quai d'Orsay, and continued walking until the now familiar vista of the broad esplanade des Invalides opened before them. When the guide headed briskly off down the sidewalk bordering the rue du Marechal Galleni directly toward the golden dome, Joe hurried to keep pace, increasingly convinced that he was about to be reunited with Yvette.

After passing through Invalides' north gate behind what appeared to be an extended French family—and again without any interference from the German soldiers standing guard—Joe could hardly restrain himself from running across the Cour d'honneur, though he could do nothing about the broad smile that creased his face. He had a brief moment of panic when his escort stopped abruptly upon reaching the southeast corner of the Dôme church and for a moment seemed to be about to head directly out through the southern gate, but it quickly became apparent that the man was simply waiting for a group of uniformed Germans—tourists, Joe assumed, based on the guidebooks in which they seemed intensely interested—to move past. Once the Boche had strolled off toward the church entrance the guide turned left and walked nonchalantly toward the eastern gate. Joe followed, silently praying that the Frenchman would turn right before reaching the portal, and when the man did so Joe almost laughed aloud. By the time the young American turned the corner himself his guide was standing at the Morins' door, speaking in a low voice with Georges and

Denise. When they saw Joe they both smiled broadly, and as he reached the threshold Denise embraced him and kissed him on both cheeks.

In response to Joe's questioning glance into the apartment, Georges winked, tapped his battered wristwatch, and in English said simply, "work." His meaning was clear: Yvette had not yet returned from the Crédit National. The news that he would have to wait a few more hours to hold the woman he loved didn't bother Joe in the least, however; until that moment he hadn't been sure he'd ever actually see her again. Despite the fact that he was in an enemy-occupied city in the middle of the greatest war the world had ever seen, Joe Cornwall was the happiest man on earth.

Chapter 6

HOME RUN

F OR JOE CORNWALL AND YVETTE MORIN, THE DAYS FOLLOWING THE
aviator's surprise August 8 return to Invalides were filled with both
happiness and a growing conviction that their earlier dreams of a
postwar life together might actually come true. Their time apart had given
each of them the opportunity to examine their feelings for one another,
and they had independently come to the inescapable conclusion that they
could and would overcome the challenges presented by their different
backgrounds, cultures, and languages. During long conversations conducted with the help of a small French-English dictionary and a growing
vocabulary of gestures, the couple began to plan in concrete terms for a
future that just days before had seemed as unlikely as it was desirable. They
even spoke half-jokingly of ultimately traveling together to Alaska to visit
Joe's mother.

Both realized, of course, that their ultimate happiness was entirely de-
pendent on the defeat of Nazi Germany and the liberation of France. They
were also equally aware that both of them still had important roles to play
in achieving that longed-for victory, and that they were certain to be separated again—likely for years—before they could finally begin building
a life together. Unfortunately, that next separation came far sooner than
either would have wished.

On Sunday, August 16, the Morins received word that on the following morning Joe would be leaving again. Whatever issues had prevented
his departure for Spain on the previous attempt had apparently been resolved, for Georges and Denise were told that an escort would take their

American guest directly to the Gare d'Austerlitz. There, Joe would presumably be handed off to a different escort for the onward rail journey to Toulouse and, ultimately, the Spanish border. The elder Morins broke the news of Joe's coming departure to him and Yvette over dinner, after which all four of them repaired to the roof of the Dôme church to watch a final sunset together.

THE MORNING OF MONDAY, AUGUST 17, BROUGHT SOMETHING OF A SURPRISE. Joe's escort to the railway station turned out to be not one person, but three. Gabrielle Wiame, the English-speaking résistant whom the aviator knew only as "Marie," was accompanied by both Maud Couvé and Germaine Mercier.[1] And, in what was almost certainly not a surprise to Joe, Yvette also insisted on going with him and the others. "Marie" was apparently aware of the emotional bond between the young Frenchwoman and the American evader and reluctantly agreed. Joe then once again said a sad farewell to the elder Morins before walking out the door with the four women.

In yet another unexpected development that morning, after leaving Invalides through the east gate "Marie" turned left and headed north toward the Seine, rather than striking off to the east and the Gare d'Austerlitz. Joe had assumed that he and his escorts would walk the roughly two and a half miles to the train station, given that all of his earlier forays through the city had been on foot. A few minutes later the reason for the detour became apparent, however, when "Marie" led the group down into a Métro station. At the bottom of the steps "Marie" motioned for the others to wait for her at a nearby kiosk, then started off toward the ticket booths. Joe watched her walk away, but noticed that before she reached her destination a thin young man in a shabby suit crossed her path and bumped into her. The man leaned close to "Marie," uttering what might have been an apology, but what looked to Joe more like a terse warning—then disappeared into the crowd. As he did so, "Marie" abruptly turned and walked back toward where Joe, Yvette, and the others were standing. Instead of stopping, she passed by and with a slight nod of her head indicated that the others were to follow her back up the stairs and out of the station. Joe's hunch that the poorly dressed young man had alerted "Marie" to some sort of danger was confirmed moments later, when after turning down a side street she stopped briefly to let her companions catch up. As they gathered around her she said the man who had bumped into her—a Turma-Vengeance lookout—had warned her the Métro station was alive with Gestapo men.[2]

"Marie" acknowledged that the agents' presence might have been part of a regular inspection of travelers' papers, but added that she could not rule out the possibility that the Boche had been forewarned of some sort of resistance activity. Security protocols forbade an immediate return to Invalides, in case the Morins had been betrayed and were under surveillance, so "Marie" told Maud Couvé to go home and then instructed Germaine, Joe, and Yvette to spend a few hours walking around the city to ensure they were not being followed. They were then to go to Germaine's apartment, she said, where she would meet them once she had further instructions to pass on. With that, she turned and hurried away.

Though understandably upset at the thought that Georges and Denise might already be in the hands of the Germans, Yvette, Joe, and Germaine did as "Marie" had instructed. For the next two hours they walked the streets of the 6th arrondissement—east of Invalides and south of the Seine—strolling as casually as they could, Joe and Yvette holding hands. Having detected no tails, they eventually made their way to the Merciers' apartment, where Germaine filled her husband in on the morning's excitement. The four of them then settled in for what they assumed would be the imminent arrival of "Marie" and her new instructions.

It turned out to be a somewhat longer wait than they had anticipated, however, for "Marie" did not appear at the Merciers' apartment until the morning of Wednesday, August 19. Her only explanation for her two-day absence was a terse reference to "security procedures," though her report that all was well with the elder Morins' was welcome news for both Yvette and Joe. The couple's spirits were further lifted when "Marie" told them that Joe could go back to Invalides "for a few more days" until the details of his next departure from Paris could be worked out. Having delivered her update, "Marie" left quickly.

Almost immediately after the woman's departure, Joe and Yvette made their way back to Invalides. While Georges and Denise were overjoyed to see them—they had assumed both had been arrested—they were also quick to voice their belief that "Marie" had in some way been responsible for the debacle at the Métro station. Nor were they alone in their distrust of her, they said, for other members of Turma-Vengeance had also begun to question the woman's loyalty. These suspicions later proved to be totally unfounded, but given the Germans' ongoing and often highly successful efforts to penetrate the French evasion networks, even the slightest uncertainty about a résistant's devotion to the cause was enough to prompt an internal investigation.[3] Until the probe into "Marie" was concluded, the elder Morins told Joe, someone else would help arrange his onward travel.

That someone turned out to be a tall, slender, and balding man who arrived at Invalides the next day, August 20.[4] Introduced to the American aviator simply as "Gotha," he was, in fact, a former Polish army officer named Andrzej Wyssogota-Zakrzewski. He'd learned the evasion trade helping fellow Polish soldiers flee from France into Spain in 1940 and 1941, and had managed to escape from German captivity several times. He ultimately founded and headed an evasion network known as Visigoth-Lorraine, but also worked closely with Turma-Vengeance, Bourgogne, Comète, and others. His careful examination of Joe's false papers on that first visit to Invalides seemed to reinforce the possibility that "Marie" was not entirely trustworthy, for though she had pronounced the documents to be fine when she looked at them, "Gotha" immediately denounced them as being "no good." He took the papers with him when he left, saying that he would return with usable ones in a few days.[5]

Not knowing how long it would take for new documents to be prepared, Joe and Yvette agreed that they would make the most of whatever time they were able to spend together. Since the Morins were not hosting other evaders at that point, Yvette was able to briefly reclaim her bedroom, and Joe slept on the couch in the downstairs living area. The first two days after their return to Invalides they ate a spare breakfast with Georges and Denise, after which Yvette walked to work at the Crédit National. Joe spent the day with the couple he'd begun to refer to as Mama and Pop, playing cards, practicing his few words of French, and occasionally strolling the grounds of Invalides or nearby streets with them or Germaine Mercier. Upon Yvette's return each afternoon she and Joe would repair to their favorite aerie—the roof of the Dôme church—and spend the hours until dark talking of the future.

The first weekend after the couple's brief sojourn at the Mercier's apartment brought an unexpected reunion. Just before noon on Saturday, August 21, Maud Couvé arrived at Invalides accompanied by Harry Eastman and Dick Davitt. The two gunners had been told that their departure from Paris was imminent, and they had lobbied Maud for the chance to see Joe a final time before beginning what was almost certain to be a challenging journey over the Pyrenees into Spain. The Gunner Trio shared a modest lunch with the Morins, Maud, and Germaine Mercier, during which Harry and Dick promised that whichever of them reached England first would brief the 94th Bomb Group's intelligence personnel on the events of July 14. They would also pass on the news that Joe had survived the downing of *Salty's Naturals* and was in the care of a resistance organization, they said, so that the terse telegram his family had undoubtedly already received notifying them that he was "missing in action" could be amended to include his current status.

With the end of the meal it was time for Harry and Dick to return with Maud to the apartment on rue de Madrid. Both aviators told Joe they hoped to see him soon in England, and after a final round of handshakes—and hugs for the Morins and Germaine—the two men followed Maud out the door. Joe watched them go with mixed emotions; while he hoped that their journey back to England would go smoothly and quickly, he fervently wished that his own "home run" might be delayed a little while longer.

Just when and how Joe would leave the City of Light—and the route he would follow to reach England—were not, of course, his decisions to make. The timing and method of the gunner's home run would be determined by the network that was sheltering him, as it would be for all the 94th Bomb Group airmen who had survived July 14 over Le Bourget and had managed to thus far avoid capture.

And though Joe didn't know it, all of his fellow Bastille Day evaders would leave Paris to begin their journeys back to England well before he had to say his final goodbyes to the City of Light and to the woman he loved.

BY THE SUMMER OF 1943 THERE WERE ESSENTIALLY ONLY TWO WAYS TO GET a downed Allied aviator out of France—by sea, or on foot.

The first entailed getting the evader to the coast of either Normandy or Brittany and putting him aboard a vessel. This was usually a fishing trawler or some other type of small commercial craft, though occasionally Royal Navy motor torpedo boats would make the dash across from England to pick up larger groups of evaders.[6] Evacuation across the English Channel or the Bay of Biscay was inherently dangerous no matter what type of conveyance was employed, however, given that both bodies of water were patrolled day and night by German ships and aircraft. Indeed, only one of the 94th Bomb Group airmen shot down on Bastille Day made his home run by sea. Second Lieutenant John Bieger, Floyd Watts's copilot, was among nineteen Allied personnel evacuated from France aboard the fishing trawler *Suzanne-Renne* in October 1943.[7]

The second and by far the most common way for evaders to leave Occupied France was to walk over the border into a neutral country. Although Switzerland may have seemed an obvious choice, in practice most French evasion networks preferred to avoid the alpine nation. Its frontier with France was heavily guarded by German, Italian, and French collaborationist troops and border police, and the Swiss themselves had erected fences and other barriers in order to prevent an influx of refugees. Moreover, to avoid antagonizing Germany, Switzerland almost always interned Allied military personnel who did manage to make it across the border. Those men who avoided internment then faced a final hurdle on the road back to England: Switzerland is landlocked and at that time was surrounded either by Axis or Axis-occupied nations, and the only viable way for an evader to leave was by air. While some high-value personnel were able to do so with the help of Allied diplomatic missions or espionage organizations such as the U.S. Office of Strategic Services, such treatment was not the norm for "average" evaders.[8]

Of necessity, then, Spain was the usual destination for evaders attempting to reach England, despite the fact that it, too, had several drawbacks.

The first of these was that, like the Swiss frontier, France's border with Spain was heavily patrolled by German and collaborationist soldiers and police. The train station in Toulouse—the main southwest terminus of rail lines emanating from Paris—was the target of frequent sweeps by

Gestapo agents and military police units. The smaller stations closer to the border—in Perpignan, Tarbes, Pau, and Bayonne—were also closely watched, as were the few roads that snaked through passes in the towering Pyrenees, the three-hundred-mile mountain range spanning the entire length of the French-Spanish border.

Soaring in places to more than 11,000 feet, the Pyrenees themselves were the greatest obstacles evaders had to overcome to reach the relative safety of Spain. The rugged valleys that are the only natural corridors through the mountains are blanketed with deep snow in winter and crisscrossed by wildly rushing streams of meltwater in the summer. Daytime temperatures can range from far below zero to well over one hundred degrees depending on the season, and the smuggler's routes most often followed by the local guides leading evaders were extremely daunting, even for very fit young men.

Nor was simply surviving the journey through the mountains the only challenge evaders faced. Despite Spain's official neutrality the nation's dictator, General Francisco Franco, was so pro-Axis that he had sent Spanish troops to fight alongside the Germans in their battle against the Soviets on the Eastern Front.[9] Many Spaniards shared their despotic leader's fondness for fascism, and evaders who managed to make it into Spain could never be sure what sort of reception they might receive. Indeed, the Spanish government's official policy regarding Allied military personnel who ended up in Spain was to arrest and intern them for the duration of the war, with their internment to be spent in prison.

Such hazards notwithstanding, Spain had much to recommend it as an escape route from Occupied France. Although the border was well patrolled, it would have required thousands of troops to seal it completely—men who were not available because they were busy fighting in Russia and elsewhere.[10] Local resistance groups on the French side of the mountains kept careful track of the movements of the German and collaborationist units that were on border-guard duty, and sympathetic Spaniards and Basques south of the mountains—people who in many cases were related to their compatriots to the north—paid equally close attention to the movements of Spanish troops and police. By coordinating information from both sides of the border, the networks substantially reduced the possibility that the evaders would be intercepted. Many networks also sought to increase the chances of a successful border crossing by funneling the aviators and their guides through neutral Andorra, a tiny principality sandwiched between France and Spain in the eastern Pyrenees. Historically a center of north-south smuggling because of its location, Andorra had some of the finest mountain guides in Europe—many of whom did heroic service leading parties of Allied personnel into Spain.

As a further hedge against the possibility that evaders would be captured after crossing the Pyrenees, the French networks' Spanish and Basque colleagues sought out soldiers and police officers who were sympathetic to the Allied cause, or could be blackmailed or bribed to look the other way. This often helped airmen and their guides to avoid police and military checkpoints and patrols, or hastened the aviators' release from confinement if they had been unfortunate enough to be arrested on arrival.

Once evaders reached Spain the goal whenever possible was to get them to the British enclave at Gibraltar. The six-hundred-mile trip across the length of the Iberian Peninsula was usually made by train, with groups of evaders using identification papers and travel documents supplied by military officials stationed at the American and British consulates in larger towns near the French border, or at each nation's embassy in Madrid. The trip south was not an easy one, for agents of both the Gestapo and the Abwehr—Germany's military intelligence service—were extremely active in Spain.[11] While they rarely resorted to violence, the German operatives would not hesitate to impede the evaders' progress in any way they could—most often by reporting them to the Spanish authorities.

Allied personnel who reached Gibraltar were screened to ensure that they were bona fide evaders and not Axis agents. Men who passed the vetting procedure were provided with new uniforms, pocket money, and travel orders authorizing their return to England. That journey was normally made by air, aboard military transports or civilian airliners operating between Gibraltar's small Royal Air Force field and British and American air bases outside London. Soon after arrival the now former evaders underwent longer and far more involved debriefings with MI9 or MIS-X, the British and American intelligence organizations tasked with supporting escape and evasion operations.[12] The returnees were extensively interviewed about their time in France, the people they encountered, any enemy activity or installations they might have observed, and any ways they believed escape and evasion training and aids might be improved. Then, interviews completed and after a stern warning not to discuss anything about their time in France with anyone, the men were returned to their units.

FOURTEEN OF THE SEVENTEEN MEMBERS OF THE 94TH BOMB GROUP WHO reached Paris after being shot down over Le Bourget ultimately made the home run back to England by following the Pyrenees route out of France.[13] The "over the mountains" group included Robert Conroy, Larry Templeton, Roscoe Greene, Kee Harrison, Floyd Watts, David Turner, Charles McNemar, Jefferson Polk, Samuel Potvin, John Carpenter, John Buice, and Joe Manos. Harry Eastman and Dick Davitt also walked out of France and into Spain, but as members of the Gunner Trio their stories require a closer look.

AFTER LEAVING INVALIDES ON AUGUST 21 HARRY AND DICK HAD RETURNED to Maud Couvé and Alice Brouard's apartment on rue de Madrid. The following day the men were told they'd be traveling separately, and that Eastman would be the first to go. That evening he was led to the Gare d'Austerlitz, where he joined a group of nine evaders that included three members of Kee Harrison's crew—Turner, Polk, and McNemar—who had spent their time in Paris with members of various networks.[14] Three other Americans were also part of the group: technical sergeants Francis Green and Edward Ruby of the 384th Bomb Group, and Staff Sergeant Donald Harding of the 95th.[15] The party was rounded out by an RAF fighter pilot and a Royal Canadian Air Force (RCAF) tail gunner, and by four escorts provided by the Bourgogne network headed by twenty-five-year-old former soldier Georges Broussine.[16]

The evaders and their escorts boarded the 8 P.M. night train from Paris to Toulouse, where they arrived on the morning of August 23. After an anxious hour in the crowded station they entrained for Foix, scattered through two third-class cars. By the time their pre–World War I vintage locomotive wheezed into Foix in the early afternoon, Harry Eastman and his fellow evaders had begun to relax somewhat.[17] That feeling was premature, however, for after the party left the station and started walking into the nearby woods one of the guides saw what looked like a bicycle-mounted policeman coming toward the group. A quick hand gesture sent everyone into the shrub-covered ditches lining either side of the road, where the evaders and their escorts lay as quietly as possible. When the coast seemed clear three of the guides hustled their charges out of hiding and down the road, apparently not realizing or caring that Harding, Francis Green, the Canadian gunner, and the fourth French guide had been left behind.[18]

Harry Eastman and his companions had little time to wonder what had become of their fellow evaders, for the remaining guides pressed doggedly on. Well after midnight the men were allowed to stop, and the group stayed under cover until a car arrived at their hiding place on the afternoon of August 25. Driven south for several hours, the evaders were eventually handed over to the man who would guide them through the mountains, and over the next five days the party made its way to and across the France-Andorra border. After a one-night stop at a small hotel in the tiny principality, Eastman and the others were on the move again on the evening of August 31, and by noon the following day had crossed the Spanish border, in the process dodging sporadic rifle fire aimed at them by border troops.

Things took a quick turn for the even worse on September 2, when the evaders and their French helpers were arrested by local police and taken to the district prison in the Catalan town of La Seu d'Urgell. As the senior officer of the group (and possibly as the result of a bribe), David Turner was paroled and he and one of the French guides immediately entrained for Barcelona, where the young American officer went straight to the British consulate. After making his report, Turner—despite his pleas that he be allowed to return to La Seu d'Urgell to be with the others—was ordered to Madrid and from there to Gibraltar. For reasons that remain unclear, on September 15 Turner was flown to Marrakesh in French Morocco. Four days later he boarded a C-47 transport bound for the RAF base at Saint Mawgan in Cornwall, and by September 21 he was enjoying his home run party at the Rougham officers club.

Eastman and the others had to wait a bit longer for their own bashes, however. As a result of Turner's report the resident MI9 officer in

Barcelona was able to get the other Allied evaders released after five days in La Seu d'Urgell jail. The men were transported to Lérida, where instead of being confined to the military stockade they were installed in the Hotel Palacio. They enjoyed the town's hospitality for two weeks, spent one night in Saragoza, and were then moved on to Alhama de Grenada, where the MI9 man was able to interview them at length. Thanks to the efforts of a U.S. Army major named Clark—an attaché from the American consulate in San Sebastian—the enlisted men reached Gibraltar on October 2. Three days later Eastman, McNemar, and Polk were flown to Bristol, and traveled from there to Rougham by train. As it turned out, Eastman was the second member of the Gunner Trio to return to Sussex.

Dick Davitt, for his part, left the City of Light on August 24. Two days earlier, just after Harry Eastman's departure, the young aviator had also said goodbye to Maud Couvé and Alice Brouard. Davitt was guided some three miles to the southwest, to an apartment only a few hundred yards from the Gare d'Austerlitz. He stayed with Gabrielle Wiame, the woman he knew only as "Marie," who on the afternoon of the twenty-fourth led Davitt to the Jardin des Plantes—the vast botanical garden adjacent to the Gare d'Austerlitz. There he joined a group of evaders that included a young RAF officer who introduced himself as Peter; five Frenchmen and one woman; and, to Davitt's surprise, three other B-17 aviators who had survived Bastille Day. First Lieutenant James Munday, a 384th Bomb Group pilot, had been shot down during the attack on Villacoublay and was still dealing with shrapnel injuries to one of his knees.[19] The other two were well known to Davitt—Sam Potvin and John Carpenter of Floyd Watts's crew, who after arriving in Paris on August 5 had sheltered with Francoise Vandevoorde and her husband, Maurice, in Fontenay-sur-Bois.[20]

The eleven evaders and their two guides left the Gare d'Austerlitz on the night express to Toulouse, where the next morning they boarded a waiting truck for the sixty-mile drive to Arignac. The small town south of Foix was the jumping-off point for the push into Andorra, which the group and two local guides began on the evening of August 25. Though things initially went well, after only a few hours of walking it became obvious that Munday's injured knee was failing him and that the young officer would not be able to keep up. One of the local résistants offered to stay behind with him, and the rest of the group pushed on.[21]

After reaching Andorra the evaders and their guides spent two days in a small hotel, but for reasons that remain unclear Peter, the young RAF officer, was not with them.[22] The others pressed on nonetheless, and after a week of hard walking reached the Spanish city of Manresa. From there the American airmen took a train to Barcelona, where they spent three days waiting for the next leg of their journey to be arranged. They were then driven to Madrid—presumably by Major Clark—where they found David Turner. By September 15 Davitt, Carpenter, and Potvin were in Gibraltar, and late on the eighteenth they boarded a transport bound for Saint Mawgan, like Turner making the journey via Marrakesh. On September 20 Davitt finally returned from what he jokingly referred to as his "unintentional European vacation."[23]

While two members of the Gunner Trio had to walk to freedom, the third, Joe Cornwall, was the only one of the Bastille Day aviators to leave France the same way he'd arrived—by air.

THE FAREWELL LUNCH OF THE GUNNER TRIO AT INVALIDES ON SATURDAY, August 21, was followed by forty-eight hours of relative quiet in the Morin household. Georges and Denise went about their normal "concierge" duties, while Joe and Yvette spent as much time as they could in their retreat atop the Dôme church.

But late on the afternoon of Monday the twenty-third the routine was interrupted by the unexpected arrival of André Schoegel. "Petrel" was accompanied by two new evaders, twenty-five-year-old Warrant Officer Roderick A. (Roy) Scott of the RCAF and thirty-year-old Sergeant James George Antony Trusty of the RAF. The men were the pilot and mid-upper gunner, respectively, of a Handley Page Halifax II bomber of the RAF's No. 138 (Special Duties) Squadron.[24] Based at Tempsford in Bedfordshire, the unit and sister Squadron 161 specialized in covert, nighttime operations in support of European resistance movements and Allied intelligence and sabotage missions in Axis-occupied countries. Scott and his crew had been engaged in a clandestine supply-drop mission over France on the night of August 13 and were flying at very low altitude when their aircraft was hit by antiaircraft fire and then attacked by a German Bf 110 night fighter.

Scott had managed to put the blazing aircraft down in a field near La Chapelle-Viel in Normandy, though two members of the seven-man crew had been killed by the enemy fire. Three more of the aviators were quickly captured, and Scott and Trusty were helped by locals until passed on to members of Turma-Vengeance. On the morning of the twenty-third Hubert and Reneé Renaudin—the same couple that had earlier aided David Turner, Harry Eastman, and Dick Davitt—put the two men on the train from Évreux to Paris, where Schoegel met them and took them to Invalides.

The arrival of the two new "guests" was not the only thing that upset the normal routine at the Morins' home, however. Schoegel was angry to find Joe Cornwall still there, and apparently had not heard about the August 17 debacle in the Métro station or the problem "Gotha" had found with Joe's false papers. Georges and Denise explained that the documents provided by Gabrielle Wiame had borne the official stamp of a coastal district from which all civilians had been evacuated months earlier, and repeated their suspicion that Wiame was working with the Germans.[25] They also told Schoegel that "Gotha" had not returned with new papers as he had said he would, nor had they received any further instructions from anyone in the network. Only slightly mollified, Schoegel promised to look into things and get back to them as soon as he could.

The two new evaders quickly proved themselves to be welcome additions to the Morins' household—despite the fact that their presence meant Yvette had to give up her room to them and go back to sleeping at the Merciers' apartment. Both aviators were polite and well mannered, and more than happy to eat rabbit in any way Denise cared to make it. On their first evening at Invalides Trusty and Scott were invited to join Joe, Yvette, and the elder Morins atop the Dôme church, and over the course of subsequent visits the newcomers became as fond of the rooftop aerie as had all its previous visitors.

Unfortunately, the sense of security the lofty perch engendered led Tony Trusty to commit a security violation that was both foolish and potentially fatal for himself and the others. On his second or third visit he used a small penknife to scratch a brief message into the outer skin of the circular metal cupola covering the small dome just behind and above the altar of Saint-Louis des Invalides:

J.G.A.T.
of the RAF Visited here 1943,
When escaping to
England, having been shot down
by German A/A Fire

Though Trusty's desire to memorialize both his survival and his presence atop one of the most famous buildings in France is understandable, the graffiti would have been a death sentence for the Morins had it been discovered and read by an enemy. That it was not borders on the miraculous.[26]

The elder Morins' status as "caretakers" of Invalides certainly made them vulnerable, in that any indication that Allied evaders were being housed within the complex would have immediately focused the Germans' suspicions on them and, by extension, on Yvette. But their unique position as "keepers of the keys" also gave Georges and Denise advance notice of special ceremonies that would bring large numbers of German or collaborationist troops onto the grounds, thereby allowing the couple to both restrict the movements of their evader guests and warn off Resistance members who might otherwise have been arriving for meetings or to pass on documents or equipment.

While many of the events were of a social nature—such as the weddings of German officers in Saint-Louis des Invalides—others were decidedly more martial. That was the case on Friday, August 27, only four days after the arrival of Scott and Trusty. Just after dawn, scores of military trucks began pulling up outside every entrance to the Invalides complex and disgorging hundreds of uniformed troops. The soldiers were not German; they were members of the Legion of French Volunteers Against Bolshevism, a collaborationist militia formed in July 1941 through the amalgamation of various right-wing parties.[27] Organized and equipped as a standard German infantry regiment, the force had fought in Russia and the Balkans and the ceremony held that day in the Cour d'honneur was intended to officially mark the second anniversary of the legion's creation, and to award medals to those who had distinguished themselves in combat. The participants had no idea, of course, that three Allied evaders were calmly playing poker less than three hundred yards from where senior German and French collaborationist officers stood on the reviewing stand.

Things were much quieter at Invalides the day after the ceremony, so much so that Joe, Yvette, Scott, and Trusty felt at ease enough to pose for Georges's camera on the lawn in front of the Dôme church. In the photo, the four sit closely together; Roy Scott looks sheepishly at the ground, while Tony Trusty—wearing an ascot beneath his shirt and jacket and looking undeniably English—peers directly at the camera. Joe and Yvette, on the other hand, lean in toward each other, their smiles and body language speaking volumes about the depth of their feelings for each other. Their relationship was no secret to Trusty and Scott, of course, and both of the newcomers later wrote of the couple with great affection and not a little envy.

Unfortunately, Joe and Yvette received some upsetting news on the same afternoon that photo was taken. "Gotha" finally returned with revised papers for Joe, and told the airman that he, Trusty, and Scott would be leaving for Spain in "three or four days." While the specter of yet another separation was understandably upsetting for Joe and Yvette, it turned out that the departure window "Gotha" had given them was wildly inaccurate. Indeed, it wasn't until the evening of September 6 that a woman arrived to lead the three evaders to their next destination. It was a moment that Joe and Yvette had been dreading, but a last-minute examination of the aviators' false papers led the guide to declare that the documents "Gotha" had given Joe days earlier were "still not in order," though she apparently did not explain the problem.[28] She told Joe to stay with the Morins until the issue could be sorted out, and after a round of handshakes and hugs Trusty and Scott followed her out the door. A week later both airmen were in Spain.

This latest reprieve for Joe and Yvette lasted until the evening of Wednesday, September 16, when a man sent by "Gotha" arrived at the Morins' door accompanied by USAAF Second Lieutenant Andrew G. Lindsay and Sergeant Percival V. Matthews of the RAF. After another round of emotional goodbyes with Yvette and her parents, Joe reluctantly followed the other three men into the night.[29] The escort led the evaders to a house near the Gare Saint-Lazare, where he said they would meet the guide who would accompany them to the Spanish border. But the guide never appeared, and after waiting for more than an hour the escort led Joe and the others to a different house in Paris. There the aviators were handed off to four Frenchmen, who took the evaders to Maurice Cottereau's Café du Moulin Rouge in the northeastern suburb of Drancy. Joe and the others stayed there two nights waiting for a guide. The fact that no one appeared made Cottereau nervous and, fearing that "Gotha" was untrustworthy, on September 19 he decided to disperse the three men. Lindsay and Matthews were sent to Bobigny, another Paris suburb, while Denise Morin came to escort Joe back to Invalides.[30]

The airman's unexpected return led to an understandably joyous reunion with Yvette, though her parents cautioned the couple that Joe would likely be leaving again as soon as his onward travel could be arranged. But that process was slowed considerably by the Turma-Vengeance network's lingering suspicions about both "Marie" and "Gotha" and, by extension, of other résistants with whom the two worked.[31] The possibility that the Germans had penetrated the Comète, Bourgogne, or Visigoth lines—or worse, had agents within Turma-Vengeance itself—prompted someone above the Morins in the network's hierarchy to start looking for a more secure way to get Joe out of France. That decision turned out to be good news for the airman and Yvette, because it allowed them to spend nearly a month more together. And during that time the couple made a momentous decision.

Joe and Yvette had pledged themselves to one another early on in their relationship, vowing that they would find a way to be together when the war ended. But following Joe's September 19 return to Invalides the couple decided to consecrate their relationship with an official engagement. Joe therefore formally asked Georges and Denise for their daughter's hand in marriage, with the ceremony to be performed as soon as possible after the liberation of France. The elder Morins happily gave their consent, and the couple's betrothal was blessed by Saint-François-Xavier's charismatic Monsignor Georges Chevrot, himself a résistant.[32] Joe, Yvette, Georges, and Denise all understood that fate might very well delay the hoped-for union far longer than any of them could then imagine, but that knowledge did nothing to dampen the joy the engagement brought them.

News that arrived at Invalides on October 15, on the other hand, did add a bittersweet note to Joe and Yvette's happiness. The airman's onward journey had finally been arranged, and he would be leaving the following afternoon.

WHEN SUSPICIONS ABOUT "MARIE" AND "GOTHA" SENT MEMBERS OF Turma-Vengeance looking for alternate ways of getting Joe Cornwall out of France, André Schoegel put them in contact with a member of the Jade-Fitzroy network who went by the nom de guerre "Trellu." It was a providential meeting, for the twenty-six-year-old former soldier—whose real name was Pierre Hentic—was arguably the man best qualified to make Joe's home run a reality.

After the fall of France Hentic had cofounded Jade-Fitzroy, which was allied directly with Britain's MI6 (Secret Intelligence Service) rather than Charles de Gaulle's Free French BCRA. André Schoegel and his wife had been among the network's first recruits. Arrested by the Germans in 1942, Hentic had escaped to England and was subsequently tapped to direct the clandestine maritime and air operations that moved agents and equipment into and out of France. He had parachuted back into his native land in May 1943, and over the next five months organized several seaborne operations (for which he used the nom de guerre "Maho"), nearly a dozen landings by British special-missions aircraft, and a score of drops of both agents and supplies. Hentic not only had the authority to decide when and where incoming covert flights would land, he also determined which passengers would be aboard when the airplanes departed for England. When told by Turma-Vengeance of Joe Cornwall's three aborted attempts to leave France, Hentic agreed to find a place for the American airman aboard an outgoing flight.

The morning of October 16 was an understandably somber one in the Morins' apartment. In the time that Joe had spent at Invalides he had come to see Georges and Denise as surrogate parents, wise and caring people with an inner strength that reminded him of his mother and grandmother. The elder Morins had sheltered him, fed him, and shared their lives with him, all at terrible risk. And, of course, it was through them that he'd found Yvette—a strong, capable, and intelligent woman in her own right. Despite the difference in their ages, languages, and cultures, the American aviator and the vibrant Parisienne had found genuine and fulfilling love in the most unexpected of places in the most dangerous of times.

And though Joe and Yvette had said their goodbyes before, that did not make this parting any easier. They had promised to spend their lives together, but they were both realists who understood the war might well last for years, and that it was entirely possible one or both of them might not survive it. While they didn't know Hentic or the details of Joe's impending journey, both assumed it would be dangerous. Nor were the Morins safe—the Germans had stepped up their antiresistance activities in Paris, making several arrests in just the past few days.[33] To help ease Yvette's fears about his safety, Joe vowed that he would get a message to her once he was back in England. And she, in turn, promised that she would write to him, entrusting the letter to a departing evader or résistant.

Finally, just after five thirty in the afternoon, the time came for Joe to leave Invalides for the last time. He, Yvette, Georges, Denise, and Germaine Mercier set off on foot for the Gare d'Austerlitz, some two and a half miles to the southeast. Joe and Yvette walked hand-in-hand, while Denise carried Joe's dinner for the trip—a shoebox bearing some roasted rabbit wrapped in a cloth. At the station the group made contact with the woman who was to be Joe's escort, and after she handed the airman his ticket they all walked toward the train's departure platform. There were no troops or police at the head of the platform, just a conductor checking tickets and glancing at identity cards, and before Joe walked through he stopped to hug and kiss Georges, Denise, and Germaine. Then Joe and Yvette embraced for several moments, tears running down their cheeks as they whispered in each other's ears. Reluctantly turning away, Joe followed his escort aboard their assigned car.

Moments later, as the train began pulling away, Joe's emotional state briefly overcame his common sense. Suddenly realizing that in the confusion of the farewells he'd forgotten the shoebox, he opened the window of the railway carriage and shouted in English, "Yvette, my rabbit!" His outburst could have had tragic consequences had it reached the ears of the German soldiers two platforms over, but as it was the din of arriving and departing trains ensured that Yvette and the others were the only ones to hear it. Though momentarily shocked, they burst out laughing in emotional release as they watched Joe's waving form disappear into the distance.[34]

THE FACT THAT JOE HAD NO SHOEBOX DINNER TURNED OUT NOT TO BE A problem, for his journey was far shorter than he had anticipated. Because neither he nor the Morins had been given any details of his journey, they had assumed that his route back to England would take him over the Pyrenees to Spain, and that he would travel by rail at least as far as Toulouse. Instead, Joe's escort motioned him to follow her off the train at a small station between Toury and Artenay, barely fifty-five miles southwest of Paris. There the aviator was handed off to a male member of Pierre Hentic's team, and the female escort returned to the capital.

After leaving the station Joe and his new guide walked some seven miles to a small farmhouse, where they stayed until October 18. "Trellu" arrived late that night, accompanied by French Colonel L. Brosse, a former army officer who had become a senior member of Jade-Fitzroy, and a second man whom Cornwall later identified as a British SIS captain named Louis.[35] The four men and three additional helpers climbed into the back of a small farm truck for a lights-out journey over several miles of back roads. The vehicle dropped them next to a vast open field nine miles northwest of Toury and less than a mile west of the village of Baudreville, and when the helpers began setting out small, unlit flashlights at intervals down the field Joe realized that he would not be hiking over the Pyrenees.

Indeed, at that very moment the agent of Joe's deliverance was just minutes away. Flying Officer James McAllister McBride of the No. 161 (Special Duties) Squadron was inbound in a single-engine Lysander IIIa, the slow yet sturdy aircraft of choice for covert landings in France. The twenty-five-year-old pilot had taken off from Tempsford three hours earlier on Operation Primrose, carrying a single Polish radio operator who was on his way to join an SOE team operating south of Chartres.[36] McBride had encountered a bit of difficulty in finding the field, but by 12:58 A.M. he was overhead and Hentic ordered his men to turn on the four flashlights that would mark the landing area. The Lysander touched down at exactly 1 A.M. on October 19, and the incoming radio operator and his equipment were quickly offloaded and Joe and his two fellow passengers taken aboard. This was not an easy process, for all three men had to clamber up a narrow metal ladder welded to the left side of the Lysander's fuselage and cram themselves into a small rear cockpit originally intended for a single gunner. But the men managed it, and less than three minutes after landing McBride was lifting the aircraft back into the night sky and pointing its nose toward England.

The flight gave Joe time to ponder the events of the previous three months, and the ways in which his time in France had changed him. He had taken off from Rougham a man convinced he had no future, living day to day in fear, his other emotions largely numbed by the death and destruction he'd witnessed on every combat mission. Yet he was now returning to England as a man in love, engaged to marry the woman with whom he planned to spend the rest of his life and happier than he had ever been. He knew that he and Yvette would likely be separated for some time, and accepted that fate might have some unpleasant surprises in store for them. What he didn't expect was one startling and totally incomprehensible bit of news he received soon after McBride's Lysander landed at Tempsford at 4:03 A.M. on October 19.[37]

After untangling themselves from the cramped rear cockpit Joe and his two fellow passengers were led into the No. 161 Squadron operations building, where a USAAF lieutenant was waiting with an enlisted driver. The RAF had notified Eighth Air Force headquarters that Joe would be returning, the man said, and he and the driver were there to take Joe to London for the standard debriefing by MIS-X.[38] As Joe settled into the staff car for the drive south, the officer turned to him and said, "Sergeant, you'll be happy to know we've sent a telegram to your wife informing her of your safe return."

Stunned, Joe could only respond, "My what?"

Chapter 7

A HOMEWARD FLIGHT AND A TRAIN TO HELL

J OE CORNWALL WAS A VERY TIRED AND EXTREMELY CONFUSED MAN during the hours-long ride from Tempsford airfield to London. Tired, because he had been awake for almost twenty-four hours, and confused—even dumbfounded—by the young officer's statement that the USAAF had contacted someone it believed to be Joe's wife. Though the lieutenant was apologetic when Joe explained that he wasn't married, the man had no further details about the notification and explained that a solution to the mystery would have to wait until they got to London. He would call the 94th Group at Rougham, he said, while Joe started the debriefing process.

Just before dawn the staff car pulled up in front of a narrow, multistory Georgian townhouse at 63 Brook Street, barely fifty feet from the famous Claridge's Hotel in London's tony Mayfair district.[1] There was no signage to indicate the smaller building's purpose, and heavy curtains blocked the view through the three-section bay window to one side of the front door. Upon walking into the marble-tiled foyer Joe and the lieutenant encountered a military police soldier sitting behind a standard U.S. Army–issue wooden desk, a stenciled sign on the wall behind him reading, "Welcome to the United States Special Reception Center." Both men signed the security log, after which the young lieutenant told Joe he would call Rougham about the mistaken next-of-kin notification. He then hurried off, disappearing through one of several doors lining a short hallway stretching toward the rear of the building.

Moments later another uniformed MP appeared and beckoned Joe to follow him up the ornate stairway just behind the desk in the foyer. They climbed several levels, ultimately reaching the landing of the top floor. The MP walked to the rear of the building and opened the door to a small bedroom, whose single dormer window looked out onto a tiny, enclosed yard. As Joe took in his new accommodations the soldier asked him his waist, jacket, hat, and shoe sizes, then returned minutes later with a complete and apparently brand-new olive-drab enlisted man's dress uniform. The left shoulder of the jacket bore an Eighth Air Force patch and the lapels carried USAAF brass, but the sleeves were devoid of rank insignia. The MP said the debriefing process would not begin until the afternoon, and suggested that Joe get some sleep. Pointing to the towel, shaving razor, and bar of soap on the room's small nightstand, the man also smilingly said that before meeting his interviewers Joe might want to avail himself of the shower room on the floor below.

For several minutes after the MP's departure Joe stood at the window, peering out at the leaden sky of a cold British morning. The journey from a deserted field in enemy-occupied France to this posh townhouse in the heart of London had been relatively abrupt, and he knew that he needed to put into some kind of order the images and sounds swirling in his head. He also needed to puzzle out why the USAAF thought he was married, and of course, he wanted the chance to savor the warmth and serenity that thinking of Yvette brought him. But all of that would have to wait, he admitted to himself, because right now, more than anything, he needed to sleep. He lay down on the narrow bed, still wearing the clothes he'd put on at Invalides four days earlier, and was instantly dead to the world.

Awakened in midafternoon by a different MP, Joe shaved, showered, and put on the new uniform before going downstairs, where he found the young lieutenant waiting for him. The man had called Rougham, he said, and been told that news of Joe's MIA status and his return to Allied control had been sent to a Clara B. Cornwall in Raceland, Louisiana. Joe was about to protest that he didn't know anyone by that name, and that he had never listed a wife as his next of kin, when the lieutenant interrupted him to explain the apparent source of the confusion.

When *Salty's Naturals* was shot down, the officer said, the 94th Bomb Group's administrative office had followed USAAF policy by generating a Missing Aircrew Report, or MACR, that listed all the men aboard the downed aircraft and their designated next of kin. The standard practice was to notify a missing man's wife, if he had one, the assumption being that the spouse would then communicate the airman's status to his other relatives. Though Joe had designated both of his divorced parents as his next of kin, a personnel clerk going through his file in Rougham had found the form he'd signed before leaving Colorado that authorized payment of a percentage of his GI life insurance to Clara Brawner Gypin. The clerk had assumed that Gypin was the woman's maiden name, and had "corrected" it to Cornwall on the MACR.[2]

Upon receiving notification of the loss of *Salty's Naturals* the War Department's adjutant general's office in Washington, D.C., had sent the standard "We Regret to Inform You" telegram to the address Joe had listed on the beneficiary form—Clara's mother's home outside San Antonio. The mother had responded to the telegram by informing the War Department by mail that her daughter's married name was Rebuck, not Cornwall, and that she was then living in Raceland.[3] For reasons no one could fathom, the young lieutenant said, the adjutant general's office had then sent the same telegram to the Louisiana address, again addressed to Clara B. Cornwall. Then, to make matters worse, on Monday, August 2, the War Department had listed the incorrect information on its weekly news release regarding service members killed, wounded, or missing in action. The following day at least two newspapers, one of them in Louisiana, reported Joe's MIA status and that his wife Clara had been notified.[4]

Joe had fond memories of his brief relationship with the woman he'd known as Clara Gypin, and he hoped that the erroneous next-of-kin notification had not caused her trouble with whomever she was actually married to. A more pressing concern, however, was the fact that the USAAF's mistaken assumption about Joe's marital status meant that his parents had never been informed that he'd been listed as missing in action, or that he had been safely returned to Allied control. That issue was being addressed, the lieutenant said, and within the next forty-eight hours Joe's mother and father would each receive a telegram saying simply that he was well and back in England.

The next-of-kin issues out of the way, Joe moved on to the next step in his postevasion processing—a thorough medical exam in the Special Reception Center's small clinic. Not surprisingly, he'd lost weight during his time in France, and he was found to need some minor dental work. On a more serious note, the physician determined that the lingering pain between Joe's shoulders and the partial loss of sensation along both sides of his lumbar spine were the direct result of his bailout from *Salty's Naturals* and subsequent hard landing in a French field.

With the medical exam concluded, Joe's hosts at 63 Brook Street were able to begin his formal debriefing. For several hours a day from the late afternoon of October 19 through midday on Friday the twenty-second, officers from both MIS-X and the Eighth Air Force intelligence section patiently questioned Joe about every aspect of the downing of *Salty's Naturals* and the time he'd spent in France. The intelligence officers focused on operational issues, including the numbers and types of German aircraft that had attacked the 94th Bomb Group's formation; any distinctive markings the enemy machines carried and the tactics employed against the bombers; the fate of Joe's crewmates; and the location of any enemy bases, units, or vehicles Joe had noticed during his time on the ground. The MIS-X interviewers' questions, on the other hand, covered two differing aspects of Joe's evasion experience.[5]

First, a three-person team of interviewers led by a Major Richard Nelson asked for all the details Joe could remember about his time on the ground. Where had he landed? How quickly had he gotten rid of his parachute and Mae West, and had he buried them or hidden them in some other way? How soon after landing had he encountered helpful civilians, and had they provided him with clothes and food? Did he know the real names and approximate ages of the people who'd helped him, and could he describe their appearance? Did any of the helpers speak English, and had any of them ever named the networks to which they belonged? Had he seen any indications of dissension within the groups that had aided him, and had anyone indicated any level of distrust in other members of their organization? Could he recall the street addresses of the places he'd stayed? Had he at any point been forced to interact with the Germans—at a random ID check at a train station, for example?

Joe told Nelson and his team all he could about the people he'd encountered, both civilians and network members, and provided the real names, noms de guerre, and physical descriptions of as many as he could remember. The interviewers were aware of the extended time he'd spent at Invalides, and in response to their probing questions Joe spoke at length about the Morins and the part they and the institution itself played in aiding Allied evaders. While he was very forthcoming about the family's resistance activities and dedication to France and the Allied cause, he was initially hesitant to tell them about his relationship with Yvette. But when one of the interviewers casually mentioned that during their own debriefings at 63 Brook Street both Harry Eastman and Dick Davitt had talked about the Morins—in glowing terms, the officer was quick to point out—Joe realized that it would be foolish for him to conceal the relationship. He therefore told the MIS-X agents that not only were he and Yvette in love, they were engaged to be married. Somewhat to his surprise, the interviewers did not chastise him for what might easily have been considered fraternization with a foreign national during wartime, and actually wished him and Yvette good luck in the future. Encouraged by this response, Joe asked if there was any way the Turma-Vengeance network could be notified of his safe arrival in England. Nelson said he would look into it, and fairly soon after Joe's arrival in England the Turma-Vengeance network was notified that he was safe, and that information was passed to the Morins.[6]

The interviewers' second line of inquiry dealt with the training Joe had been given regarding escape and evasion techniques, and about the utility of the escape aids provided to USAAF combat crews. Had the E&E lectures he'd received both in the United States and following his unit's arrival in Britain been helpful when he was actually on the run? If not, how could the training be improved? Had he used any of the items in his escape kit? If so, which had he found most useful, and which did he think could be eliminated? Was the amount of currency in his escape purse adequate, and was the silk map accurate?

Though Joe's interviews at 63 Brook Street were not adversarial and were conducted in a relatively relaxed atmosphere, the extraordinary period of time he'd spent in France compared with most of the other July 14 evaders guaranteed that the questioning he underwent was unusually lengthy and particularly thorough. By the time the process ended on the afternoon of October 22 the MIS-X interviewers led by Major Nelson had amassed a significant amount of information, which over the following two days they edited into the multipage Escape and Evasion Report No. 125.[7]

Classified SECRET, the document followed a standard format. The first section gave the names, ranks, and crew position of each man aboard *Salty's Naturals,* followed by their status: except for Joe and the already returned Larry Templeton, all were listed as MIA. Next came an abbreviated, five-paragraph synopsis of Joe's experiences up through his first interaction with French civilians connected to an evasion network. As in all E&E reports, the final sentence of the synopsis read simply, "My journey was arranged." Since the first two pages of the E&E report would normally be circulated to a variety of Allied organizations, the brevity of the synopsis and the lack of any substantive information regarding the individuals and organizations that aided the evader was intended to protect what in today's intelligence parlance are referred to as "sources and methods."

The real meat of the E&E report was found in the three appendices that followed the abbreviated synopsis. Appendix B listed all the enemy activity and installations the evader had either personally observed or heard about during his time in occupied territory. In Joe's case, this included the extensive damage caused by the repeated Allied air raids on the Luftwaffe airfields at Le Bourget and Villacoublay and the Renault vehicle factory outside Paris; and the fact that the increasing numbers of American bombers appearing over the greater Paris area had prompted the Germans to increase the number of large-caliber antiaircraft guns dedicated to the capital's defense. Appendix C of Joe's E&E report contained a vastly expanded and far more detailed account of his activities while evading. Handwritten by one of the MIS-X interviewers as Joe spoke, the three-page section listed all the specific names, networks, and addresses missing from the synopsis. In Appendix D Joe addressed the value of his E&E training and equipment, and provided an accounting of when and how he had spent the money in his escape purse.

The final document in the E&E report was a standard form warning all returned evaders not to talk to anyone about their time in German-occupied territory, because "information about your escape or evasion from capture would be useful to the enemy and a danger to your friends."

The returned service member was told to be "particularly on your guard with persons representing the press," and ordered to "give no account of your experiences in books, newspapers, periodicals, or in broadcasts or in lectures." At the bottom of the form Joe's signature acknowledged that he would abide by the restrictions, and that he also understood that the disclosure of any information regarding his evasion to any unauthorized person would make him liable to disciplinary action.[8]

When his debriefing concluded on Friday afternoon, Joe was informed he could remain at the Special Reception Center through the weekend. He would be allowed to come and go as he pleased, he was told, but was required to return to the facility each evening by midnight. He was also issued travel orders directing him to rejoin the 94th Bomb Group at Rougham by no later than 4 P.M. on Monday, October 25. The orders authorized him to travel by train, and he was provided with a one-way, third-class London & Northeastern Railway ticket and some spending money.

It is unclear how Joe passed his free weekend in London, but it's safe to assume that he spent much of the time thinking about Yvette. The woman he loved, to whom he was engaged and with whom he planned to spend the rest of his life, was trapped behind the formidable walls of Adolf Hitler's "Fortress Europe." She and her parents were in constant danger from the Germans and even from possible spies within the ranks of their own network, and there was absolutely nothing he could do to help or protect them. Nor could he communicate with them, or they with him. His feelings of sadness, helplessness, and longing would likely only have been magnified by the fact that Yvette had turned twenty-two on Thursday, October 21, and he had been unable to celebrate it with her.

All those thoughts and feelings would still have been clouding Joe's mind and heart when he set out for Rougham on the morning of Monday the twenty-fifth. The journey was blessedly uneventful, and when he stepped off the train at Bury St. Edmunds station his mood was undoubtedly lifted by the sight of the two other members of the Gunner Trio, Dick Davitt and Harry Eastman. Upon hearing from the 94th Group admin officer that their friend was due to arrive from London, they had talked the man into allowing them to sign out a jeep so they could be the ones to meet him. Having been evaders themselves, they knew how disorienting it would be for Joe to have spent days at Brook Street talking in detail about his experiences in France, only to be jolted back into the reality of daily duty in an operational squadron. And because both Harry and Dick had spent time at Invalides, met the Morins, and knew of Joe's relationship with Yvette, they also would have clearly understood just how emotionally bereft their friend would be after having to leave both the woman he loved and the couple he had come to see as surrogate parents. The two gunners therefore likely intended the drive back to Rougham to be an opportunity for Joe to vent his feelings, and the trio obviously stopped along the way—at the Sword in Hand, perhaps—because the three-mile journey from the station to the airfield took nearly four hours. No official mention was made of the gunners' state of sobriety upon finally reaching Rougham, however, and Joe signed back onto the 94th Bomb Group's rolls late in the afternoon.[9]

The unit had changed significantly over the three months since the Bastille Day mission to Le Bourget, having lost an additional nineteen Fortresses and fifteen crews in combat.[10] Many familiar faces were missing from Rougham's mess hall and NCO Club, and the influx of replacement personnel meant that Joe felt as though he were a newcomer to the organization he'd joined almost a year earlier. That sense of being an outsider was further reinforced by the fact that he'd been "evicted" from his previous quarters. As had happened to both Eastman and Davitt, once Joe had been declared MIA his bunk had been assigned to someone else, and upon his return he was assigned to sleep in a Quonset hut full of strangers. Worse, in the days after *Salty's Naturals* went down, the footlockers containing the individual crew members' uniforms and personal belongings had been inventoried, and those items deemed appropriate for return to their next-of-kin had been boxed and placed in storage pending an official determination as to whether they had been killed in action. It took Joe several days to cut through the red tape that resulted from his not being dead in order to retrieve his belongings, though upon finally opening the box he was pleased to find that several letters from his mother had arrived in his absence.

Different living arrangements and missing personal items were not the only surprises Joe encountered on his return to Rougham. Two days after rejoining the 94th Bomb Group he was promoted to technical sergeant, and at the same ceremony was awarded the Purple Heart in recognition of the injuries sustained on bailing out of *Salty's Naturals*.[11] On a less positive note, however, he was told that USAAF regulations prohibited a returned evader from participating in further combat missions in the theater in which his evasion occurred, lest he be captured again and reveal under torture the individuals and networks that had facilitated his earlier escape. As a result, Joe was removed from flight status and assigned to the group's armament section where, he was assured, his expertise as an aircraft armorer would be put to good use until his return to the United States could be arranged.

Although Joe was not upset about being taken off flight status—he knew that a bomber crewman's life expectancy grew shorter with each mission, and he was now a man with something to live for—he was appalled at the thought of having to leave England. Even though he couldn't communicate directly with Yvette, before they'd parted she had said she would try to get a message to him. She knew that he was based at Rougham with the 94th Group, and believed that another American evader passing through Invalides might be able to act as a courier. Joe was afraid that if he were transferred back to the States he might never receive word from Yvette, that he wouldn't know whether she and her parents were safe. He knew it was foolish, but even though she was on the other side of the English Channel and in the heart of German-occupied Europe he still felt that they were connected. Would that connection remain intact if he were on the other side of the Atlantic, or worse, on some Godforsaken island in the Pacific?

In the weeks following his return to Rougham, Joe sought to submerge his anxieties about Yvette's safety and his fears about their future beneath a tidal wave of work. He spent nearly every waking hour in the armament shop, maintaining and, when necessary, repairing machine guns, turrets, ammunition-feed chutes, bomb racks, and a host of related systems. The only time off he allowed himself was the occasional pub crawl in Bury St. Edmunds, usually in company with Harry Eastman and Dick Davitt. The trio's time together lasted barely a month, however, for Davitt left for the United States on November 14, and Eastman followed a week later. According to a clerk in the 94th Group headquarters Joe's own departure was imminent, so he put in a request for some time off. On the same day Harry boarded a C-54A transport in Prestwick, Scotland, for the trans-Atlantic flight, Joe was granted a four-day pass to London.[12]

On arriving in the British capital on the morning of November 21 Joe headed for the Columbia Club at 95–99 Lancaster Gate, just across Bayswater Road from the north edge of Kensington Gardens and Hyde Park. Built in the mid-1800s as a series of upscale townhouses, in 1920 the structures were consolidated and converted into a hotel. After America's entry into World War II the building had become the U.S. forces' primary London billet for both transient personnel and those on leave in the city. Each room contained from two to eight metal bunk beds, with a certain number of beds allocated every week to each of the major U.S. military organizations based in Britain. The free accommodations were basic (less so, of course, for officers), but guests could eat and drink in the club's dining rooms and bars for far less than it would have cost elsewhere in the city. The building's central location and the presence of the Lancaster Gate tube station less than three hundred yards away made it an ideal base from which to explore London, and service members could obtain reduced-price tickets to theaters and other entertainment venues.

Joe had timed his trip to London perfectly, for when he returned to Rougham on Thursday the twenty-fifth—just in time for Thanksgiving dinner in the mess hall—his travel orders were waiting for him. They directed him to report to the USAAF Air Transport Command detachment at RAF Prestwick no later than 4 P.M. on Wednesday, December 1, for "onward movement to the Zone of the Interior," the official military term for the continental United States. Joe initially thought he would be taking the train on the three-hundred-mile journey to Scotland, but on the day before his departure from Rougham he was told that he and a few other men also bound for the States would be flown to Prestwick. Joe assumed the aircraft would be the 94th Group's "station hack," a small, twin-engine C-45 utility transport used to ferry people, equipment, and spare parts between Rougham and other fields.

But on the following morning the jeep carrying Joe and the other homeward-bound aviators rolled to a stop in front of a B-17 whose engines were already running. The Fortress was on its way to Prestwick to pick up some incoming replacements, and someone in base operations had decided the bomber might as well carry Joe and the other departing airmen on its way north. The aircraft carried no bombs, but because German fighters were known to stage surprise raids into the skies over northern England and Scotland, the Fortress's gunners were all on board and their weapons were provided with full combat loads of ammunition. Joe and his fellow passengers packed themselves and their duffle bags into the bomber's waist, from just aft of the ball turret to just ahead of the right-side crew entry hatch, and settled in for the flight. Though Joe left no record of his thoughts about the trip to Prestwick, it was his first time aloft in a B-17 since the day *Salty's Naturals* had gone down over France, and we may assume that the flight had something of a déjà vu quality. The acrid smell of burning Avgas, the bomber's bumping and swaying in reaction to turbulence, and especially the movements of the waist gunners as they scanned the surrounding skies for any hint of trouble would certainly have reminded Joe not only of how that previous flight had ended, but also of those who had not survived it.

The journey to Prestwick passed without incident, and after a night spent in the base's transient NCO quarters Joe joined twenty-two other U.S. servicemen aboard yet another four-engine aircraft, this one a Douglas C-54A Skymaster transport fitted to carry a mix of cargo and passengers.[13] Though the plane carried USAAF markings it was operated by an eight-man crew from Trans World Airlines, which provided flight personnel for many of the noncombat military aircraft routinely transiting the North Atlantic ferry route. Just as the 94th Bomb Group's B-17s had done on their flight to England, the Skymaster leap-frogged the Atlantic, though in the opposite direction. Following overnight stops in Greenland and Newfoundland the C-54A landed at National Airport outside Washington, D.C., on December 5.

The travel orders Joe had been issued before leaving Rougham directed him to report to Mitchell Field on New York's Long Island, but upon arrival there on December 6 he was immediately put aboard a military bus for the one-hundred-mile trip to the U.S. Army Air Forces Personnel Redistribution Center in Atlantic City, New Jersey. Opened just four months earlier, the facility's purpose was to receive all USAAF members returning to the continental United States from overseas and "after examination and re-evaluation assign them to appropriate stations, detail them to rest camps or effect their separation from the service."[14] The weeklong process included an intensive records check intended to correct any problems with the returning airman's pay, legal affairs, or allotments; a thorough medical examination; and mental-health screenings.

Joe's status as a returned evader ensured that during the course of several mental-health interviews he was questioned closely about the emotional effects of being shot down, losing crewmates, and being forced to go on the run in enemy-occupied territory.[15] Joe was required by regulations to discuss any personal relationships he might have formed while in France, so he spoke of Yvette and the fears he had for the safety of her and her parents. The Army psychiatrists doing the interviews would not have been surprised by the fact that Joe had fallen in love while overseas, since many thousands of American service members had romantic or sexual liaisons while deployed, but his actual engagement to someone inside German-occupied Europe may well have struck them as a new facet to an otherwise fairly common theme.

Joe's chats with the psychiatrists obviously did not raise any red flags, for he was ultimately classified as fit for further active service. In keeping with the USAAF policy mandating special treatment within the redistribution system for former prisoners of war, escapees, and returned evaders, after being cleared for duty Joe was given his choice of available postings. He requested assignment as a flexible gunnery instructor somewhere in the western United States—presumably to be closer to his father in Washington and his mother in Alaska. No such positions were immediately available, however, and Joe was instead ordered to USAAF Redistribution Center No. 3 in Santa Monica, California, for fifteen days of rest and recuperation. Following his time there, he was told, he would be granted four weeks of home leave. Upon his return to duty he would be given the first available assignment that matched his preferences.

At the time of Joe's arrival just before Christmas, the Santa Monica facility comprised three oceanfront resorts—the Del Mar Beach Club, the Edgewater Beach Club, and the Grand Hotel—as well as associated warehouses, parking lots, and vacant land later developed as additional recreation areas.[16] The Santa Monica Redistribution Center's purpose was the same as the facility in New Jersey—to evaluate the mental and physical status of personnel returning from overseas in order to determine whether they should be retained on active duty or discharged. While treatment was available for those recovering from wounds or psychic injuries, the emphasis for the majority of the service members was on rest and recreation. The latter came in a variety of forms—long days on the beach, arts and crafts classes, horse-riding lessons, dances, band recitals, and organized tours to Hollywood and other parts of California. The regimen was intended to reduce any symptoms of combat stress—what we now know as post-traumatic stress disorder—and to make an individual's transition back into stateside military life as easy as possible.

Despite his longing to be with Yvette and his continuing anxieties about her safety and that of her parents, Joe managed to find some tranquility during his stay in Santa Monica. By the time he left the Redistribution Center on January 12, 1944, he had decided that the only way to get through the months and possibly years that would elapse before he and Yvette could be together would be to do just as he had done following his return to Rougham—focus on work in order to help the time pass more quickly. His return to duty would not happen immediately, however, for on his last day in Santa Monica he was given orders mandating a month's home leave. The orders further directed that at the end of the four weeks he was to report to the 1178th Flexible Gunnery Training School at Buckingham Army Airfield near Fort Myers, Florida. There Joe would attend an instructor's course, after which—in keeping with his assignment preference—he would join the 420th Army Air Forces Base Unit's gunnery training cadre at March Field near San Bernardino, California. While Joe had been hoping for a posting to McChord Field in order to be close to his relatives, March was at least on the right coast.

At the end of his home leave Joe reported as ordered to Buckingham Army Airfield, and it was while undergoing training there that he was surprised to receive a letter from Jeff Dickson's wife, Louise. Though Major Nelson—one of Joe's interviewers at 63 Brooke Street—hadn't revealed it, he had known the Dicksons before the war. Nelson first heard the story of Jeff Dickson's time aboard *Salty's Naturals* while participating in Larry Templeton's debriefing, and had promptly written to Louise Dickson—who at that point had only been told Jeff was missing in action, not that he was presumed dead. In what would appear to be both a clear security violation and a monumentally insensitive act, Nelson told her that though

Templeton had not actually seen Jeff after the B-17 collided with the German fighter, the tail gunner was convinced that he and Joe Cornwall were the only survivors. Nelson also provided Louise with Templeton's stateside address, and in late October 1943 she wrote to him, saying she "would be grateful if you would tell me what you know about my husband."[17] In his reply, Templeton said, "I really did not know what happened, but I do know that Joe Cornwall did get out and is back in England."[18]

That piece of information prompted Louise Dickson to write to Nelson asking how she could contact Joe, and the MIS-X officer responded with the APO address of the 94th Bomb Group. While Louise apparently wrote to Joe, he did not receive the letter before returning to the United States, and it was only after Nelson's transfer from London to MIS-X's headquarters at Fort Hunt, Virginia, in early March 1944 that he was able to provide Louise with Joe's address in Florida. In her subsequent letter, Louise told Joe that she had still not been officially informed of her husband's death, but had accepted the fact and wanted to hear Joe's account of the loss of *Salty's Naturals*. Joe responded that he would be happy to speak with her, and in a March 31, 1944, letter to him Louise said she was planning to be in Florida the first or second week in April and wanted to speak with him face to face.[19] Joe agreed, and in their subsequent meeting he told her all he could about her husband's final hours. It was obviously difficult for Louise to listen to Joe's account, but she appreciated his willingness to speak with her and thanked him for helping to provide the details that no one else could give her.[20]

Upon his May 4 completion of the training course in Florida Joe traveled back across the country to March Field, where for the next two months he immersed himself in work as a flexible gunnery instructor. The only break in his daily routine came on July 5, when he marked his twenty-ninth birthday by drinking a few solitary beers in the March Field sergeants club. He was feeling particularly melancholy, for the Allied landings in Normandy in June had not resulted in the swift liberation of Paris he'd been hoping for. It had been almost nine months since he'd said goodbye to Yvette, and the passage of time had done nothing to lessen his longing for her. Moreover, July 14 would mark the one-year anniversary of the downing of *Salty's Naturals*, and the thought of the friends he'd lost that day still filled Joe with an ineffable sadness.

When he returned to his room in the NCO barracks after work the next day he was surprised to find a large official envelope thumbtacked to his door. From the many APO postmarks and scribbled forwarding instructions scrawled across its front it was obvious the envelope had been following Joe for some time, and when he noticed that it had originated from Rougham he wondered idly if it contained some official form he'd forgotten to sign before returning to the States. When he opened it he realized it contained a second, smaller envelope, unmarked save for his name written in a delicate hand he at once recognized as Yvette's. His heart racing, he carefully unsealed the envelope and pulled out a two-page letter written in French.

The undated missive began "Mon cher Joe," and with the help of a small French-English dictionary he'd bought in a used book shop in Santa Monica he spent the next few hours laboriously translating the body of the letter. Yvette had written it on behalf of herself—whom she referred to as Mickey—and three other network members whom Joe obviously knew, Roger, Bob, and Paul.[21] It was obvious that Yvette had penned it not long after Joe's departure from Paris, for one of the first lines read, "We were very glad to hear that you arrived across the Channel. No need to tell you the pleasure that news brought us." It was also apparent that Yvette had been aware that Joe would likely not be the only person to read her words, for though warm and caring in tone the letter contained no protestations of love or yearning. "We are gathered tonight at Mama's," it said simply, "to reminisce about the good and bad memories that brought us together. . . . Life is still the same here, and we hope for the arrival of our American and English friends. . . . Don't forget your promise to joyously celebrate the peace to come, the liberation of our dear country, in the company of all your Parisian comrades who are not forgetting you."[22]

Though Joe was disappointed that the letter had not been of a more personal nature, he was nonetheless delighted to have a long-awaited and tangible connection to Yvette. She had held the paper in her hands, and the fact that she had been safe and thinking of him when she wrote it helped ease the ache of missing her. The missive's arrival, he admitted to himself, was the best belated birthday gift he could have hoped for.

What Joe did not know, however, was that by the time he read the letter Yvette and her parents were already in the hands of the Gestapo.

FOLLOWING JOE'S DEPARTURE FROM PARIS IN MID-OCTOBER 1943 THE Morins had continued their work with Turma-Vengeance and their liaisons with the Bourgogne, Shelburn, and de Larminat organizations. The family home remained a key meeting place for senior leaders of those and other networks, as well as a central "post office" where important messages between resistance members and among the various groups were received and passed on. The Morins also oversaw the storage of weapons, equipment, and false documents in various places around Invalides.

Yvette and her parents continued to aid Allied aviators passing through Paris, primarily by escorting the men between safe houses and to and from the city's various train and Métro stations. While several of the evaders spent a few hours at Invalides—some even enjoying a meal of roasted rabbit—none stayed overnight. The leaders of Turma-Vengeance and the other networks had come to see the complex as a vital logistics and administrative hub, and believed that housing non-French-speaking Allied airmen there was an unnecessary risk. There were, after all, many other locations in the city where evaders could be safely and discreetly lodged—places that, unlike Invalides, did not routinely play host to hordes of German military tourists.

The decision to stop boarding Allied servicemen with the Morins did not affect the aid and shelter the family provided to resistance members. In the weeks and months following Joe's return to England the family hosted several French "guests" for periods ranging from a few days to several weeks.

Among the first visitors was Paul Durin, a member of the Paris metropolitan fire service. When war broke out in 1939 Durin was a sergeant working in the fire station on rue du Vieux Colombier, less than a mile east of Invalides in the 6th arrondissement. Called up for army service, he took part in the fighting that followed the Germans' May 1940 invasion of France. After the armistice Durin went into hiding, and by August 1941 he was the head of a resistance organization composed primarily of still-serving firefighters. He also became a member of Turma-Vengeance, and by mid-1943 was among the network's senior leaders. He was briefly detained by French police late in 1943, but was released and immediately returned to his resistance activities. In early January 1944 both he and his wife, Cécile, were almost snared by the Germans, and at that point the couple moved in with the Morins. They stayed for just over three weeks before moving on to another safe house, but returned frequently to Invalides for network meetings.[23]

Another of the Morins' French "guests" was more than familiar with his hosts and with Invalides. In 1940 the family had for several weeks sheltered a teenaged refractor—the term used to describe those seeking to avoid forced labor in Germany—named Michel Bourgeois, who was attempting to flee to England. He ultimately succeeded, and in late February 1944 the now twenty-two-year-old agent of de Gaulle's BCRA returned to France bearing the nom de guerre "Maxime" and accompanied by his radio operator, thirty-five-year-old Martin Mary ("Jacques").[24] The pair had been sent to aid in the establishment of aircraft landing fields and parachute drop zones—apparently in preparation for the eventual Allied invasion of Europe—in cooperation with Georges Broussine's Burgundy network. After moving into Paris from the countryside the duo spent nearly six weeks with the Morins, and during that time "Jacques" put his considerable radio skills to work on behalf of Turma-Vengeance and some of the other réseaux. He did not broadcast from Invalides, however, but from varying locations in the city in order to prevent the transmitter's discovery by German radio-direction-finding efforts.

Those operations—which used multiple receivers to pinpoint the source of clandestine transmissions through triangulation—were an important part of the Germans' increasingly effective antiresistance activities in the greater Paris region. That covert war was carried out by the Abwehr and the Gestapo, though the two organizations had dissimilar objectives and different ways of attaining them.

As a military intelligence service the Abwehr was ultimately subordinate to the high command of the German armed forces, and was organized into three main abteilungen, or departments. In Paris, the Abwehr was headquartered in the commandeered Hôtel Lutetia on boulevard Raspail, from which its Abteilung III-F worked to search out Allied agents and penetrate resistance groups. The goal was to gain information and, if possible, take control of the networks, their radios, and their members in order to co-opt incoming operatives while also feeding false information to their controllers in Britain. While Abwehr agents were certainly not averse to using violence, intimidation, or coercion to attain their goals, they were generally loath to "roll up" a hostile network while it was still producing actionable intelligence.

The Gestapo in Paris, on the other hand, was headquartered in various buildings along avenue Foch—and normally acted with a far simpler and decidedly more brutal mandate than did the Abwehr.[25] Under the terms of Adolf Hitler's 1941 Nacht und Nebel ("Night and Fog") decree, the Gestapo was directed to locate and eliminate anyone guilty of committing offenses against the Reich, whether within Germany or in the occupied territories. After their arrest and once all usable information had been extracted from them through torture, offenders were to be "disappeared"—either executed outright or sent to concentration camps to be gassed or worked to death—with no information regarding their whereabouts or ultimate fate provided to their relatives.

By late 1943 German efforts to use collaborators and "turned" résistants to penetrate the Paris-based networks had begun to bear fruit, with the number of arrests steadily increasing. Among those taken was Dr. Victor Dupont, one of the three founders of Turma-Vengeance, who was captured at the Gare de Montparnasse on October 9.[26] A month and a half later, on November 25, Andrzej Wyssogota-Zakrzewski—the man Joe Cornwall knew as "Gotha"—was arrested aboard a train in southern France as he was shepherding a group of evaders toward the Spanish border.[27] Another victim was Mme. Madeleine Melot, the Bourgogne member and friend of Gabrielle Wiame who had hosted the impromptu luncheon for Joe, Harry Eastman, and Dick Davitt on July 30. The elderly widow was seized at her home on rue Larrey, thrown into the back seat of a black Citroën Traction Avant—the elegant yet sinister roadster favored by the Gestapo in France—and driven away.[28]

With the advent of the new year, other résistants with whom the Morins had interacted also disappeared into the night and fog. Germaine Bajpai and Fernande Onimus, cochiefs of the Comète safe-house system, were both arrested on the night of January 17–18, 1944, and on May 14 Paul and Cécile Durin were swept up in what resistance members called a *souriciere* (mousetrap). The fireman and his wife had been on their way to deliver some documents to a safe house—which had been secretly taken over by the Germans—when they were surrounded by leather-coated Gestapo agents and quickly hustled into the back of a waiting truck.[29]

The Durins' sudden arrest was certainly painful for the Morins on a personal level, but it was also a stark reminder that Gestapo and Abwehr penetration of the various networks operating in the capital was both extensive and highly effective. Yvette and her parents became even more cautious in their dealings with other network members, especially with the more recent recruits, and it was this increased vigilance that in late June led to their realization that two members of Turma-Vengeance were working with the Germans.

The pair, Spanish- or possibly Moroccan-born brothers who used the family name Dérida, had joined the group in early 1944.[30] They worked primarily as couriers, delivering messages among the network's various "post offices," including the one operated by the Morins. Yvette still performed occasional "postal duty" for Turma-Vengeance, despite having become the secretary to Jean Delore ("Jean de la Lune"), the head of the Darius network, after leaving her job at the Crédit National in mid-March.

On Saturday, June 24, one of the Dérida brothers appeared at the Morins' door, saying that he had an urgent message for Jean. Something about the man's behavior made both Yvette and her father suspicious, and though they accepted the sealed envelope he proffered, Yvette pointedly told the courier that she would not be seeing Jean for several days. The man nonetheless returned on Monday the twenty-sixth, asking if Yvette had conveyed the message. When she replied that she hadn't, the courier said that he needed to take back the original envelope because some important detail had been left out of the message it contained. He then handed Yvette a different, heavily sealed envelope, saying that it was extremely important that she carry it forward as soon as possible. When asked if the second message was also intended for "Jean de la Lune" the man demurred, saying only that it was urgent and needed to move quickly.

Dérida's continuing odd behavior prompted Yvette and Georges to devise a simple security check. Yvette would indeed set out on foot carrying the envelope, but instead of transporting it to the usual next "mail box" in the chain—a nurse at the nearby Hôpital Necker—she would walk in the opposite direction. As she aimlessly strolled the streets of Paris she would check for any sign that she was under surveillance, peering into reflective shop windows, glancing nonchalantly around her before crossing a street, and occasionally turning down narrow alleys that would make a "tail" instantly obvious.

Yvette set out on the morning of Thursday, June 29, the envelope bearing the second message tucked into a zippered compartment in her purse. She had anticipated that it might take some time to spot any followers, assuming that they would likely be experienced Gestapo or Milice agents, but when she stopped to look into a shop window barely twenty minutes after leaving Invalides she was astonished to see one of the Déridas a block behind her. Peering closer at the scene reflected in the glass, Yvette was astounded to also see the man's brother, the same distance back but on the other side of the street. For the men to undertake the surveillance themselves was a foolish lapse in basic clandestine practice, and Yvette found herself hoping that the Déridas were equally inept at whatever other duties they might be undertaking for the Germans.

After strolling casually along for another half hour to ensure that the brothers were the only ones tailing her, Yvette turned a corner and then hurried to the end of the short block. She dashed across a narrow street, rounded another corner in the opposite direction, and was on her way back to Invalides before the Déridas even realized they'd lost her. When she told her parents that the brothers themselves had been tailing her, they were equally surprised at the men's incompetence. Georges then decided that they should open the sealed envelope, in order to see just what sort of information the brothers were attempting to pass up the chain.

The sheet of paper Georges pulled out stunned the Morins, both because it was written in plain text instead of code and because it outlined in detail virtually everything the family did as résistants. It was the sort of document that could put all of them in front of a German firing squad, but even that was not the most shocking thing about it. Georges, Denise, and Yvette all realized that the Déridas had intended the message for someone within Turma-Vengeance or one of its partner networks. That clearly meant that the brothers were not the only ones working for the Germans—somewhere along the chain a spy was collecting information, compiling the names and addresses of people to be arrested.

And yet, as Georges pointed out, by not delivering the envelope Yvette had likely bought them all some time. It would take a few days for the Déridas to realize that the message hadn't reached its intended recipient, and as soon as Georges informed others in the network of the brothers' treachery the traitors would be interrogated and then executed—or perhaps even "turned" against their Germans handlers. News that the damning message was intended for someone else in one of the networks would also spark an intense hunt for the unknown spy who, if found, would face the same fate as the Déridas. With luck, Georges said, the Allied armies advancing out of the Normandy beachheads would reach Paris before the Germans could roll up the capital's numerous resistance networks.

Events quickly seemed to prove Georges right, for within days the Dérida brothers had vanished and Turma-Vengeance and the networks with which it closely operated were undergoing intense internal-security reviews.[31] The Morins cautiously went back to work, and on Monday, July 3, were told that the following day their home would be the site of an important equipment hand-over. Early on Tuesday morning several members of the firefighters' network established by Paul Durin appeared at Invalides, their nondescript haversacks stuffed with large flashlights. They left the bags with the Morins, saying that some people would soon be around to pick them up.

Those people turned out to be Michel Bourgeois and his radio operator, "Jacques," who arrived late on Tuesday afternoon. The need to mark fields for covert landings by Allied special operations aircraft and parachutists had not ended with the landings in Normandy, the men explained, and the lights provided by the firemen were ideal for the task. Bourgeois, whom the Morins affectionately called "Bébé," and "Jacques" stayed for an austere dinner and a few glasses of wine, then left for their current safe house before curfew.

Just after six the next morning, July 5, Yvette and her parents sat down to their usual breakfast of black bread, cheese, and ersatz coffee. They were talking about Joe—and how they hoped he would enjoy his birthday, wherever he was—when their conversation was interrupted by someone pounding on their door and shouting "Open Up!" in German. In an instant the Morins knew that the day they had long dreaded was finally upon them. But even as that realization was sinking in, several strong kicks from outside sent the door crashing open, and in rushed several Gestapo agents waving pistols and yelling "Hands up! Stay where you are!" As two of the men rushed up the stairs to clear the other rooms, the man apparently in charge told Denise and Yvette in passable French to remain seated. When Denise asked if she and her daughter could put on something over their nightgowns the man responded with a gruff "No," but then allowed them to put their hands down.

Over the next thirty minutes, as the Morins sat in stunned silence, the Germans tore the house apart searching for any incriminating evidence. They found nothing, and the man in charge ordered Georges, Denise, and Yvette to get dressed—all under the watchful eyes of an armed agent. When the three were ready they were brusquely led out the door and shoved into the windowless back of an unmarked van. Two of the Gestapo men climbed in after them, and as soon as the van's rear doors were closed the vehicle headed north on the boulevard des Invalides. The journey lasted only minutes, for the Morins were taken not to avenue Foch, but straight across the River Seine to 11 rue des Saussaies. The prewar home of the Sûreté Nationale, France's national police force, the building was now the headquarters of the Paris Gestapo.[32]

The van carrying Yvette and her parents drove in through the building's central street entrance, then halted abruptly. When the rear doors slammed open the Morins were hustled down a flight of stairs into the building's basement, where Yvette and Denise were led off in one direction and Georges in the other. The women were placed in separate cells, and over the following seventeen hours were individually questioned several times about their resistance activities. Their interrogators already knew many details about Turma-Vengeance's operations and members, and about the Morins' activities, and though the women were screamed at, threatened, and slapped around they were not tortured. Sadly, the same was not true for Georges. The disabled World War I veteran was subjected to electric shocks, submersion in a bathtub full of ice, suspension from the ceiling by his wrists while Gestapo men beat him with metal rods, and a variety of other brutal techniques. Despite it all he told his captors nothing, enduring the torture in silence.

The following morning Yvette and her parents were transported from the rue des Saussaies to the capital's military prison. Known by Parisians as Centre pénitentiaire de Fresnes, the facility was some six miles south of Invalides and was used to house captured résistants and Allied POWs awaiting transfer to other facilities. Georges was confined in the men's wing, and Yvette and Denise in the women's block. Conditions were horrific throughout the former civilian prison, with severe overcrowding, appalling sanitation, rampant disease, starvation-level rations, and frequent violence against prisoners by the guards. Executions were a daily occurrence, as was torture during interrogations.

Even as the Morins were struggling to survive at Fresnes, their friends and fellow résistants were also falling prey to the Gestapo.[33] Michel Bourgeois was arrested not long after the family, followed by Mme. de Larminat on July 13. Gustave Salomon was seized the next day, and Joseph and Yvonne Gorjux—an older couple who had aided Larry Templeton and Roscoe Greene—were taken into custody on August 3. While Mme. de Larminat was ultimately released, the others followed the Morins into captivity.[34]

As bad as conditions were at Fresnes, things were destined to get far worse for Yvette and her parents. On August 7 each of the Morins was sentenced to death, but before their executions could be carried out they were instead designated for slave labor and ordered deported to concentration camps in Germany—Georges to Buchenwald, near Weimar, and Yvette and Denise to the all-female camp at Ravensbrück, north of Berlin. Early on August 15 they and several hundred other prisoners from Fresnes and Fort de Romainville—another prison on the outskirts of Paris—were put aboard requisitioned civilian buses and driven to the Gare de Pantin. The station in the capital's northeast suburbs had been the site of many deportations during the German occupation of France, and by the summer of 1944 was one of the few rail hubs in the capital region that had not yet been obliterated by Allied bombs. On a siding sat a train comprising a locomotive, a tender, and twenty-eight closed freight cars. German troops wielding truncheons forced 543 female prisoners aboard the eleven carriages at the forward end of the train, while 1,654 male captives were packed into the seventeen cars that brought up the rear. Just before noon the locomotive belched smoke and steam and slowly moved away from the station. It was the last deportation train to leave greater Paris before the city fell to the Allies just ten days later.[35]

The journey from Paris to the train's first destination, the station at Weimar (for Buchenwald), took four terrible days. The prisoners were not fed, and were given little water. Each freight car held between fifty and one hundred people, with just a single ten-gallon can in each carriage to serve as a communal latrine. The only ventilation came from four small, barred, ceiling-level windows—two on each side of the car, front and back—and the summer heat and closely packed occupants ensured that the atmosphere in the carriages remained stifling. The train stopped briefly each morning and evening, when those prisoners who had died were offloaded and the living were allowed to empty the latrine cans. Several individuals who attempted to escape during the halts were shot by the guards, and on the second day of the journey the prisoners were told that any further escape attempts would result in the immediate execution of ten people from the escaper's freight car.

On the afternoon of the third day the train entered a tunnel, but about halfway through suddenly screeched to a halt. The exit was blocked by rubble from an Allied air raid, and for the next three hours the train sat in the dark—the engine still belching smoke and steam—as the Germans tried to decide what to do. By the time the train backed out of the tunnel more than a dozen prisoners had died of asphyxiation, and their bodies were unceremoniously dumped along the tracks. The remaining captives were forced to disembark from their cars, and were then marched almost five miles through heavy woods until reaching the other side of the mountain. A second train was waiting, and after the prisoners boarded their hellish journey continued.[36]

When the train rolled to a stop in the small station at Buchenwald on the morning of August 20 the cars bearing the male prisoners were uncoupled and shunted to a siding. As the locomotive pulled the remaining carriages back onto the main line and set off on the 170-mile journey to Ravensbrück, Georges Morin and his fellow captives were marched at gunpoint to a huge shed-like structure. The men were made to strip and hand over their wedding rings, after which their heads were shaved and they were herded into group showers. Upon emerging each man was handed his striped prisoner's uniform, the rough woolen shirt bearing a triangular piece of fabric color-coded to denote the individual's status. For Georges and most of the other new arrivals the symbol was red and carried a large letter "F"—the combination indicating French political prisoners. The triangle also bore each man's prisoner number—Georges's was 77549—which was repeated on the inmate record that identified his pre-arrest profession as "beamter schriftsleiter," or official clerk.[37]

That document and a few other surviving German records are the only account we have of Georges Morin's sojourn in the nightmare world that was the Nazi concentration-camp system. At the time of his arrival at Buchenwald, many of the camp's prisoners were being used as slave labor in the armaments factories that dotted the surrounding area, and we may assume that Georges was so employed. We know that on September 3 Georges was transferred to the nearby camp known as Mittelbau-Dora, whose inmates were used to dig tunnels in which V-1 flying bombs and V-2 ballistic missiles were manufactured.[38] Prisoners also assembled components for the so-called "vengeance weapons," and it is possible that Georges was involved in that effort. For reasons that remain unclear, on November 1 he was transferred to another Mittelbau subcamp, Ellrich-Juliushütte.

While we don't know what sort of labor Georges was forced to do at Ellrich, we can be certain that the working conditions sapped his already greatly diminished health. Malnourished, abused, and likely suffering from a host of maladies, he was sent to the camp's woefully inadequate "hospital," which consisted of little more than lice-infested straw pallets on a cold, wet floor. At thirty minutes after midnight on December 23, 1944, Georges Jules Morin—war hero, husband, father, résistant, and proud son of France—died of what his SS-issued death certificate listed as enterocolitis. Two days later he was one of fifty deceased prisoners cremated in Mittelbau's ovens.[39]

By that point his wife and daughter were well and truly immersed in their own living hell.

Chapter 8

LIBERATION, LOVE, AND LOSS

FTER LEAVING THE STATION AT BUCHENWALD THE TRAIN BEARING Yvette, her mother, and the other surviving female prisoners rolled on for another 195 miles through central Germany, working its way steadily northeastward toward Ravensbrück. At noon on August 21 the train groaned to a halt at the small station in Fürstenberg, some forty-five miles north of Berlin. When the doors of the freight cars were unlocked and jerked open from the outside, the women were greeted by the barking and growling of leashed guard dogs and the bellowing of truncheon-wielding SS troops. Yvette, Denise, and the others were ordered out of the cars and made to form up five abreast in a single long column. The hundreds of thirsty, weakened women were then marched down a long, dusty road, through the village of Fürstenberg, around a lake known as the Schwedtsee and into the camp that only a few would be lucky enough to survive.

The sight that greeted them was a true vision of hell. As Virginia d'Albert-Lake, one of the new arrivals, later described it:

> As we entered the camp, we saw long, bottle-green barracks, with window facings painted white; narrow plots of grass surrounding the buildings with, here and there, a few bushes or scraggly trees. . . . Then we saw some of the inmates, strange, gnome-like looking women, with shaved heads, dressed in blue and grey-striped skirts and jackets,

with heavy wooden-soled galoshes on their feet. Some were struggling under the weight of huge soup kettles; others went by pushing a cart piled high with long, narrow wooden boxes, followed by eight or ten others pulling and pushing an immense wagon full to overflowing with garbage. Then, a detachment of others dragged by, horrible-looking creatures, thin and haggard, with huge open, festering sores on their stocking-less legs. . . . We were made to stand in the broad main street, awaiting we didn't know what. . . . We were so exhausted after a week of sleepless nights. We stared at each other in dull incomprehension. A woman SS [guard] kept parading back and forth. We cried out to her for water. . . . But no water was brought.[1]

Yvette and the others were forced to stand at attention in the glaring sun for hours as their captors counted and recounted them, trying to square the numbers of prisoners before them with the figures on the manifests that had accompanied the women on the hellish trip from Paris. As night fell and the counting continued, dozens of women dropped to the ground, unconscious or dead.

Once the male and female guards were satisfied with their counts, the women were marched by groups into a warehouse-like processing building. There Denise, Yvette, and the other new arrivals were forced to turn over any valuables they might still be carrying, including watches, wedding rings, and other jewelry. After having their heads shaved, the women were subjected to a humiliating "physical examination." Forced to strip naked, they were led one by one before a panel of SS doctors. After a cursory look down each woman's throat the men examined their teeth—not to ascertain the state of the individual's oral health, but to note whether there were any gold fillings that could be harvested after death. Sadistically painful vaginal and anal examinations followed—again, not to detect signs of ill health, but to ascertain whether the prisoners were trying to hide any valuables.

Following the "examination" the women lined up to receive the thin woolen skirts and jackets and rough wooden clogs that would be their only clothing for the remainder of their time in the camp. Sewn to the sleeve of each striped jacket was the same sort of colored fabric triangle that had adorned Georges Morin's uniform at Buchenwald: red for political prisoner, an "F" for French, and the prisoner's individual number—50515 for

Denise and 50516 for Yvette.[2] After the women had dressed, all of them were herded down the narrow, coal-dust-covered "streets" to an empty barracks building. Female SS guards used whips and clubs to force the new arrivals into the structure, which had originally been constructed to house one hundred prisoners but within moments was crowded with more than five hundred. Rows of crude wooden, shelf-like bunks were stacked floor to ceiling, each four-foot-wide space intended for three or four women. Yvette and Denise managed to claim a spot on a lower tier, and as they settled in they wondered aloud about what had become of the barrack's previous inhabitants.

Mother and daughter spent their first night in Ravensbrück huddled together for warmth and mutual reassurance on the rough planks of their lice-infested bunk, listening as the other two occupants of the cramped space cried, coughed, and prayed. Those noises were intermittently drowned out by the sudden, wolf-like baying of guard dogs set free to roam the camp, and, more ominously, by the occasional loud crack of a pistol or rifle shot. At 3:30 A.M. a far more terrifying sound jerked all the women in the barracks from their fitful sleep—the loud, discordant shrieking of a high-pitched siren announced the start of the camp-wide morning roll call. The new arrivals from France did not have to rush from the barracks—they were all quarantined for ten days—but they would soon come to know only too well the special horrors of standing at attention for two or three hours while the guards undertook their seemingly endless count.

At the end of the quarantine period the recently arrived French prisoners were introduced to the grueling routine that was daily life at Ravensbrück. Following the morning roll call and a hurried "breakfast" of ersatz coffee and a single piece of moldy black bread, the women were assigned to duties that ranged from kitchen work to construction to assembling field radios and other military equipment at the nearby Siemens factory. While the labor varied day to day, the length of the workday did not—eleven backbreaking hours was the norm, with the only interruption a fifteen-minute break for a meager "lunch" of thin soup and another slice of moldy bread. Though the newly arrived French women began their stay at Ravensbrück in relatively good health, within weeks the punishing conditions—hard labor exacerbated by malnutrition, dehydration, and the prevalence of such diseases as typhus, typhoid, and diphtheria—began taking a toll. And then there was the physical abuse meted out by the Germans. Prisoners who were slow in responding to a guard's order would be horsewhipped or beaten with a cudgel. More severe instances of non-cooperation would see the woman being set on by the guard dogs, or being tied to a wooden frame and lashed repeatedly across the back and buttocks with a stick. In the tremendously unsanitary conditions that prevailed in the camp the wounds from such a whipping quickly became infected, inevitably leading to septic shock.[3]

But Yvette and the other arrivals from Paris soon realized that there were prisoners in Ravensbrück who were subject to even more horrific abuse, though not as punishment for perceived infractions of camp rules. Relatively healthy teenaged girls and young women, most of them Polish, were purposely maimed and crippled in ghastly and macabre medical experiments carried out by SS doctors, ostensibly to help the Germans better understand and treat combat wounds suffered by their troops. The unfortunate victims were subjected to a range of horrific "tests"—all of which were conducted while the women were awake and fully conscious. Some had their leg bones shattered or their calf muscles or nerves torn out, with the resultant wounds being intentionally infected with bacteria or foreign objects. Others had limbs crudely amputated, still others were exposed to toxic chemicals, and several were shot at point-blank range and left untreated to see how long it would take for them to bleed out. With pity and affection Yvette and her fellow French prisoners referred to the experiment subjects as "lapins" (rabbits), because the Germans treated them as nothing more than human laboratory animals.[4]

Yvette and her mother assumed that they would remain in Ravensbrück until they died or were liberated, but on September 18 they were among five hundred French prisoners chosen for transfer to the Buchenwald *Aussenkommando* ("external detachment") called Arbeitslager (labor camp) Torgau.[5] In preparation for the relocation, the women were allowed to shower and were given clean uniforms bearing new individual numbers—31903 for Yvette and 31904 for Denise. On the morning of the nineteenth the entire group marched to the train station in Fürstenberg, where the women were packed aboard waiting railcars. A three-day, 120-mile journey brought them to the station at Torgau, some 120 miles south of Ravensbrück, in Saxony. After disembarking from the freight cars on the afternoon of the twenty-first the women were marched through the town, where they were amazed to find hundreds of French prisoners of war. The men called to them from the barred upper windows of buildings and from small barbed-wire enclosures that dotted the town.[6] The chance to speak to their countrymen, however briefly, cheered the women prisoners immensely, as did the first sight of their new home.

Set in a small forest clearing a half-hour walk outside the town, Arbeitslager Torgau looked more like a commercial factory than a Nazi prison. Though circled by tall fences, the facility consisted of many stucco buildings separated by concrete walkways lined with bushes and small areas of well-tended lawn. The new arrivals were struck by how pleasant the surroundings seemed in comparison to those they'd left behind at Ravensbrück, an impression that was further enhanced when the women were ushered into their quarters. As Virginia d'Albert-Lake later wrote:

There were three small dormitories and one large one. The floors were of cement; the bunks had three tiers; there were steam heat radiators; the straw mattresses and pillows were new, and everything was clean. There were two washrooms, down the center of which ran two troughs and a water pipe, with spouts at regular intervals. Outhouses were the only non-modern feature. . . . What a change from Ravensbrück! It looked as if we were going to be treated like human beings! We lined up for our blankets and were given two apiece—clean wool ones. Each of us had her own bed! That same evening food arrived, which included good fresh bread, not the black sawdust of Ravensbrück. There was sauerkraut soup too, and a piece of sausage for each of us.[7]

The women's initially positive impression of Torgau changed abruptly the following morning, however. After roll call on Sunday the twenty-second they were marched to a large factory-like building, where it quickly became obvious that the *Arbeitslager* was, in fact, an army munitions plant. The women were immediately put to work retrieving spent copper shell casings from huge basins of acid, a process intended to make the casings reusable. Workers had to wear heavy protective aprons made of thick rubber, and the acid basins produced fumes that made breathing difficult.

But it was not the working conditions that ultimately incensed the French prisoners to the point of revolt. Within an hour of arriving in the work hall dozens of women—including Yvette, Denise, and Virginia d'Albert-Lake—simply took off their aprons, dropped them on the floor, and announced to their startled German overseers that as résistants they were soldiers of France and they refused to help produce tools of war for the enemy.[8] An SS adjutant's threat to send back to Ravensbrück anyone who refused to work sparked an intense debate among the prisoners:

> Many of the women changed their decision at this threat, while those who were willing to take the risk were scornful of their comrades' cowardice. What a morning that was! There was no semblance of order. . . . Women were lecturing and arguing, fighting and weeping. Leaders were making up lists, drawing up petitions. It was all madness; everyone was caught up in the wild excitement and nervous intensity of the situation. . . . We all suffered that day. Friends, enemies. We were torn between courage and fear, idealism and realism, pride and shame.[9]

The Germans, for their part, seemed temporarily uncertain how to respond to the revolt. The French women were ultimately sent back to their dormitories, where most spent the night wondering what the morning would bring. To their surprise and relief, what sunrise did not bring was firing squads. At the dawn roll call the camp commandant announced that two hundred of the prisoners would be required to work in the munitions halls, but the others would be divided between food preparation in the facility's several kitchens and agricultural work outside the fences. Anyone who refused to do labor of any kind, he announced ominously, would immediately be returned to Ravensbrück. For reasons known only to themselves, the requisite number of women decided that the munitions work was their best option. Yvette and Denise, on the other hand, stuck firmly to their refusal to help the German war effort, instead opting for agricultural work.[10]

Their decision kept them out of the munitions hall, but it also guaranteed long days of backbreaking labor. The fields that surrounded the camp not only provided food for the prisoners, the guards, and the guards' families, they also fed the several hundred German civilian workers—mostly women—assigned to other aspects of the ammunition-production process. Yvette, Denise, and the other agricultural workers therefore spent eleven hours a day in the fields, tending to and harvesting crops planted earlier in the season. As August turned to September increasingly cold weather and frequent rain added to the physical challenges of the work, though the "field women" were at least able to supplement their increasingly meager diet with fresh vegetables.

Yvette and Denise had been at Torgau for just over seven weeks when, on October 15, they and about half of the original number of female prisoners sent to the camp were marched to the railway station and loaded aboard waiting freight cars. The women were understandably worried that they were about to be sent back to Ravensbrück, but their actual destination was a small village known as Abteroda, just over fifty miles southwest of Buchenwald.[11] Until the 1920s the community had been the home of the Kalischachtanlage Abteroda, a potash salt mine, and it was the extensive network of disused tunnels that made the otherwise unremarkable village strategically important to the German war effort.

From 1938 onward many of the tunnels had been enlarged and equipped with machinery used in the production of ammunition ranging from rifle and machine-gun cartridges to artillery shells, while other tunnels were used as storage areas. New buildings were constructed above ground to house offices, shops that built the wooden crates used to ship the ammunition, and barracks and orderly rooms for the soldiers who guarded the complex. By early 1944 the Allied bombing raids began seriously impeding the manufacturing of jet engines for the Luftwaffe at the BMW plant in nearby Eisenach and the production facilities were moved underground at several locations, including Abteroda.[12] Much of the ammunition-production machinery was moved elsewhere, and work crews from the Organisation Todt—the huge civil and military engineering firm—further expanded and improved the tunnels beneath and around the village and installed the infrastructure required for engine production. Though BMW provided some administrators and technical staff, the bulk of the labor force comprised concentration camp inmates. Because the Abteroda facility had been designated an *Aussenkommando* of Buchenwald, that camp's commandant, SS-Colonel Hermann Pister, was required to provide the necessary workers—preferably females, he was told, because their hands were thought to be better suited to detail work. Having been informed that the women in Torgau's munitions hall had been so debilitated by exposure to acid that they were essentially useless, Pister simply ordered that roughly half the female prisoners at that camp be sent to Abteroda to work until they died—an SS policy known as *Vernichtung durch Arbeit* (extermination through labor). The other women were returned directly to Ravensbrück.[13]

Yvette, her mother, and the others selected for labor in the engine facility spent four days locked in the unheated freight cars without food or water, and when they finally arrived at the station that served Abteroda it was in the middle of a swirling snowstorm. Still wearing only the thin clothes and wooden clogs they had been issued on arrival at Torgau, the women were packed into the back of open-top troop trucks for the frigid, four-mile journey to the BMW work site. On arrival the newcomers were forced into the 180-foot by 60-foot, two-story building that was to be both their workplace and barracks.

The structure's ground floor was almost wholly taken up with rows of crude wooden worktables, all of which had long benches along each side. Atop each table were boxes of small aluminum parts and various bundles of colored wire, items that made it immediately obvious to the new arrivals that they would be expected to work on military items of some sort. When many of the women began muttering that they were résistants and would not aid in the production of war materiel, the SS adjutant standing in the middle of the room blandly informed them that anyone who refused to work would immediately be taken out and shot. Given the stark choice between work or death, the women wisely decided to hold their tongues—at least for the time being.

The new arrivals were then herded up a narrow flight of stairs to the building's second floor, which was stacked to the ceiling with tiers of the now familiar crude wooden bunks. At either end of the room were rows of buckets to be used as toilets, and the women were told they were responsible for emptying the containers each evening. Guards then handed out new fabric triangles the prisoners were to sew on in place of the ones issued at Ravensbrück before the transfer to Torgau. Still red to indicate the wearer was a political prisoner and still marked with a large "F," the triangles bore new numbers—Denise was now 50515 and Yvette 50516.[14]

For the next three and a half months the daily schedule for the French prisoners working at Abteroda never varied. After a meager breakfast at dawn the women spent the next eleven hours in the first-floor workshop, with only an equally meager lunch at midday to break up the monotony of assembling small subcomponents for the BMW jet engines. Strands of delicate wire had to be threaded through minute holes in various aluminum stampings, and each completed component had to meet stringent quality-control parameters. If a German inspector found a flaw in any part, the women who'd produced it would be beaten or whipped in front of the others. Such punishment was fairly common when the workers were first learning the process, but as the weeks went on assembly errors ceased being the result of inexperience or inability, and instead resulted from intentional sabotage.

Rather than refusing to work and suffering the extreme consequences such a refusal would certainly trigger, Yvette, Denise, and many of their fellow prisoners decided the best way to aid the Allied war effort was to build flaws into the BMW engines, hopefully causing the power plants to malfunction or even fail catastrophically in operational use. It was a dangerous game to play, for any woman suspected of committing overt sabotage would be summarily executed—and several were. The faults built into the subcomponents had to be significant enough to cause the engine to eventually fail, but small enough to pass muster during the quality-control inspection. The women used different methods, but the most common was to scrape away a tiny bit of outer insulation from two or three adjacent wires within a bundle. The heat and vibration produced by the running engine would hopefully cause the damaged wires to break or arc, either of which could potentially cause the engine to malfunction.[15]

Over time, the sabotage effort proved successful enough that a detachment of some twenty SS troops arrived from Buchenwald to carry out an extensive investigation. All the French women were interrogated, the upstairs dormitory was torn apart in a search for engine components the women might have stolen, and already completed parts were disassembled and closely examined for any sign of tampering. Despite these efforts the Germans were unable to determine exactly how the parts were being sabotaged and by whom. Under pressure to resume production, the plant managers restarted the assembly process with double the number of overseers in the workshop. Yet the tighter security at Abteroda did little to decrease the number of engine components that failed under operational conditions and in early February 1944 the camp commander, SS-First Sergeant John, asked officials at Buchenwald to remove all of the surviving 249 French female prisoners on "suspicion of collective resistance." He requested that they be replaced by other—presumably more obedient—inmates from Ravensbrück, and suggested that the appropriate punishment for the recalcitrant French prisoners would be execution.[16]

Buchenwald commandant Pister granted John's request for new workers, and 125 of the French women left Abteroda aboard railway freight cars on February 12. The remaining 124 individuals were kept at work until the arrival of 125 replacement female prisoners from Ravensbrück, after which the last French women—including Yvette and Denise—left Abteroda by train on February 26.

While there are some indications that Pister had initially agreed with John's suggestion that the sabotage of the BMW engines perpetrated by the French workers warranted a summary death sentence, the intervention of another German aircraft company saved the women from immediate execution. That firm, Junkers Flugzeug und Motorenwerke (Aircraft and Motor Works), had established a small production plant in Markkleeberg, a town nestled between two small lakes some four and a half miles due south of Leipzig. The facility's primary purpose was to produce the Junkers Jumo 004 turbojet engine—the power plant used in the Messerschmitt Me 262 jet fighter and a competitor to BMW's 003. A designated subcamp of Buchenwald, the Markkleeberg plant's existing workforce—comprising primarily Hungarian Jewish women—was unable to keep up with production quotas and Junkers desperately needed more slave laborers.

It is unclear why Pister agreed to send the French women to Markkleeberg. At Abteroda they'd proven themselves to be unreliable workers who found ingenious ways to damage machinery desperately needed for the German war effort, and logic should certainly have indicated they would probably attempt the same sort of sabotage at the Junkers plant. Perhaps by that late point in the war, with the Allies relentlessly advancing on the heart of the Reich from both west and east, the Buchenwald commandant simply didn't see industrial disruption as all that important an issue. Or, possibly, Pister knew he would soon have to start moving prisoners out of Buchenwald and its major subcamps to prevent advancing Soviet forces from liberating them, and believed that by sending the French women to Markkleeberg he was effectively reducing the number of prisoners he would have to personally deal with. Whatever the reason for his decision, the Buchenwald commandant knew that the women would ultimately suffer the fate the Abteroda commander had suggested for them—Markkleeberg was also a *Vernichtung durch Arbeit* facility, and the chances that any of the French prisoners would survive their time there were vanishingly slim.[17]

Denise and Yvette arrived at the camp on February 26 with the second group of women from Abteroda, and their introduction to the punishing conditions was almost immediate.[18] The new arrivals were herded into a warehouse-like building, where they were forced to strip off the rags they had been wearing for months and then issued the thin, one-piece, gray work overalls that would be their only clothing. The prisoners were assigned to one of two twelve-hour shifts—6:15 A.M. to 6:15 P.M., or vice versa—and from then on their lives were dominated by work, hunger, pain, and disease.[19]

The Morins were fortunate to be assigned to the same work shift, which initially saw them doing essentially the same labor they'd performed at Abteroda. Along with hundreds of other women, Yvette and Denise assembled stamped-aluminum subcomponents for the Jumo 004 engine, a task that required each prisoner to do very precise work with a small metal tool. As at the BMW facility, each completed subassembly was quality-control checked by a technician, and if a woman's work was deemed unacceptable she was beaten. And, also as had happened at Abteroda, many of the French women began finding ways to introduce undetectable flaws into the components, again despite the very real threat that should their sabotage be detected they would almost certainly be executed. That threat ultimately receded for Yvette and Denise, however, for after several weeks in the engine plant mother and daughter were reassigned to the group of prisoners tasked with delivering wheelbarrows full of heating coal from a storage area to the camp's workshops and offices.[20]

The change in jobs was likely the result of Denise's failing health, which was itself largely the consequence of the malnutrition that affected all the prisoners at Markkleeberg. In keeping with the *Vernichtung durch Arbeit* policy the women were fed just once a day, at the midpoint of their work shift, and the fare consisted only of a cup of thin soup and a few ounces of stale and moldy bread. The starvation-level rations affected all the inmates, but older women like Denise tended to be far more likely to exhibit the physical manifestations associated with malnourishment—among which were the sort of hand tremors that would hinder the fine detail work the Junkers technicians demanded in the engine plant. But the transfer to the "coal commando" had one small benefit—the women delivering the coal among the camp's various buildings had the opportunity to dig up edible bulbs or tubers. They had to be careful though; one woman was poisoned when she ate what she thought was a radish, but was actually a belladonna root.[21]

Hunger was not the only thing that caused pain for Markkleeberg's slave laborers. Though the fenced camp's main gate and guard towers were manned by a score of Wehrmacht troops, the barracks and work areas were the domain of brutal, whip-wielding female overseers collectively known as *Aufseherinnen*. As one prisoner later remembered, the uniformed, booted women "hit us for the slightest cause—or even without any cause. They beat us even for looking at them or for not looking at them. They always found an unfortunate woman who attracted their attention. She might have been too pretty or too ugly, too tall or too short, or just something about her look made the girl the target of their rage and torment. For any little thing they did not like, they slapped us or copied down the numbers on our overalls to call us later for further punishment."[22]

In addition to backbreaking labor, starvation, physical abuse, exposure to the elements, and the constant threat of execution, Markkleeberg's female prisoners also had to confront the panoply of diseases that ravaged the Nazi concentration camps. Typhus, typhoid, and dysentery were endemic, and tuberculosis, malaria, and meningitis were common. Prisoners were also prey to pneumonia and other infections, and it was one of the latter that would have taken Denise's life had it not been for help she received from an unexpected quarter.

In mid-March 1945 Yvette noticed that her mother's throat was swelling, and that the older woman was having trouble swallowing. The symptoms quickly worsened, with Denise developing a wracking cough and raging fever and having increasing difficulty breathing. While Markkleeberg had a small camp infirmary it was for the staff, not the prisoners, and the Germans executed any slave laborer incapable of working. Fortunately, one of the other members of the "coal commando," a Hungarian Jewish woman who had been a nurse before the war, was able to diagnose Denise's malady as a severe case of diphtheria.[23] The bacterial infection was widespread in the camp, and without treatment was often fatal. Understandably concerned about her mother, Yvette hatched a bold but extremely dangerous plan. While ostensibly delivering coal to the infirmary—and obviously at the risk of their lives—she and the Jewish woman stole several vials of sulfonamide antibiotics and a syringe. Given by injection over the course of several days, the drugs brought about a significant improvement in Denise's condition. She had not completely recovered, however, when Germany's worsening military situation forced her, Yvette, and the other female prisoners to confront one last great threat.

By early April 1945 the Third Reich was in its death throes. Advancing from the east, Soviet forces had taken most of Poland and were moving farther into Austria, eastern Czechoslovakia, and East Prussia. In the west, the British, American, and French armies were driving ever deeper into Germany's heartland, with the leading U.S. 12th Army Group making a determined push for the Elbe River. In response to the two-front Allied offensive the Nazi hierarchy had begun closing and in many cases attempting to dismantle hundreds of concentration camps and their satellite facilities as part of a larger effort to destroy the evidence of the Reich's heinous crimes against humanity. Not wanting prisoners to be liberated by the Allies—and still needing slave laborers—the Germans executed those people deemed too debilitated to be of further use and evacuated the others to camps deeper within the Reich. Though some evacuations were conducted by rail or ship, most were death marches in which prisoners were forced to walk vast distances under unbelievably harsh conditions. Tens of thousands died of starvation, exposure, and exhaustion, and anyone who attempted to escape or lagged behind was murdered by the accompanying SS or Wehrmacht guards.[24]

On April 6 the approach of U.S. forces prompted the Germans to begin the evacuation of the vast Buchenwald camp system. On Friday the thirteenth Markkleeberg's commandant, SS-Lieutenant Colonel Wiegand, was ordered to empty the facility immediately and march the prisoners to the still-operating camp at Theresienstadt in occupied Czechoslovakia, a little over one hundred miles to the southeast.[25] The women were hastily called together and told they would be leaving in twenty minutes, that no one would be left behind, and that anyone who attempted to hide would be shot. The guards then organized those prisoners who could walk into a long column and put the sick aboard small wagons, and when the sad procession wound its way out of the camp and through the streets of Markkleeberg, Yvette was pulling the cart bearing Denise and four others.

Over the following days the German guards accompanying the column harried and threatened the emaciated women, forcing them to keep up a brutal pace with only a few minutes' rest every four hours. The still-frigid weather and lack of food and water quickly began taking a grim toll, with dozens of the prisoners simply dropping to the ground either dead or too exhausted to continue. The guards shot those stragglers who were still breathing, then tossed their bodies into the underbrush. Several women who attempted to escape were also killed, though others managed to slip away unseen during the frequent rainstorms that engulfed the column.

It was one such cloudburst that allowed Yvette, Denise, and the others aboard the cart to make good their escape. As the column was approaching the Elbe River near the town of Meissen, twelve miles northwest of Dresden, the skies opened and torrents of rain cut visibility to only a few feet. With an almost superhuman effort given her poor health, Yvette pulled the cart off the road and onto a narrow dirt track that led off to the south, into thick, fog-shrouded woods. Pulling the small vehicle as quickly as possible, she followed the track for what she estimated to be several kilometers, only slowing down when the shape of a single person materialized out of the fog ahead. With nowhere to go—the forest on either side of the track was too dense to pull the cart through—Yvette and the others could only wait to see if the apparition was friend or foe. As the wraith slowly resolved into a slender, dark-haired man, the women were stunned to hear him speaking softly in their language. He was a Frenchman who had escaped from a German POW camp, he said, and he was on his way to help liberate his comrades. When the women explained that they too were escapees, the man gave them directions to the abandoned barn where he had been staying since gaining his freedom. They should remain there, he said, because the Russians would soon arrive and liberate them.

The man's forecast about the Russians' imminent arrival was somewhat optimistic, as it turned out. The women spent more than a week in the abandoned barn, an interlude during which they rested as much as possible between forays into the woods in search of food and potable water. The pickings were slim, however, and by the time they were discovered by members of a Soviet patrol the women were in decidedly poor condition. Yvette and the others were taken to a Russian field hospital in Tharandt, where on admittance all were found to be suffering from exposure and extreme malnutrition. Denise weighed barely eighty pounds, while the otherwise gaunt Yvette had an abdomen swollen with more than twenty pounds of edema.

After nearly a month in the Russians' care—during which time Adolf Hitler committed suicide and Nazi Germany surrendered unconditionally—Yvette and Denise were judged stable enough to be sent home. The first part of that journey took place aboard a flatbed railcar, on which the two women and a score of other concentration camp survivors were transported west to the "Line of Contact"—the demarcation between the areas then occupied by Russia and those held by American, British, and French forces.[26] Transferred to the care of U.S. Army medics, Yvette and Denise were given another thorough physical examination before being transported to the French border and turned over to their country's Red Cross. That organization aided the women in their homeward journey, and on June 6, 1945, mother and daughter returned to Paris.

Their homecoming was understandably bittersweet. The city had survived the war essentially unscathed and now, ten months after its liberation, the streets were once again bustling with raucous life undimmed by the shadow of the swastika banners that had once adorned Paris's grandest buildings. The French tricolor was everywhere, and the crowds of soldiers touring the museums and packing the sidewalk cafés and climbing the Eiffel Tower—and, yes, scuffing the marble floors of the viewing platform encircling Napoléon's Tomb—now wore Allied uniforms.

But for Denise and Yvette, a pall hung over the slowly re-illuminating City of Light. Still in poor physical health and grappling with the severe psychological trauma inflicted by their time in the camps, they were also confronted by other challenges. Where would they live? How would they earn a living? And, most importantly, what had happened to Georges, and to Joe?

To their great relief, within days of their arrival in Paris Yvette and Denise were able to return to their home at Invalides. The directors of the Invalides-based veterans' organization decreed that out of respect for the still-absent Georges and in recognition of the family's resistance work the women could stay in the apartment for the foreseeable future. Old friends also provided aid, bringing food parcels and helping mother and daughter get to their appointments at the clinics offering free care to concentration-camp returnees. One former résistant proved especially helpful, both in easing Yvette and Denise into a semblance of normal life and in helping to alleviate their financial worries.

André Schoegel had avoided arrest by the Germans, and after the liberation of Paris he made contact with the British and American military agencies seeking to identify and reward those French civilians who had helped Allied personnel either evade capture or reach safety after escaping from captivity. Those organizations—the IS9 section of Britain's MI9 and the Awards Branch of MIS-X—had both opened offices in Paris almost as soon as the Germans had pulled out of the capital. The two groups worked closely together, using names and addresses culled from evaders' and escapees' reports to locate and interview helpers. Those civilians whose assistance could be verified were eligible to receive both awards and cash payments from the American and British governments, and it was with the latter in mind that on June 14 Schoegel escorted Denise and Yvette to the MIS-X office in Room 504 of the Hotel Majestic.[27]

That first meeting was relatively brief, with the officer conducting the interview spending most of the time reading to the women from the E&E reports of the various aviators the Morins had helped. Denise and Yvette promised to write a full account of the assistance the family had provided, and asked if there were any way to determine whether Georges was still alive. The MIS-X officer vowed to do what he could to find out, and then gave mother and daughter a food parcel for which, he noted, "they seemed most appreciative."[28]

Over the following days Denise and Yvette worked to produce the "full account" of the family's wartime activities the MIS-X officer had requested. The result was a highly detailed, two-page document listing the various *réseaux* for which they worked or which they assisted; the other résistants with whom they interacted, by name and nom de guerre; the names, ranks, and nationalities of all the evaders they aided, either directly or indirectly; and the names or aliases of anyone they believed to have been in the service of the enemy. Denise delivered the account to the MIS-X office on June 20, and the officer who interviewed her about its contents observed that while still physically frail, she was "an admirable woman, having done a considerable work." The man added that Denise was "very proud of having done her duty as a Frenchwoman," and noted that while "she desires nothing" in return for her service, she "would be very happy to see General De Gaulle."[29]

Over the following weeks MIS-X and IS9 evaluated Denise and Yvette's accounts, the information contained in relevant American and British evasion reports, and the statements of other helpers. On July 11 Major John F. White Jr., deputy head of the Paris MIS-X office, wrote to his IS9 counterpart, Donald Darling, confirming that the women would each receive 22,000 French francs as initial recompense for their arrest and deportation—with both payments shared between the two organizations. The type of awards and amount of possible cash payments to be made in recognition of their service as helpers was still being determined, he wrote.[30]

WHILE THE INITIAL "DEPORTATION AWARD" FROM MIS-X AND IS9 CERTAINLY helped ease Denise and Yvette's financial situation, it did nothing to calm their fears regarding the whereabouts and well-being of Georges and Joe.

Though the women had been told upon their return to Paris that men who had spent time in Buchenwald believed Georges had died or been executed the previous December, neither mother nor daughter was willing to accept that he was dead until they were provided with some sort of official, tangible proof. After all, they reasoned, many people believed to have died in the camps had returned. Until someone could convince them otherwise, they would assume that "Papa" was alive and trying to find his way back to them.

Yvette's longing for news of her father was matched by her intense desire to have word of Joe. Before leaving Paris the final time to return to England he'd confided to her that he would likely be sent to the Pacific to fight the Japanese, and she was haunted by the thought that while she and her mother had been in the camps the man she loved, the man she hoped to spend her life with, had died in combat above some nameless island on the other side of the world. Two pieces of information she'd received just after she and her mother returned to Paris had stoked Yvette's fears regarding Joe.

First, Germaine Mercier told her that soon after the Allies arrived in the capital someone—she could not recall who—had told her with absolute certainty that Yvette and her parents had died and Germaine had passed the sad news around among their acquaintances. The second piece of information came from Madame de Larminat. The older woman told Yvette that after the liberation of Paris several of the friends Joe had made during his time in the city had written to him care of the 94th Bomb Group at Rougham, and the letters might have included the report of Yvette's death. In a way, Madame de Larminat reasoned, the fact that Joe had not responded to any of the letters was good news—if the missives hadn't reached him, he would not have heard of his beloved's "death." On the other hand, the woman said, if the letters were reaching Joe he would know that she and her mother were alive. Indeed, on June 4, just two days before Yvette and Denise returned to Paris, an English-speaking Frenchwoman named Gladys Oriot had written to Joe at the behest of Germaine Mercier and Madame de Larminat herself, telling the airman that his fiancée and prospective mother-in-law were on their way home, but that Georges Morin "died last December in captivity."[31]

Yvette's desire for information about Joe only increased as the weeks went by, and on July 9 she opened another avenue of inquiry. She and her mother had been asked to visit the IS9 Awards Branch at 4 rue de Valois in the 1st arrondissement as part of the agency's effort to further explore the extent of the aid the Morins had provided to Commonwealth evaders.

The interview was to help determine what level of formal recognition the women—and the still missing Georges—would receive from the British government, as well as the amount of any cash payment coming to them in thanks for their evasion work. In his postmeeting report the IS9 representative, RAF Flight Lieutenant Howard, noted that mother and daughter had "had no word" about Georges. He then added that Yvette was "anxious to have news of airman Joseph Cornwall."[32]

Over the following weeks Yvette and Denise got on with life the best they could, trying to regain a sense of normalcy and using the "deportee" payments they'd received to support themselves. Despite their continued requests for information through French, British, and American channels they learned nothing more about Georges's fate, nor was Yvette able to find out whether Joe was alive. Indeed, the young woman had begun to believe that her fiancé had likely perished in the Pacific, and in her growing grief found solace in remembering the short but intense time they had spent together. If indeed Joe was gone, she swore, she would dedicate herself to caring for her mother until—God willing—her father came home.

Then, a few days after Japan's September 2, 1945, surrender in Tokyo Bay formally ended World War II, Joe came back into Yvette's life—by mail.

THE LETTER FROM YVETTE THAT FINALLY REACHED JOE AT MARCH FIELD in July 1944 had done wonders for the airman's morale, and the fact that no others followed did not particularly concern him. He understood how difficult it must have been for her to get even that one short note out of occupied Paris, and with the Allied armies closing in on the French capital he knew it would only be a matter of weeks before Yvette and her parents—and indeed, all the friends Joe had made in France—would be free once more. Then, he vowed to himself, he could contact the woman he loved, and they would begin the next phase of their life together.

But things did not turn out as Joe had hoped. In the weeks following the August 25 liberation of Paris he had written repeatedly to Yvette at the avenue de Tourville address, but had gotten no response. He'd then reached out to Germaine Mercier, but had not heard from her either. Joe's worst nightmare—that something terrible must have happened to the

Morins—seemed to come all too horribly true when in late December 1944 he received a much-forwarded and redirected letter from Paris informing him that Yvette and her parents had been arrested by the Gestapo and subsequently executed.[33]

Devastated by the news, Joe fell into a deep depression. He sought to bury his sorrow in work, but even twelve-hour days in the classroom or on the March Field gunnery ranges did little to assuage his grief. In what was likely an attempt to give some purpose to what he saw as a now hopelessly empty life, Joe began applying for transfer to the Pacific. Arguing that his status as both an airplane armorer and a combat-experienced flexible gunner more than qualified him for a position in one of the remaining B-24 units operating against Japan, he submitted at least four requests for what was officially defined as a "voluntary permanent change of station." Unfortunately, the very expertise and experience that Joe cited as factors qualifying him for a return to combat also made him the ideal instructor, and each of his applications for transfer was denied "for the good of the service"—he was just too valuable where he was, his commander told him.

Denied the chance to return to combat, Joe had no choice but to carry on at March Field. He decided that when the war ended he would do exactly as he had told Yvette he would do in the event something happened to her—he would go to Alaska, spend time with his mother, then find some way to lose himself in the territory's vastness. He could hire himself out as a hunting guide, he thought, or maybe go back to work on a commercial fishing boat. It didn't matter, really, since the goal would simply be to give his broken heart a chance to heal in a land virtually devoid of people.

But in late July 1945 Joe's melancholy reveries came to an abrupt halt when another envelope bearing multiple forwarding addresses finally found him. The letter was the one written on June 4 by Gladys Oriot on behalf of Germaine Mercier. Though Joe was deeply saddened by the seeming confirmation of Georges's death, he was understandably elated by the news that Yvette and Denise were alive and on their way home. He immediately wrote a long and joyous letter, pouring out his love for both of them and his intense relief that God had spared them. As soon as he was free to do so he would return to Paris, he said, and he and Yvette could embark on the life they talked so much about on those evenings atop the Dôme church.

Sadly, the arrival of Joe's letter prompted Yvette to make a decision that would break both their hearts.

THOUGH DENISE AND YVETTE ADAMANTLY REFUSED TO ACCEPT THE IDEA THAT Georges was really gone, by late August 1945 it had become obvious to both women that even if he were still alive he was probably dealing with memory loss or severe psychological issues—why else would he not have found his way home? And if by some miracle he were to actually return to Paris, his wife and daughter agreed, he would likely require long-term, comprehensive care—a large part of which they themselves vowed to provide.

And then there was Yvette's intense devotion to Denise. Always close, mother and daughter had developed an even deeper bond during their time in the camps, and that connection had only grown stronger as they faced the physical, emotional, and financial challenges of life in postliberation Paris. Yvette knew that her mother would need her continuing love, support, and assistance—especially if her beloved husband Georges never returned. Because Yvette had come to believe in her heart that Joe was dead, she had decided to dedicate herself to caring for her mother for as long as Denise might live.

Such was Yvette's frame of mind when she received Joe's letter. Though ecstatic that he was alive and that his love for her was apparently undimmed despite the time they'd been apart, she was torn between the unexpectedly renewed prospect of life with him and the vow she had made to herself to devote her life to caring for her mother. As much as she wanted to experience in reality the dreams she and Joe had shared, Yvette could not put her own happiness before Denise's well-being. A new life in America with Joe would be impossible, Yvette knew, for she would not leave her mother and Denise would not leave France as long as there was even the faintest hope that Georges might be alive. Nor would it be fair to ask Joe to come back to Paris, for despite her love for him their life as husband and wife would not be her primary focus as long as her mother was alive.

With Gladys Oriot's help Yvette put all of these thoughts on paper in her response to Joe, who replied that he understood and accepted the fact that Yvette needed to put her mother first. In subsequent letters the couple spoke of their love for one another, of how life-changing their time in Paris had been for both of them, and of how the memories of that time, and of each other, would stay with them forever. But, in the end, like many of their contemporaries who had found love during the tumultuous war years, they agreed that the realities of the postwar world would make it impossible for them to live out their dreams of a life together. They wished each other well, and with heavy hearts went their separate ways.

Neither could have foreseen the subsequent courses their lives would take.

EPILOGUE

O N OCTOBER 1, 1945, JOE CORNWALL WAS DISCHARGED FROM THE USAAF at San Bernardino Army Airfield in Southern California and placed on the inactive reserve list. He received $4,370.29 in final pay, and days later was on his way to Alaska.[1]

Joe's sojourn in what was then still a U.S. territory first took him to Juneau, where his mother was running a hair salon. Joe then spent several months working as a hunting guide in southeast Alaska, but by May 1946 had made a significant career change. On the twentieth of that month a letter from the office of the regional director of the U.S. Fish and Wildlife Service in Juneau notified Joe that his application for the position of engineer on the FWS's patrol vessel *Auklet* had been granted.[2] Joe served aboard the forty-eight-foot-long, tugboat-like vessel for the next four years, as it undertook fisheries-protection operations in southeast Alaska from its home port in Wrangel.

The Fish and Wildlife Service's announcement in the fall of 1950 that it would sell the thirty-three-year-old *Auklet* out of government service prompted Joe to make yet another momentous decision. On December 27 he rejoined what by then had become the U.S. Air Force.[3] After several months of training he was designated a weapons-maintenance specialist with the rank of master sergeant, and over the following seven years was stationed at various bases both in the United States and abroad—including an assignment with a combat fighter-bomber squadron in Korea. On February 26, 1957, Joe was posted to the field that had been so much a part of his earlier USAAF time—the now renamed Lowry Air Force Base in

Denver. And it was there that yet another aspect of his World War II years reappeared.

Joe had been working as a weapons-maintenance instructor at Lowry for some time when, under circumstances that remain unclear, he ran into Clara Gypin Rebuck. The woman whom the USAAF had in 1943 mistakenly believed to be Joe's wife had divorced her second husband, Clarence "Smokey" Rebuck, and was living in the Denver area. The renewed acquaintance between Joe and Clara ultimately evolved into something deeper, and on March 24, 1959, the couple married at the First Methodist Church's Lehmberg Chapel in Colorado Springs.[4]

Joe stayed in the USAF after his marriage, and was eventually promoted to senior master sergeant. He spent the bulk of the next seven years at Lowry—except for one year at Thule Air Base in Greenland and another at Glasgow AFB, Montana. He had hoped to remain in the service long enough to attain the rank of chief master sergeant—a promotion for which his performance reports and other documents indicated he was more than qualified—but his career goals were derailed by increasingly poor health. Joe began showing symptoms of Parkinson's Disease in the early 1960s, and the attendant tremors, muscle stiffness, and speech difficulties ultimately led the Air Force to declare him medically unfit for further duty. At the time of his retirement on June 30, 1966, Joe was credited with twenty-six years of service (which included his time in the inactive reserve). In addition to the aerial gunner wings he proudly wore throughout his military career, the decorations credited to him included the Purple Heart, the Air Medal, the World War II Victory Medal, and the United Nations Service Medal.

After his retirement from the Air Force Joe went to work as a maintenance supervisor for the local school district, a position he held until his Parkinson's symptoms grew so pronounced that he could no longer walk or drive. With Clara's loving help he struggled against the disease as best he could, but by 1992 he was also dealing with congestive heart failure. On January 29, 1993, Joseph Ellison Cornwall died of a heart attack in the emergency room of Presbyterian-St. Luke's Hospital in Aurora, Colorado, at the age of seventy-seven.[5] His beloved wife Clara died at eighty-nine on July 30, 2003, and both are interred at the Fort Logan National Cemetery in Denver.

In August 2017, during a visit with Clara Cornwall's son Nate Gypin, the author was privileged to be allowed access to a trunk full of Joe Cornwall's possessions. Among them were documents and photos pertaining to his USAAF and USAF service, uniform items, pictures of him and Clara, and other family memorabilia. The trove also included the simple black billfold Joe was carrying on the day of his death. In addition to his driver's license and other usual items, the wallet contained something unexpected: Folded neatly and tucked into an inside compartment was a faded and obviously old piece of paper. When opened, it proved to be the letter Yvette had sent Joe soon after his departure from France, the one beginning "Mon Cher Joe."

He had apparently kept it with him for fifty years.

THOUGH YVETTE AND DENISE MORIN CONTINUED TO HOPE THAT GEORGES was alive and would ultimately return to them, in the spring of 1946 the MIS-X office in Paris issued an official death certificate that stated he had perished in German custody, though an exact date was not given. The determination that Georges had died as a direct result of his arrest and deportation was considered when IS9 and MIS-X set about deciding what sort of compensation should be paid to his wife and daughter in recognition of the family's work on behalf of Allied evaders. In a May 14, 1946, letter to Denise, Major John White of MIS-X informed her that the British and American governments took pleasure in awarding her 349,000 francs in return for the aid she and her family provided to Allied airmen during the occupation.[6]

Nor was money the only recognition the Morins received for their wartime work. On December 26, 1946, Denise and Yvette each received the U.S. Medal of Freedom—the former with Silver Palm and the latter with Bronze Palm. The citations accompanying the awards acknowledged each woman's "exceptionally meritorious achievement, which aided the United States in the prosecution of the war against the enemy in Continental Europe." Both were lauded for their "heroism, ingenuity, and outstanding determination in the performance of hazardous missions." They disregarded their own personal safety, the citations read, and assisted directly in the evasion of fifty Allied airmen, until they were arrested by the Gestapo and deported to Germany. The women's courage and devotion to the Allied cause "contributed materially to the success of the war effort, thereby meriting the praise and recognition of the United Nations."[7] The following day Georges was posthumously awarded the Medal of Freedom with Silver Palm. His citation acknowledged the same "heroism, ingenuity, and outstanding determination in the performance of hazardous missions," and noted that he aided the Allied evaders at the "risk to his life."[8]

The United States was not the only nation to honor the Morins for their wartime service, of course. On January 30, 1947, the British government awarded Denise the British Empire Medal and Yvette the King's Medal for Courage, citing both for the aid they provided to Commonwealth evaders despite the enormous risks to their own safety. Because Georges had been officially declared deceased, Britain presented his wife and daughter with a "Certificate 17," honoring him with the civilian equivalent of a "Mention in Dispatches."[9] The French government subsequently awarded all three Morins the Médaille de la Résistance, and over the following decades appointed both Denise and Yvette to the Légion d'honneur, the former ultimately progressing to the rank of commandeur and the latter to officier.[10]

While these many prestigious awards were certainly well deserved, they had little practical effect on the life Yvette and Denise led in the decades following the end of the war. The cash payments they received from the British and American governments were helpful, of course, but evaporated with alarming speed as the women faced the realities of life in postwar Paris. Fortunately, as a war widow Denise was offered the opportunity to operate a news kiosk in front of the Saint-Pierre de Chaillot church on the rue Marceau in the 16th arrondissement. The stand sold newspapers, magazines, books, cigarettes, and snacks, and though a humble enterprise it was to provide the women with a modest but steady income for decades. It was not an easy life, however, for Yvette and her mother had to be at the stand by four thirty every morning—seven days a week—to receive the day's delivery of newspapers and other goods. The stand usually remained open until seven in the evening, and the long hours took a heavy toll on bodies still suffering the effects of wartime imprisonment.[11]

In 1948 Yvette married a man named Raoul Claerebout, and the following year the couple had a daughter. Named Denise, after her grandmother, the child grew up in the same Invalides home as her mother had. It was not an ideal childhood, unfortunately, for at the age of three young Denise was diagnosed with polio, which required long hours of treatment each day, much of it undertaken at Paris's Hôpital Necker children's hospital. The illness was also hard on the family's finances, since young Denise was not eligible for care under the war deportees' health insurance program and her parents thus had to pay cash for her treatments. Those payments were made even more of a burden by the fact that Raoul Claerebout was an inveterate and not at all successful gambler who also had a severe drinking problem and, when drunk, was prone to violence.[12]

When young Denise was nine years old her father died in a car accident, an event that made life even more difficult for Yvette and her mother. The women had to alternate work at the kiosk with caring for young Denise, a routine that made for long hours and little sleep. Not long afterward the architect of Invalides told Yvette and her mother that he had been asked by his superiors why the two women were still living in the "concierge" apartment, since neither worked on the grounds. It looked as though the women would have to find somewhere else to live, until the director of what by then had been renamed the Office national des anciens combattants et victimes de guerre provided a solution. If the women agreed to clean the agency's offices at night, they would be able to stay in the apartment. Though the arrangement would mean even less sleep for Yvette and her mother they readily agreed, and they and young Denise were able to stay in the home until 1983, a year that marked a watershed in the lives of all three women.

In the late 1930s one of the chief architects of France's historic monuments, Jean-Pierre Pacquet, had developed a plan intended to reveal the "true majesty" of the southern part of the Invalides complex—a project that called for the removal of the fences facing the place Vauban, and for the demolition of what he termed the "parasitic" buildings at the corner of the boulevard des Invalides and avenue de Tourville.[13] Those included the apartment long occupied by the Morins but not, oddly enough, the combination gatehouse and Architect's office right next door. Though Pacquet died in 1975 his plan lived on, and its implementation meant that the home that had meant so much to the Morin family—and to Joe Cornwall, for that matter—was torn down in the late 1980s.

Before that sorry event Yvette, her mother, and young Denise moved to an apartment in Massy, nine miles southwest of Invalides and just to the west of Orly Airport. By that point both of the older women were retired, and they lived there together until Denise's death in 1994 at the age of ninety-six. Yvette's daughter, now Denise Weil, had purchased a house outside Angoulême, in the same département de la Charente where her grandmother was born. After buying land around the building Mme. Weil and her husband developed the property into a horse farm, and in 2004 Yvette moved in with them.

It was there in the summer of 2017 that the author and his wife shared a wonderful day—and a delightful home-cooked meal—with a still spry, engaging, and tremendously welcoming ninety-six-year-old Yvette. Her green eyes alternately sparkling and tearing up, she spoke at length and in detail about her parents, the family's role in the Resistance, the people they'd worked with and sheltered, and of the memories of that time that remain with her.

Later, in an email in which she answered a series of follow-on questions about her time with Joe Cornwall, Yvette echoed the sentiments shared by many couples during those dark days of world conflict.

"The war had brought us together," she said simply, "and peace separated us."

Appendix: After the War

IN THE YEARS FOLLOWING THE END OF WORLD WAR II, AS THE SURVIVING participants in the 94th Bomb Group's Bastille Day raid got on with their lives, the remains of those who died aboard *Salty's Naturals* underwent a somewhat circuitous journey to their final resting places.

The bodies of eight crew members—Purdy, Jones, Lichtenberger, Marquardt, Smith, Dickson, Harris, and Sprague—were recovered either from the wreckage of *Salty's Naturals* or from the surrounding area.[1] Those remains were initially interred as unknowns in adjoining graves in the French military section of Évreux's Saint-Louis Cemetery. A ninth body—Santangelo's—was buried with the others about three weeks later, though the official records do not indicate the reason for the disparity in burial dates.

Following the end of the war in Europe the nine bodies were disinterred and transferred to the French communal cemetery at Saint-André-de-l'Eure, part of which was being used as a temporary collecting point for the remains of Allied service members initially buried in other locations. In March 1948 all of the remains were again disinterred and prepared for shipment to what was then designated the Saint-Laurent U.S. Military Cemetery, which eventually became the Normandy American Cemetery and Memorial in Colleville-sur-Mer. The nine sets of remains underwent extensive forensic examination, and despite being in what was termed "a state of advanced decomposition" each was ultimately identified by dental records. Those identifications were supported by the fact that several of the remains wore identification bracelets, and all of the remains were still "comingled" with pieces of uniform and flight equipment that either bore the individual's name or a unique serial number that could be matched against 94th Bomb Group records. Five sets of remains were permanently interred at Saint-Laurent, while those of Ed Purdy, Chuck Sprague, Rick Marquardt, and John Smith were returned to the United States at the request of their families. Purdy was buried in Colorado, Sprague in Oregon, and Marquardt and Smith in Wisconsin.

As to those who survived the Bastille Day raid:

LAWRENCE H. TEMPLETON

Following his return from France, the only other surviving member of the *Salty's Naturals* crew besides Joe Cornwall was transferred back to the United States. After undergoing evaluation at the U.S. Army Air Forces Personnel Redistribution Center in Atlantic City, New Jersey, Larry was found fit for further overseas duty. He was ultimately tapped to join the 485th Bombardment Squadron, 501st Bombardment Group, a very heavy bomber unit flying the B-29B Superfortress. The organization trained in Nebraska and in January 1945 Larry was part of the "ground echelon" that took ship for the group's new Pacific Theater duty station, Guam's Northwest Field. Larry served as an assistant armament crew chief until the end of the war, and was separated from the USAAF at Camp McCoy, Wisconsin, on November 24, 1945.

After returning to civilian life, Larry worked at various jobs and designed and built a home for his family. The major focus of his life—in addition, of course, to his wife and three sons—was the Wisconsin Evangelical Lutheran Church. He was elected to the Board of Elders, and also served as a representative of the congregation at regional and national conventions.

Lawrence Templeton died March 3, 1999, at the age of eighty-three.

HARRY L. EASTMAN

Harry's bailout on the Le Bourget raid ended up causing him increasingly serious orthopedic problems that exacerbated his already existing arthritis. The second member of the Gunner Trio was medically discharged from the USAAF at Drew Field in Tampa, Florida, on June 10, 1944. He married the former Josephine Ryan in 1948, though the marriage ultimately ended in divorce. For several years after returning to Michigan Harry owned and operated a sporting goods store in Ludington, then managed the Lincoln Hills Golf Club until retiring in 1974. He died on November 25, 1991, at the age of eighty-one.

RICHARD S. DAVITT

Following his separation from the USAAF on June 16, 1945, the third member of the Gunner Trio initially returned to Ohio. When his first marriage ended in divorce he moved west, settling in California. He became an investigator with the Burns International Detective Agency in Los Angeles, and in March 1958 married Joy Cook, a beautician. Dick Davitt—former gunner and successful wartime evader—died February 24, 1978, in Inglewood, California. He was sixty-two years old.

RODERICK A. SCOTT

After the war Roy returned to his hometown of Toronto, married, and became a teacher in the public school system. He attained BA and MA degrees in education, and ultimately retired after twenty-two years as a school principal. Following his retirement he became very active in the Royal Air Force Escaping Society, traveling throughout Ontario speaking about his wartime experiences. He edited the newsletter of the RAFES's Canadian branch, and was instrumental in raising funds for former helpers.

Late in life Roy suffered from both cancer and Parkinson's, and died on June 28, 2005, at the age of eighty-seven.

JAMES GEORGE ANTONY TRUSTY

Upon his return to England Tony Trusty was awarded the Distinguished Flying Medal. He remained on active RAF service for the remainder of the war, though it is unclear in what capacity. After demobilization he returned to his wife, Evelyn, and their three daughters, in Stamford, Lincolnshire. He died in 1989 at seventy-six.

RALPH H. SALTSMAN JR.

After his release from the Germans' Stalag Luft III POW camp—where he spent twenty-two months—"Salty" Saltsman remained in the USAAF. Shortly after his return to the United States, while on the beach in Atlantic City, New Jersey, he met Cornelia Janeway. They married in August 1945 and ultimately had four children.

Saltsman commanded the 18th Fighter-Bomber Group in combat during the Korean War, and his last assignment before retiring in 1960 was as secretary to U.S. Air Force Chief of Staff General Curtis LeMay. After leaving the USAF Saltsman worked for the Martin Marietta corporation on the Titan rocket program, and later at the United Airlines Training Center in Denver.

Following his death at ninety-five on July 22, 2012, Ralph H. Saltsman Jr. was interred at Colorado's Fort Logan National Cemetery, the same final resting place as Joe Cornwall.

KEE HARRISON

In keeping with the USAAF dictum that aircrewmen were not to fly combat missions in the theater from which they had evaded or escaped, following his return to Rougham in mid-September 1943 the redoubtable Harrison was transferred to the Delaware-based 2nd Ferrying Group. For the remainder of the war in Europe he flew C-47 transports on the trans-Atlantic ferry route, moving people and equipment between Britain and the United States. After his discharge in September 1945 Kee followed a decidedly different path, becoming an ordained Episcopal priest in 1951. He served as rector of several churches in Florida, and following his 1979 retirement he settled in Naples. The Reverend Kee Harrison died on February 10, 2005, at the age of ninety.

Acknowledgments

Writing an accurate, informative, compelling, and hopefully enjoyable work of history is a complex and lengthy process—in my case, at least. The most time-consuming and arguably the most important aspect of that process is the preparation. Finding and examining vital documents, locating and interviewing people who took part in the events being written about, and, whenever possible, walking the ground the story covers are all essential prerequisites to the actual telling of the tale.

I am very fortunate that in undertaking the research for this volume I was ably and generously assisted by many people both in the United States and abroad. I sincerely appreciate their help, without which *Escape From Paris* would not have been possible. Any errors or omissions in this book are, of course, mine alone.

Above all, I wish to thank my wife, Margaret Spragins Harding. This book—like those that preceded it—would not have been possible without her enduring love, consistently wise counsel, and seemingly boundless patience and enthusiasm. Her skills as a French linguist were especially important on this project, as was her amazing ability to put people at ease in any situation. She is a tremendously insightful and perceptive human being, and quite simply the most remarkable person I have ever encountered. I am blessed beyond measure to be able to spend my life with her.

I am also tremendously indebted to Ellen Hampton. An American-born journalist, educator, and author who has lived and worked in France for thirty years, she was absolutely indispensable when it came to locating and evaluating key records held in several French archives. Moreover, it was she who found and first interviewed Yvette Morin-Claerebout on my behalf, and then arranged for my wife and I to visit and speak at length with that courageous and indomitable woman. We are very pleased to also call Ellen a friend, and this book has benefited immeasurably from her help and guidance.

My warmest and most heartfelt thanks—as well as my profound respect and great admiration—go to Yvette Morin-Claerebout. She willingly and honestly shared her memories of the war years, of her parents, of the other brave résistants with whom the Morins worked, and of the evaders the family sheltered and aided, despite the pain many of those recollections still evokes. I also sincerely appreciate the help and hospitality of Yvette's daughter and son-in-law, Denise and Jacques Weil.

I would also particularly like to thank Michael LeBlanc, Canadian historian par excellence of the Allied evasion experience in World War II, for his willingness to share information, sources, and guidance. Thanks also to Nate Gypin Sr., for sharing his memories of his stepfather, Joe Cornwall, and for giving me access to a trove of letters, photos, and other memorabilia pertaining to Joe's life.

Thanks to my agent, Scott Mendel, for his continuing excellent advice and guidance, and especially for his suggestion that World War II Paris would make an interesting locale for a book; and to Robert Pigeon, my editor at Da Capo, for his friendship and assistance in shaping and improving the manuscript that became *Escape From Paris*.

I am also indebted to:

IN THE UNITED STATES:

My colleagues Paraag Shukla, David Lauterborn, Brian Walker, and Claire Barrett at *Military History* magazine, for their friendship, understanding, and support, and for their patience with my frequent absences—both mental and physical—while I was researching and writing this book.

Jennifer Berry, longtime friend and hands-down the best photo researcher on planet Earth.

Steve Walkowiak, an excellent graphic designer on whom I depend for both my own books and for the high-end illustrations that are so important to the look and quality of *Military History* magazine.

Marguerite Brouard-Miller, daughter of Alice Brouard, for her memories of her mother, of Maud Couvé, of life in wartime Paris, and of those evaders who sheltered with the women and their children.

Thomas E. Buffenbarger, library technician at the U.S. Army War College Library, for his help in tracking down the very obscure volume *Der Weg der 87. Infantrie-Division*.

Ron Coleman of the Library and Archives Reference Desk at the United States Holocaust Memorial Museum, for his patience in responding to my many questions and his guidance in researching the deportation records of the Morin family.

Thomas Culbert and Geoff Gentilini, for their immensely helpful research work at the National Archives and the National Personnel Records Center, respectively.

Alicia M. Flickinger and Tifanie L. Cropper of the U.S. Army Human Resources Command's Freedom of Information and Privacy Act Office, for their assistance in locating the Individual Deceased Personnel Files and other records pertaining to several of the U.S. airmen involved in the July 14, 1943, raid on Le Bourget.

Caroline Godwin, for her excellent translations of obscure French documents.

Satu Hasse-Webb, for her excellent German translations and her help in researching the U.S. National Archives files pertaining to French women deported to, and held in, Ravensbrück concentration camp.

Byron Higgins and Roger and Mary Ellen Lynch, for very useful information about Harry Eastman.

Christine and Tom Hilger, for their generous help in providing letters and photographs pertaining to Christine's father and mother, Jeff and Louise Dickson.

Sylvester Jackson of the U.S. Air Force Historical Research Agency, for providing the VIII Bomber Command Narrative Mission Report for the July 14, 1943, raid on Le Bourget.

Don Lasseter, author of *Their Deeds of Valor*, for his very helpful suggestions about locating key escape and evasion reports.

Ted Panken, for his fast and accurate interview transcriptions.

Vivian Rogers-Price of the National Museum of the Mighty Eighth Air Force, for her help in locating excerpts from Harry E. Slater's *Lingering Contrails of the Big Square A.*

Chris Saltsman and George Saltsman, son and nephew, respectively, of Ralph Saltsman, for their willingness to share incredibly useful documents, photos, and maps pertaining to Salty's World War II experiences.

Bruce Templeton, son of *Salty's Naturals* tail gunner Larry Templeton, for sharing information about his father's wartime service.

Roger Watts of the 94th Bomb Group Association, for his help and guidance in researching the unit's personnel, history, and operations.

IN FRANCE:

Abigail Altman of the American Library in Paris, for her help in the search for Yvette Morin-Claerebout, and for recommending Ellen Hampton as a Paris-based researcher.

Mickaël Blasselle, Siriane Chartier, and Cécilie Poulet of the Musée de l'Armée, Invalides, for their help in locating information on the Morins, Turma-Vengeance, and resistance activities in Paris, and for arranging a fascinating private tour of the attic of the Cathédrale Saint-Louis des Invalides and the roof of the Dôme church.

Fabrice Bourrée and Frantz Malassis of the Fondation de la Résistance, for their assistance in researching the origins and operations of key Paris-based evasion *réseaux,* and for information on the specific activities of the Morin family.

Alice Bouteille and Christine Minjollet of the Musée de la Légion d'honneur et des Ordres de chevalerie, for their help in locating the files pertaining to Denise Morin and Yvette Morin-Claerebout.

Marc Chantran, administrator of the site chantran.vengeance.free.fr, for providing valuable background information on Turma-Vengeance's founders, organization, and operations.

Author Loïc Lemarchand, for his vital help in researching the events of July 14, 1943; for his friendship; for supplying fascinating photos not only of some of the key American, German, and French individuals in this book, but also for searching out the exact location of the wreckage of *Salty's Naturals;* and for providing me with a copy of his delightful and engrossing book, *Bel atterrissage capitaine!*

Stefan Martens of the Institut historique allemand in Paris, for his assistance in determining which German military units were assigned to the Hôtel des Invalides in 1943 and 1944.

Jean-Baptiste Ordas, for providing wartime photos of the Hôtel des Invalides from his extensive collection.

Fr. Philippe Ploix of the Diocese of Paris, for providing information on the life and works of Msgr. Georges Chevrot.

Isabelle Thomas of France TV, for help in finding wartime photos of the Morins and some of the evaders they sheltered.

Sylvie Zaidman, director of the Musée du Général Leclerc de Hauteclocque et de Libération de Paris—and Guilem Touratier of the same organization—for research advice and guidance.

IN GERMANY:

Axel Braisz of the International Tracing Service's Referat Nutzservice in Bad Arolsen, for his help in locating World War II German military, SS, and police documents pertaining to the deportation of the Morin family, details of their time in the camps, and the circumstances surrounding Georges Morin's death.

Daniel Schneider of the Bundesarchiv-Abteilung Militärarchive in Freiburg, for his help in locating records for the Abwehr office in Occupied Paris.

Lutz Moser of the Bundesarchiv Koblenz, for his help in researching the records of the SS, SD, and Kripo offices in the French capital.

IN GREAT BRITAIN:

Ray Bowden of the USAAF Nose Art Project, for his help in determining the various names carried by Captain Edward Purdy's two aircraft.

Cliff Hall and Graham Sage of the Rougham Control Tower Museum, for arranging a delightful and extremely helpful visit to the former home of the 94th Bomb Group. And additional thanks to Cliff for providing me with a copy of his fascinating and very informative book, *Pictorial History of the Men and Aircraft of the 94th Bombardment Group,* and for sharing his memories of being a young boy interacting with the B-17 crews that flew missions from the base.

Ciara Harper of the renowned Shuttleworth Collection, for her help in arranging a wonderful visit to get a close-up look at a Lysander of the type that carried Joe Cornwall back to England.

John Harding, author of *Lansdale's Belt,* for his help in tracking down information on Jeff Dickson's career as a sports promoter, especially the events he organized in England.

Chris McCairns, for allowing me to use the photo taken in 1943 by his father, F/O J. A. McCairns, of F/O James McBride and his Lysander; and to Ian Titman for helping find and reproduce the image.

The research staff at the National Archives in Kew, for their help in tracking down the evasion reports of Commonwealth military personnel.

IN MALTA:

Bob Body, for his help in researching the history and operations of the Tempsford-based 61 and 138 (Special Operations) Squadrons.

Notes

CHAPTER 1

1. The USAAC was redesignated the U.S. Army Air Forces, USAAF, on June 20, 1941.

2. Mollie's subterfuge worked far better than she might have imagined. In the 1910 federal census the head of the Campbell household is M. S. Campbell, who is clearly marked as female. Yet even some descendants have made the mistake of assuming that the entry referred to Marion S. Campbell, and that it was Mollie who had deserted the family.

3. The headquarters for Air Corps technical training was at Chanute Field, Illinois.

4. Joe Cornwall's successful completion of the Flexible Gunnery Course resulted in the changing of his MOS from 911 to 612, Airplane Armorer-Gunner.

5. The Minnesota-based prepared-foods firm George A. Hormel and Company introduced a canned beef stew in 1935 under the Dinty Moore brand. Like the company's later canned meat offering—Spam—Dinty Moore beef stew was a staple in American households (and in many military mess halls) throughout the late 1930s.

6. A unit's TO&E lays out in exhaustive detail the number of people to be assigned to a specific unit, by rank and job title. And, as the name indicates, the same document also details every piece of equipment the unit is required to have, by designation and nomenclature for such larger items as aircraft and vehicles, and by individual part number for smaller items.

7. USAAF planners had decided that most Britain-bound multi-engine aircraft would be flown across the Atlantic by their combat crews, rather than by ferry pilots.

8. As we shall see in the following chapters, the nickname applied to the Fortresses flown by Ed Purdy and his crew evolved over time.

9. Racially insensitive by today's standards, the artwork was in keeping with the cultural mores of its time. It was also far tamer, and far less offensive, than many other examples of nose art to be found at that time on American military aircraft.

10. Andover is now known as Perth-Andover.

11. There were two guns in each of the B-17's two manned, power-operated turrets (top and ball); two in the tail position; one in each of the waist positions; one firing upward from the radio operator's position; and three in the navigator/bombardier position in the aircraft's nose. Of the latter, two weapons were fixed to fire out either side of the compartment and were referred to as "cheek" guns, while the third was fitted into a flexible mount in the upper center part of the glazed Plexiglas nose. This single nose weapon was added as a "field modification" in order to give Fortress crews a better chance of successfully engaging enemy aircraft attacking from directly ahead.

12. Clarence "Smokey" Rebuck was a patient on the same tuberculosis ward at Fitzsimons hospital as Jesse Gypin. Details of Clara's first and second marriages, and of how she and Joe Cornwall met, were provided during interviews conducted by the author with her son, Nathan Gypin. The interview is hereafter cited as Harding-Gypin 2017.

13. In February 1942 then Brigadier General Eaker—having been tapped to lead VIII Bomber Command—arrived in England with a small team of officers to begin laying the groundwork for the arrival of the men and aircraft tasked with carrying out the United States' planned daylight precision bombing campaign against Germany. Eaker's team included thirty-three-year-old Major Bernie Lay Jr., who had been an Air Corps bomber pilot in the interwar years before transferring to the reserves in order to pursue a civilian career as an aviation writer. His autobiographical book *I Wanted Wings* was turned into a popular 1941 movie, which brought Lay to the attention of Eaker, who himself held a degree in journalism. Lay had returned to active duty in 1939 after the outbreak of war in Europe, and Eaker sought him out and added him to his staff. Initially assigned to head the Army Air Forces in Great Britain (AAFGB) history and film office, Lay flew several combat missions and was eventually tapped to command a B-24 group. He was ultimately shot down but evaded capture and returned to England. After the war he and another Eighth Air Force veteran, screenwriter Sy Bartlett, cowrote *Twelve O'Clock High*, a fictionalized account of the birth and early operations of the USAAF's Britain-based bomber force that was made into a 1949 hit motion picture starring Gregory Peck. Lay's nonfiction account of his time on the run in Occupied France, published in 1945 as *I've Had It* and later reissued as *Presumed Lost*, is both excellent history and a great read.

14. For a very thorough and enjoyable recounting of the 94th Bomb Group's formation and wartime experiences, see Harry E. Slater's excellent *Lingering Contrails of the Big Square A,* from which much of the 94th-specific material in this chapter was drawn.

15. Eighth Air Force crews used two main terms to refer to enemy antiaircraft fire. The first, "ack-ack," was borrowed from the British and was more commonly used during the early USAAF missions over the Continent in 1942. The second term, flak, was a contraction of the German *Flugzeugabwehrkanone,* literally anti-aircraft cannon, and was more popular among later-arriving crews.

16. Though initially thought to have been killed in action, Rosener survived the downing of his aircraft and spent the remainder of the war in Germany's Stalag Luft III POW camp—where he was eventually joined by his younger brother, Niel, who was also a B-17 pilot. Maurice Rosener went on to serve in the postwar U.S. Air Force, and died in 2004 at the age of eighty-five.

17. Pinetree was opened by then Brigadier General Ira C. Eaker in mid-May 1942 as the headquarters of VIII Bomber Command. The organization occupied the former Wycombe Abbey girls' school in High Wycombe, Buckinghamshire, some thirty miles northwest of London.

18. Though designated Saint-Omer-Longuenesse in Eighth Air Force records of the period, the airfield is usually referred to as Saint-Omer-Wizernes in World War II German documents. It is actually closer to Longuenesse than to the Saint-Omer suburb of Wizernes.

19. Drawn from Lawrence Templeton's article "If Memory Serves Me Correctly," published in the March 1980 issue of *Nostalgic Notes,* the 94th Bomb Group Association newsletter.

20. When Anderson moved up to take over VIII Bomber Command in July 1943 his replacement was a pugnacious, cigar-chewing colonel named Curtis E. LeMay, who had arrived in Britain in October 1942 as commander of the 305th Bomb Group (Heavy) and who is widely credited for developing the combat box formation. LeMay did not believe in opulent quarters for servicemen of any rank, and of his lodgings at Elveden Hall he later wrote, "Now I found myself with a copper dome over my head and God knows how much 'richly veined marble' staring me in the face." LeMay would go on to play a leading role in the USAAF bombing campaign against Japan (and ultimately become head of the U.S. Air Force's Strategic Air Command). For more on his career, see Warren Kozak's *LeMay: The Life and Wars of General Curtis LeMay.*

21. For a more detailed overview of the Kiel mission, see Ralph H. Saltsman Jr.'s "Air Battle at Kiel" in the Summer 1989 issue of the journal *Air Power History.* Hereafter cited as "Air Battle at Kiel."

22. Drawn from Saltsman's original typewritten manuscript for what became his article "Air Battle at Kiel."

23. Built to a standard RAF design in 1941–1942, the field had three intersecting runways laid out in a roughly triangular pattern. The 2,000-yard-long main runway ran east to west and was fifty yards wide. The second runway was 1,400 yards from north to south, and the third was also 1,400 yards north to southeast. While the station was officially called Bury St. Edmunds, local people always called it Rougham Airfield (and still do). With the arrival of the 94th the field was extended to fifty hard-standings and dispersal areas, three of which were diamond shaped to give capacity for fifty aircraft.

The 94th was not the only group involved in the July 13 mission that had been directed to change base locations. The 96th had moved into its new airfield on June 11, and the 95th was scheduled to relocate on June 15. The swaps were intended to give the B-26 and B-17 groups operating locations that better suited each, in terms of runway length, personnel accommodations, and so on.

24. "Air Battle at Kiel."

25. Despite the extent of the damage inflicted on 42-29711, the Fortress was eventually repaired (but only after Larry Templeton convinced one of the mechanics undertaking the restoration to remove its nose art, which remained in Templeton's family until after his death in 1999). The former *Natural* was transferred to the 91st Bomb Group's 322nd Bomb Squadron, and returned to combat duty with the name *Chief Sly II*. Unfortunately, its reprieve did not last long—the Fortress was shot down into the Baltic Sea on September 10, 1943, with the loss of its entire crew.

26. The story of Cornwall and Davitt's encounter with the MP was written up by a USAAF public affairs officer (who managed to misspell Joe's last name as "Cronwall") and distributed to several British and American wire services. The article ran in some forty newspapers across the United States during the first week of August.

CHAPTER 2

1. There is often confusion between this first, impromptu parade reviewed by Bock, and a later and far more lavish parade—complete with bands—reviewed by one of Bock's subordinate commanders, General der Infanterie Kurt von Briesen. Though newsreel images of the mounted World War I veteran and holder of the Knights Cross of the Iron Cross taking the salute of his passing troops were seen around the world, Briesen didn't have long to savor his triumph—he was killed in action on the Russian Front in November 1941. Bock, for his part, died on May 4, 1945, the day after the car in which he was a passenger was strafed by an Allied fighter.

2. A pejorative term used by the French to refer to Germans, especially soldiers.

3. Though during the Nazi period the term *Wehrmacht* referred to Germany's unified military forces—Heer (army), Luftwaffe (air force), and Kriegsmarine (navy)—it is commonly used to refer to the combined Heer-Luftwaffe forces that undertook most of Germany's ground offensives. It is so used throughout this volume.

4. Between May 15 and 17 French tanks—largely the heavily armored Char B1-bis—had managed to hold the line against the advancing Germans, inflicting heavy casualties and surprising General Heinz Guderian, Germany's preeminent armor commander. The small village of Stonne changed hands repeatedly, finally falling to the Germans on the afternoon of the seventeenth.

5. At that point in time, of course, most people in France were unaware that Operation Dynamo, the evacuation at Dunkirk, also moved more than 120,000 French troops to Britain. Many of those soldiers would later form the core of the Free French forces that would liberate Paris in 1944.

6. Having fled Paris for Tours, Reynaud and most members of his government moved on to Bordeaux on June 13.

7. For an in-depth look at the turmoil within the Reynaud government on the eve of France's collapse, see the author's 2014 book *The Last Battle: When U.S. and German Soldiers Joined Forces in the Waning Hours of World War II in Europe.*

8. The railcar was historic, of course, in that it was the same carriage in which Germany had signed the 1918 armistice. The car had been on display at Invalides' Musée de l'Armée for several years, until ultimately being refurbished and housed in a purpose-built museum building at Compiègne. The Germans had it moved back to the exact spot where the World War I event had been held, their intent being to both underscore their victory and thumb their collective nose at the French. Following the 1940 ceremony the carriage was moved to Germany, where it was ultimately destroyed. A replica was built after the war and installed in the small museum at Compiègne.

9. As John Goldsmith recounted in his wonderful memoir *Accidental Agent: Behind Enemy Lines With the French Resistance,* "The Nazi bureaucrats inflicted many humiliations and indignities on Occupied France, but this was one of the most stupid. Wine is part of a Frenchman's soul. It is indispensable. It is sacred. . . . Only the dull, humourless Master Race could have been so insensitive to a national characteristic as to invite the further wrath of an oppressed people."

10. Created Marshal General of France by King Louis XIV, Henri de la Tour d'Auvergne, Vicomte de Turenne (1611–1675) was arguably France's most able military commander of the pre-Napoleonic period. Turenne's remains, like those of Napoléon, reside at Invalides.

11. Following France's defeat by Prussia and the North German Confederation in the 1870–1871 Franco-Prussian War, the regular French army was disbanded in accordance with the armistice terms agreed to by the leaders of the French

Third Republic. The largely working-class members of the National Guard—the militia force tasked during the war with the defense of Paris—refused to accept disbandment and rebelled. Popular elections in Paris brought the revolutionary Commune to power in the city. The national government, based temporarily in Versailles, reformed elements of the regular army and, on May 21, 1871, sent them into the streets to put down what was seen as a proletarian rebellion; thousands were killed in the resulting battles throughout Paris.

12. The story of Georges's early life and service in World War I as presented here is built upon information provided by his daughter during in-person interviews with Ellen Hampton in February 2017 (hereafter cited as Hampton-Claerebout 2017) and with the author in June 2017 (hereafter cited as Harding-Claerebout 2017), as well as upon service records held by France's Service historique de la défense, Fondation de la résistance, and la Bibliothèque de documentation internationale contemporaine.

13. Within the Morin family it is popularly believed that Georges enlisted at the age of seventeen, having lied to recruiters about his age. However, his military records—held at the Service historique de la défense in Vincennes—clearly indicate that he enlisted in 1917, at eighteen.

14. Hampton-Claerebout 2017.

15. The organization was created in 1916 and attached to the Ministry of Labor.

16. This line of structures had originally been built as workers' quarters during the construction of Invalides, and had been modernized over the years. Details on the Morins' apartment and the surrounding structures are taken from *Justification du Projet et Definition des Travaux Proposes* (the 1988 document outlining the extensive alterations made to the southwest corner of the complex, which among other things resulted in the demolition of the Morins' former home), and from Hampton-Claerebout 2017.

17. Though the Morins lived within the Invalides complex, the address of their apartment was listed as 2, avenue de Tourville. The street runs parallel to the southern side of the Invalides complex, beginning at the place de l'École Militaire in the west and ending at the boulevard des Invalides in the east—some 200 feet south of where the Morins' home was located.

18. The author was honored to be given a rare personal tour of both the attic of Saint-Louis-des-Invalides and the rooftop area between the cupola and the dome, and can attest to both the fantastic view and the potential hazards of the latter.

19. In 1946 the organization was again renamed, becoming the Office national des anciens combattants et victimes de guerre (National Office for Veterans and Victims of War), which it remains as of this writing.

20. The Anschluss ("joining") saw Austria annexed to Nazi Germany. Renamed the province of Ostmark, the country was divided into seven administrative districts and its armed forces became part of the Wehrmacht.

21. The 1924 "Treaty of Alliance and Friendship" between France and Czechoslovakia was one of three similar treaties Paris concluded with the smaller central European states that were attempting to resist the growing power of Hungary and the possible rebirth of a Hapsburg empire.

22. Harding–Claerebout 2017.

23. *Paris at War*, 15.

24. The mass confusion that engulfed France's road network as a result of the Luftwaffe attacks resulted in many of the Musée de l'Armée's treasures being abandoned along a stretch of road near Étampes, some thirty miles southwest of Paris. Two trucks bearing such priceless items as the hat Napoléon wore during the 1812 retreat from Moscow, his medals, Empress Josephine's jewels, and pistols inlaid with gems and ivory were among a group of vehicles attacked by Ju 87 Stuka dive-bombers on June 13. Both trucks were disabled in the assault, and the following day they were abandoned by their panic-stricken drivers. A Wehrmacht officer, Lieutenant Colonel Oberneburg of the predominantly Austrian 44th Infantry Division, discovered the scattered items. An apparently cultured individual, he recognized some of them. When his guess about their provenance was validated by the words "Hôtel des Invalides" stamped on a section of destroyed crate, he immediately ordered his soldiers to secure the items and load them aboard a Wehrmacht truck. The items were temporarily stored at the hospital in Étampes, and eventually turned over to Versailles mayor Gaston Henry-Haye, who safeguarded them until they were returned to Invalides. (Henry-Haye, a longtime politician and former member of the French Senate, was later named Vichy France's ambassador to the United States.)

25. Among the objects Denise was able to hide in the days before the Germans arrived were dozens of large, ornate, porcelain apothecary jars that had been kept in the hospital's pharmacy. The pharmacist, Madame Ferré (sometimes rendered as "Ferret"), had not had time to crate the jars for shipment and was afraid the antique and very valuable containers would be stolen by the Germans. Over the course of a very long day Mme. Ferré and Denise moved the jars into an out-of-the-way storeroom and locked them in. Harding-Claerebout 2017.

26. Panzerjäger Abteilung 187 was a specialized antitank unit assigned to the 87. Infanterie-Division. Oehmichen and his men were among the first German troops to enter Paris, and in addition to Invalides the unit's companies were tasked to secure the Eiffel Tower, the École Militaire, the military barracks facing the Champs de Mars, the government ministries along the quai d'Orsay, and the Hôtel de Ville (Paris city hall) on the Right Bank.

27. Evacuated during the Germans' June advance on the capital, the veterans began trickling back to Invalides following the June 22 signing of the Franco-German armistice.

28. It is unclear whether the Germans chose the tune, or just continued using an existing one. The irony, of course, is that beginning in 1941 the Allies used the

four notes as an audible representation of the "V for Victory" hand gesture and slogan—*dit-dit-dit-dah* being the letter "V" in Morse code. Harding-Claerebout 2017.

29. Oehmichen related the story in detail in his postwar memoir *Der Weg der 87. Infanterie-Division.*

30. There is an ongoing debate among historians regarding the date of Hitler's June visit to Paris. In his postwar memoir, Albert Speer said the visit took place on Friday, June 28, yet Breker, Giesler, and others in attendance remembered it as June 23. The latter date is the most likely, given that most sources agree the visit took place on a very quiet Sunday morning.

31. The group also included General Hans Speidel, 18th Army chief of staff, and General Wilhelm Keitel, chief of the Oberkommando der Wehrmacht (supreme high command of the German armed forces). Contrary to popular belief, Keitel was not a field marshal at the time of the Invalides visit; he was not promoted to that rank until July 19, 1940.

32. *The Rise and Fall of the Third Reich*, 223.

33. *Hitler's Propaganda Pilgrimage*, 108. SS-General Martin Bormann was head of the Reich Chancellery and also acted as Hitler's private secretary. He was tried for war crimes in absentia at Nuremberg and sentenced to death, though in 1998 it was conclusively proven that he had died in Berlin in 1945. In his postwar memoir *Paris, Hitler et Moi*, Arno Breker remembered the events at Invalides slightly differently, saying that Hitler spoke of the Duke of Reichstadt while the party was still staring down at Napoléon's sarcophagus and issued the order at that point.

34. For the complete story of the political machinations—both French and German—behind the transfer of the young duke's remains from Vienna to Paris, see Georges Poisson's *Hitler's Gift to France: The Return of the Remains of Napoléon II.*

35. Louis XVIII came to the throne in April 1814 after spending most of his life in exile. The king was briefly replaced by Napoléon after his return from Elba, but following Waterloo Louis XVIII returned to Paris and reigned until 1824. Marie-Louise was Napoléon's second wife.

36. In keeping with Hapsburg tradition, the young duke's heart and intestines were removed during his embalming; the silver urn containing his heart is in the Loreto Chapel of Vienna's Augustinian Church (along with some fifty other urns containing the hearts of various Hapsburgs), and the copper vase containing his intestines is in the Ducal Crypt beneath Vienna's Saint Stephen's Cathedral.

37. Harding-Claerebout 2017. Denise's exploit is also recounted in slightly different forms in *Hitler's Gift*, 93, and *Histoire des Invalides*, 291–293. The latter incorrectly cites Denise's father as the one who buried the wire frame; he died on November 17, 1940.

38. Gestapo is an abbreviation of *Geheime Staatspolizei*, literally secret state police. It was considered a sister organization to the Sicherheitsdienst, the security

service of the SS. Both organizations were administered by the Reichssicherheit-shauptamt (Reich Main Security Office), itself subordinate to Heinrich Himmler in his capacity as the chief of all German police forces and the head of the SS.

39. *Hitler's Gift*, 103–104; *Histoire des Invalides*, 292–293.

40. The story of Denise's discovery of the rabbit, and the importance it and its descendants made in the Morins' lives, is chronicled in *Histoire des Invalides* and other sources. It was also recounted to the author in Harding-Claerebout 2017. As a point of interest, the rabbits that are found around Invalides to this day are believed to be descendants of that first pregnant female.

CHAPTER 3

1. Loss numbers are drawn from *Lingering Contrails*, 358 (though the author listed the nine Kiel losses as having occurred on June 6, rather than the correct June 13); *Pictorial History of the Men and Aircraft of the 94th Bombardment Group (H), 1943–1945*, pp. 370-371, hereafter cited as *94th Pictorial History;* and figures given in *War Diaries, 331st Bomb Squadron, 94th Bomb Group*, May and June 1943, hereafter cited as *94th War Diary May 1943* and *94th War Diary June 1943*.

2. *Natural* had been built in Seattle by Boeing, whereas its replacement was built under license by Douglas Aircraft in Los Angeles. The former was a B-17F-65-BO, and the latter a B-17F-45-DL; so many incremental changes were made to the Fortress throughout its production life that production block numbers—the second numeral in each designation—were added so that mechanics could properly maintain the slightly different systems on each variant. The final two-letter combination simply indicated the company that built the aircraft—Boeing (BO), Douglas (DL), and Lockheed-Vega (VE), the latter in Burbank, California.

3. While the name was enclosed in painted quotation marks on the nose of the B-17, we will dispense with them from this point on in the text.

4. Colonel John G. "Dinty" Moore served at 4th Wing headquarters until October 1943, when he was given command of Base Air Depot No. 3 in Wharton, England. In December 1943 he returned to the United States, where he served in the office of the chief of the air staff for the remainder of World War II. He retired in 1947, and died in Colorado Springs on September 27, 1975.

5. *Lingering Contrails*, 48–49.

6. Castle was one of the inspirations for the character "Brigadier General Frank Savage" in *Twelve O'Clock High* by Bernie Lay Jr. and Sy Bartlett. Like Castle, Savage replaced a beloved group commander and was tasked with straightening out a "hard-luck" unit. Initially resented by the men in the unit, Savage proves himself in combat and succeeds in winning his men's respect. He eventually has a nervous breakdown, however, and is himself replaced.

Castle's story ended differently. He left the 94th Bomb Group on April 17, 1944, to take command of the 4th Bomb Wing and was promoted to brigadier general the following December 14. Ten days later Castle was shot down and killed while flying as copilot on a B-17 of the 487th Bomb Group during a mission against the airfield at Darmstadt, Germany. He was posthumously awarded the Medal of Honor for his actions that day, and California's now closed Castle Air Force Base was named for him.

7. *The Combined Bomber Offensive, April Through December 1943*, 8.

8. Ibid., 203. Owing to the transfer of all Britain-based B-24 groups to North Africa, there were no Liberators flying bombing missions from the United Kingdom at that time.

9. Ibid., 210.

10. Most of the airman from the east side of the airfield (332nd and 333rd squadrons) would walk or cycle to the Fox and Hounds in Thurston, just down Mount Road. Those from the west side of the field (331st and 410th squadrons), like Joe Cornwall, favored the aforementioned Sword in Hand or the fifteenth-century Fox on Eastgate Street.

The African-American troops assigned to the 94th—most of whom handled the transport and unloading of ordnance in the Bomb Storage Site to the east of the perimeter track—were billeted away from the main airfield, in Tostock and Drinkstone, and drank in the Bear pub in Bayton. In keeping with then current American racial attitudes and segregation policies, the USAAF designated the Bear as a "colored only" establishment and the Fox and Hounds as "white only."

11. Le Bourget was also the eastern terminus of Charles Lindbergh's epic 1927 trans-Atlantic solo flight.

12. *Narrative Mission Report, VIII Bomber Command Mission*, 72.

13. Interview with Nathaniel Gypin, 2017. Hereafter cited as Harding-Gypin 2017.

14. While the overwhelming majority of USAAF aerial gunners were enlisted men, it was not unheard of for officers to complete the required training and win gunner's wings. Among the officers who did so was Captain Clark Gable, a member of the Hollywood-based 1st Motion Picture Unit who earned his wings as part of his preparation for making a film about gunners in action. On personal orders from USAAF commander General Henry H. Arnold, Gable traveled to England in early 1943 and was embedded with the 351st Bomb Group at Polebrook, Northhamptonshire. He flew at least five combat missions, and he and his camera operator shot some fifty thousand feet of film. While the resulting movie—*Combat America*, released in January 1945—was overshadowed by William Wyler's better-known *Memphis Belle*, many of the images Gable and his team captured have become staples in any film about the Eighth Air Force in World War II.

15. Jefferson Davis Dickson was being modest in saying he'd done "pretty well" for himself in France, for in the interwar years he had become a millionaire and perhaps the best-known and most successful sports promoter in Europe—indeed, as of the summer of 1943 he was still the owner of record of the Palais des Sports complex in German-occupied Paris. Widely and respectfully referred to as the "ringmaster of Paris," he was fluent in French and spoke passable Spanish and Portuguese, was personal friends with members of several royal houses, and was respected and admired throughout the upper levels of European society. He had happened to be in New York when the United States entered the war, and despite his age—and the fact that he had a wife and infant daughter—had immediately offered his services to the USAAF. Though initially trained as an air intelligence officer, his considerable skills in both still and motion-picture photography had brought him to Anderson's attention and led to his current position.

Details surrounding Jeff Dickson's USAAF service in England and his participation in the July 14 mission are drawn from several sources, including a June 20, 1943, letter Dickson wrote to his wife, Louise; a March 26, 1945, letter to Louise from Major David F. Doyle, who had served with Dickson on the 4th Wing staff; Dickson's *Individual Deceased Personnel File; Missing Air Crew Report No. 116; USAAF Escape and Evasion Report No. 125;* and various newspaper articles reporting on Dickson's participation in the July 14 event.

16. This account of Jeff Dickson's pre-mission introduction to, and interactions with, Purdy's crew is taken from an April 18, 1944, letter written to Louise Dickson by an officer in the 331st Bomb Squadron. Unfortunately, the person's identity is unclear, since there is no salutation that might indicate whether the writer was known to Mrs. Dickson, and because the bottom half of the second page is missing, there is no signature or title. Hereafter, this letter will be cited as Unknown, to Mrs. Dickson.

17. Harry Lewis Eastman had been a Michigan State Police officer at the time of Pearl Harbor. He resigned and enlisted in the USAAF, and was trained as an aerial gunner at Las Vegas Army Airfield, where he first met Joe Cornwall. Eastman was initially posted to Biggs Army Airfield, Texas, as a flexible gunnery instructor. When the 94th Bomb Group arrived at Biggs in November 1942, one of the 331st Bomb Squadron crews was short a gunner due to illness, and Eastman talked his commanding officer into letting him fill the vacancy. Eastman, Cornwall, and Davitt became fast friends, and tended to spend a lot of off-duty time together. Details on Eastman's life, USAAF career, and time as an evader were provided to the author by his nephew, Byron Higgins, and by Roger Lynch, a lifelong friend of Higgins who also knew Eastman. The interviews are hereafter cited as, respectively, Harding-Higgins 2017 and Harding-Lynch 2017.

18. Details on the July 14 raid—including numbers of 94th Bomb Group aircraft involved, routes to and from the target, bomb loads, and so on—are drawn

from *HQs., VIII Bomber Command Tactical Mission Report for Mission No. 73, July 14, 1943,* hereafter cited as *Tactical Mission Report 73.*

19. Because they were not normally exposed to the harsh cold that flooded the rear part of the B-17, the officers in the front of the aircraft tended to favor their dress caps rather than fleece-lined flying helmets. The officers would remove the stiffeners that gave the cap its clean, rounded shape, allowing the sides of the cap to be "crushed" downward so that the wearer's radio earphones would fit over it.

20. *Tactical Mission Report 73,* "Bombing Data."

21. All times used in this chapter are drawn from *Tactical Mission Report 73.* The times mentioned in conjunction with Luftwaffe aircraft movements are based on Allied intercepts of German radio communications—both between the German intercept controllers and the fighters, and among the individual fighter pilots themselves—and the intercepts are quoted in *Tactical Mission Report 73*'s "Enemy Air Action" section.

22. While brief, an Fw 190's firing pass could be catastrophic for the target aircraft. In a three-second burst, each of the German fighter's four MG 151 20mm cannon spat out 130 explosive rounds, while in the same few moments the aircraft's two MG 131 13mm machine guns each added forty-five bullets to the lethal mix.

23. Descriptions of the events aboard *Salty's Naturals* are drawn from the accounts rendered by Joe Cornwall and Larry Templeton in *Escape and Evasion Reports 125* and *86,* respectively (hereafter cited as *E&E 125* and *E&E 86*); and from Templeton's "If Memory Serves Me Correctly." Ralph Saltsman's recollections of both the July 14 air battle and its aftermath are drawn from his unpublished 1945 typescript "My Story" and his two postwar, self-published accounts, *Good Time Cholly II* and *Return to Normandy.*

24. In his various accounts of the collision, Saltsman identified the German fighter as a Bf 109, but official after-action reports based on the observations of other aviators in the formation state categorically that it was an Fw 190. While the identity of the German pilot is not known for certain, the most likely candidate appears to be JG 2 enlisted pilot Gerhard Nuss. He was wounded in action against B-17s on that day in that area, and bailed out of his Fw 190 in the vicinity of Louviers—not far off the 94th Bomb Group's flight path. Most of the German fighter fell to earth on the rue des Jardins in Tourneville, barely one mile north of the *Salty's Naturals* crash site.

25. Purdy's heroic efforts were seen by many of the other pilots in the formation, who reported their observations upon return to England. As a result, Purdy was posthumously awarded a second Distinguished Flying Cross, under authority of Eighth Air Force General Order No. 226 of December 16, 1943. In a sad irony, the ceremony for the award of his first DFC had been scheduled for July 15, 1943.

26. As outlined in *Pilot's Flight Operating Instructions for Army Models B–17F and G,* the standard bailout procedure consisted of two steps. If it became necessary to abandon the aircraft in flight, the aircraft commander was to give three short rings on the aircraft's alarm bell, at which point the members of the crew were to don their parachutes and move to their designated exit points. A second, long ring on the bell was the signal to jump. Most actual bailouts in combat were not conducted in quite so orderly a manner, of course.

27. While it might seem more logical for the gunners to simply dive out their respective waist windows, to do so would have run the very real risk of getting entangled in the long metal belts of .50-caliber cartridges feeding each gun, or of damaging the parachute.

28. *E&E 125.*

29. In *E&E 125* Joe Cornwall stated that he and Santangelo had been trapped in *Salty's Naturals* until the bomber had fallen to about 1,000 feet, at which point the two airmen bailed out. However, the narrative mission report compiled by the 94th Bomb Group Intelligence Office and accounts by other airmen on the July 14 mission to Le Bourget state categorically that the first two jumpers to leave Purdy's aircraft did so at about 15,000 feet. The discrepancy in Cornwall's account is likely due to the confusion, stress, and anoxia-caused disorientation he experienced in the minutes following the collision with the German fighter. Indeed, in later years Cornwall told relatives that the drop from the doomed bomber seemed to go on forever.

30. "If Memory Serves."

31. German troops arrived on scene fairly soon after the crash of *Salty's Naturals,* but not soon enough to prevent two local French hooligans—Bouteloup and Serin—from looting the bodies of wallets, cigarette lighters, and watches. When tried after the liberation, the thieves claimed they had only been collecting the dead men's valuables to prevent their theft by the Germans.

The Germans recovered five bodies from within the wreckage—Purdy, Jones, Lichtenberger, Marquardt, and Smith. The body of Carroll Harris was laying about twenty feet from the remains of the bomber, while Jeff Dickson's body was found in a stand of trees about 100 yards from the crash site—whether thrown clear by the explosion of the aircraft's bombs or during the B-17's descent is unclear. Sprague's body was discovered in a field about a mile from the wreckage. Eight bodies were buried late on July 14 as "unknowns" in the French military section of Évreux's Saint-Louis Cemetery, in graves 208 to 215. Santangelo's body was buried with the others about three weeks later. Details drawn from the May 14, 1945, letter to Louise M. Dickson from John Harding.

32. Sprague's horrific fall to earth was reported by several of the 94th's aviators in their postmission reports. In parachuting circles, the malfunction the radio operator experienced is known as a "streamer."

33. Harrison's B-17F, serial 42-3190, is often incorrectly said to have carried the name *Mr. Five by Five*. That was actually the name of Harrison's usual bomber, serial 42-29717, which had been badly damaged during the 94th's June 22 mission against the German rubber-production facilities at Hüls. *Mr. Five by Five* was eventually repaired and transferred to the 92nd Bomb Group at Alconbury. It was shot down on February 25, 1944, during a mission to Stuttgart, Germany.

34. Details of Harrison's encounter with Mayer, and the ultimate crash-landing in France, are drawn from *Escape & Evasion Reports 91* (Harrison) and *98* (Turner). They are hereafter cited as *E&E 91* and *E&E 98*, respectively. French author Loïc Lemarchand's *Bel atterrissage capitaine!* is a delightful in-depth look at the Harrison crew's postcrash exploits.

35. Among the other JG 2 pilots believed to have taken part in the attack on Harrison's aircraft was Leutnant Horst Zettel. The young pilot was killed on July 27, 1943, when his Fw 190 was shot down by a Spitfire during a swirling dogfight that also claimed the lives of three other JG 2 pilots.

36. "My Story," 3; *Good Time Cholly II*, 2.

37. Frank's colorful abandon-ship announcement figures prominently in a 1976 letter from bombardier Burnett to Ralph Saltsman. Details on Burnett's and Wholley's actions during the event are drawn from the same letter.

38. Davitt's recollections are included in his *Escape & Evasion Report No. 99*, hereafter cited as *E&E 99*.

39. "My Story," *Good Time Cholly II*, op. cit.

40. To "salvo" bombs means to emergency release them before the bombardier has sighted the intended target. This was done both to lighten the aircraft and to make it possible for crew members to bail out through the bomb bay without obstruction.

41. Credit for downing Watts's aircraft is usually given to Egon Mayer, who claimed two B-17s that day, though JG 2's Leutnant Wilhelm Flegel von Farnholz has also been mentioned as the responsible pilot.

42. While the 94th Bomb Group was the only participant in the Le Bourget raid to lose aircraft, the groups attacking Villacoublay and Amiens/Glisy lost a combined total of five B-17s. The four groups attacking Le Bourget, for their part, claimed a total of forty-one German aircraft destroyed, twenty-eight probably destroyed, and thirty-two damaged, according to *Tactical Mission Report 73*. The actual number of enemy aircraft shot down during the course of the Le Bourget raid is unclear, though it was certainly far fewer than forty-one.

CHAPTER 4

1. The Fortress crashed in La Californie, a small valley under cultivation about a mile to the southwest of the township of Saint-Germain-des-Angles, about four miles northwest of Évreux.

2. *E&E 125*. Additional details on Cornwall's experiences after his bailout are drawn from Harding-Gypin 2017.

3. Some sources indicate that the woman who first helped Joe Cornwall was a Mme. Quelevee.

4. Details on Templeton's activities are drawn from *E&E 86*, from his undated letter to Louise M. Dickson, and from "If Memory Serves."

5. Details of Harrison's crash-landing and of the subsequent activities of him, David Turner, Jefferson Polk, and Charles McNemar are taken from, respectively, *Escape & Evasion Reports 91, 98, 109,* and *110*—hereafter cited as *E&E 91, E&E 98, E&E 109,* and *E&E 110.*

6. Harrison stood about five feet ten inches tall and weighed 245 pounds—all of it muscle.

7. The German ace's visit to Harrison's aircraft was photographed by a Luftwaffe propaganda team, and the images were splashed across military and civilian newspapers throughout Germany and the occupied countries. The Germans repaired the damaged B-17 (serial 42-3190) and put it into service with the special-operations unit Kampfgeschwader 200. The aircraft was reportedly used in the Mediterranean area to drop agents behind Allied lines. Its ultimate fate is unclear.

8. The account of Saltsman's postlanding activities is based on "My Story" and *Good Time Cholly II*, op. cit.

9. Houlbec-Cocherel is just over ten miles east of where *Salty's Naturals* crashed.

10. Davitt's account is drawn from *Escape & Evasion Report No. 99*, hereafter cited as *E&E 99.*

11. Eastman and Davitt were not told the family's name for security reasons. Ralph Saltsman learned it during his 1993 visit to the Normandy crash site of *Good Time Cholly II*, and mentioned it in *Return to Normandy.*

12. The priest was Alphonse Pasco, the doctor was Suzanne Huet, and "Merlin" was Louis Maury.

Trying to determine an individual's membership in a particular *réseau* can be challenging for several reasons. First, there was an obvious need for secrecy, so many people never identified themselves as having worked for a particular network, even after the war. Second, many people worked on behalf of more than one network—indeed, several individuals who after the war were listed as members of Turma-Vengeance were also identified as having been members of the Bourgogne (Burgundy) and Comète (Comet) escape lines. Information in this and following chapters regarding the creation, organization, activities, and membership of Turma-Vengeance is drawn primarily from *Fonds Turma-Vengeance. Réseau Turma-Vengeance. Listes, Rapports et Comptes-rendus des Activiteés des Membres du Réseau,* and *Vengeance: Histoire d'Un Corps Franc.*

13. *E&E 98*. Additional details are drawn from Turner's obituary in the March 2013 issue of the Air Forces Escape & Evasion Society's newsletter.

14. Henriette was Henriette Nantier-Morin. As far as can be determined, she was not related to the Morins of Invalides. She and the Renaudins were members of Turma-Vengeance.

15. Just three miles west of central Évreux, in July 1943 the base was home to Bf 109s and Fw 190s of the 1st Group (I. Gruppe) of Egon Mayer's Jagdgeschwader 2. As of this writing the base hosts several French air force transport squadrons.

16. The woman was Mme. Roger Moreau, who lived just a mile away in the village of Huest.

17. It has proven impossible to determine the man's identity.

18. Watts needn't have worried about the possibility of civilian casualties. The Fortress crashed into a section of railway line leading into the Louvres train station (just over two miles northwest of modern Charles de Gaulle Airport). The crash destroyed a signal hut and disrupted rail traffic on the line for several days, but no one on the ground was injured. The two Americans still aboard the Fortress when it hit the ground—waist gunners Staff Sergeants Lawrence Phillips and Burton Reppert—were already dead, killed by 20mm rounds before the bomber started its final plunge. The remains of the two airmen are buried at the city's military cemetery, beneath a monument placed by the people of Louvres. The stele bears one of the twisted propeller blades recovered from the crash, as well as a small English-language plaque commemorating the airmen.

The account of Watts's postcrash activities is based on *Escape and Evasion Report No. 92*, hereafter cited as *E&E 92*.

19. Several sources indicate that the young woman was Jacqueline Barron, and that her father, Pierre Barron, was the mayor of Louvres.

20. The two other surviving members of Watts's crew—navigator Second Lieutenant Allan Eastman and bombardier Second Lieutenant Richard Manning—also reached Paris, though under distinctly different circumstances. Both were wounded in the downing of their Fortress and were captured by the Germans. They were transported to Beaujon hospital in the French capital for treatment, after which they were sent to POW camp Stalag Luft VII A in Bavaria, where they spent the remainder of the war.

21. SNCF stands for Société nationale des chemins de fer français. For more on the railwaymens' role in the Resistance, see *La SNCF sous l'Occupation Allemande, 1940–1944: Rapport Documentaire*.

22. Based upon the later reports of their arrival in Paris, Cornwall, Davitt, and Eastman were led from the Gare Saint-Lazare to the boulevard Haussmann, and from there past the Le Madeleine and on to the place de la Concorde.

CHAPTER 5

1. Details on Schoegel's life and resistance activities are drawn primarily from documents in his personal file in Container 1167 of *Case Files Relating to French Citizens Proposed for Awards for Assisting American Airmen*. Additional information is from the various escape and evasion reports that mention him, and from *Demande d'Attestation d'Etat de Services, Mouvement de Résistance "Vengeance," André Auguste Schoegel*.

2. Suzanne Schoegel survived her time in the camp, and was reunited with her husband in July 1945.

3. The account of the dead child, and other details of the Morins' daily life during the first year of the occupation, are drawn from Harding-Claerebout 2017.

4. The younger Salomon, an engineer by training, would go on to serve in the Vengeance organization under the nom de guerre "Corentin." He was arrested by German military police in the town of Ploërmel on February 26, 1944, and executed by firing squad on June 30, 1944. The elder Salomon was also arrested, on July 14, 1944, in Paris, and was deported to Buchenwald. He survived, and was liberated on April 11, 1945, by troops of the U.S. 6th Armored Division.

5. *Fonds Turma-Vengeance*; and *Vengeance: Histoire*, op. cit.

6. Details on the Morins' resistance activities up to 1943 are drawn from *Case Files Relating to French Citizens Proposed for Awards for Assisting American Airmen, Container 1118, Names Moreau-Morin*.

7. Though she hadn't known it at the time she took the position, the bank's personnel manager was the uncle of one of her childhood friends. Yvette was later able to recruit the man into Turma-Vengeance. The director of Crédit National at the time Yvette was hired was Wilfrid-Siegfried Baumgartner, a well-known and highly respected economist and financier. Although he was not Jewish (the family name is Alsatian), Baumgartner was arrested in 1943 after repeatedly resisting German attempts to transfer his bank's holdings to Nazi-run institutions. He spent time in both Buchenwald and the Füssen-Plansee labor camp, but survived and enjoyed a long and successful postwar career until his death in 1978.

8. Harding-Claerebout 2017.

9. Information on Brown and Houghton and their time with the Morins is drawn from *Escape & Evasion Reports Nos. 52* and *53*, hereafter cited as *E&E 52* and *E&E 53*.

10. The three captured airmen—navigator Second Lieutenant Leonard J. Fink, engineer/top turret gunner Staff Sergeant Otho E. Masterson, and tail gunner Staff Sergeant Lee Lewis—spent the remainder of the war in a POW camp. In addition to Houghton and Brown, the men sent to Paris included pilot Second Lieutenant Joseph Rosio, copilot Second Lieutenant George W. Evans, and

waist gunners Staff Sergeant John Kuberski and Staff Sergeant Anthony Cu-cinotta. The evasion experiences of the latter four—all of whom made it back to England—are detailed in, respectively, *Escape & Evasion Reports Nos. 54, 55, 56,* and *71.* The Fortress's bombardier, Second Lieutenant Sidney Casden, was assisted by the François-Shelburn escape line and was evacuated to England by boat in January 1944. His experience is detailed in *Escape and Evasion Report No. 355.*

11. Dr. Mercier had served in Georges Morin's regiment in World War I, and from the 1920s onward had been the Morins' family physician and close friend. Yvette Morin thought of him as an "uncle," and was close friends with the doc-tor's wife. Indeed, it was apparently Yvette who brought Germaine Mercier into the Turma-Vengeance network, mainly as an escort for evaders moving around the city. Dr. Mercier, for his part, helped the network when he could, but as far as can be determined was never an official member.

12. With the aid of the Bourgogne network, Brown and Houghton left Paris and arrived in Spain on July 14, the same day Joe Cornwall's odyssey in France began.

13. While it took Cornwall, Eastman, and other American evaders some time to put names to the various places, monuments, streets, and buildings they en-countered in Paris, in the interests of clarity we will use the names from the outset.

14. Several sources indicate that the woman was Francoise Vandevoorde. She and her husband, Maurice, were members of the Bourgogne network and often sheltered evaders in their home on avenue de la Republique in the Paris suburb of Fontenay-sur-Bois.

15. As is often the case with escape and evasion reports—and with witness statements made to police and interviews recorded by reporters—accounts by dif-ferent people who participated in the same events can differ widely. While most documents dealing with Turner and Davitt, including their E&E reports, agree that they stayed with Schoegel in Orly, at least one other states that they were housed by a woman named Marie Sauvage, an acquaintance of Schoegel's. I have elected to follow the most commonly accepted accounts.

16. The garden was referred to as the Cour de la Boulangerie on eighteenth-century diagrams of Invalides. In 1987 the Hospital Garden was replaced by the much larger and more formal Jardin de l'Abondance (Garden of Abundance), which was intended to be the counterpart to the Jardin de l'Intendant, installed in 1980 on the southwest corner of Invalides.

17. Yvette's stays with the Merciers piqued the interest of the concierge in the couple's building, who seemed intensely interested in the young woman's iden-tity. Concerned that the concierge might be an informer, Dr. Mercier made a point of telling the woman that Yvette was his "niece from Bordeaux." Harding-Claerebout 2017.

18. Harding-Higgins 2017 and Harding-Lynch 2017. Harry Eastman's awareness that he looked like a harmless middle-aged Frenchman led him to do something that likely scared Germaine Mercier half to death. As the two were walking one afternoon along the northern end of the boulevard de la Tour-Maubourg—the street that marks the western boundary of Invalides—several off-duty German soldiers were playing volleyball on a narrow patch of lawn that lay between the street and the buildings that housed their barracks and various administrative offices. One of the players mis-hit the ball, which soared over the sturdy wrought iron fence separating Invalides from the wide boulevard and rolled to a stop at Harry's feet. Without a second thought, he bent over, picked up the ball, and walked a few feet closer to the fence. As the ball-less Germans watched him expectantly, he took a beat, then nonchalantly tossed the ball over the fence. The soldier who caught the ball smiled and said "Merci," at which point Harry gave the troops a cheerful wave and walked back to a visibly shaken Germaine. The remainder of their walk was uneventful.

19. Harding-Claerebout 2017.

20. While it is likely that first turn took the trio east on rue de Babylone, it is impossible to chart their subsequent course with any accuracy. "Marie" would have wanted to avoid streets that were home to German offices or French police stations, yet would have also wanted to follow routes that were fairly busy with other pedestrians.

21. The reunion of the three friends is recounted in various levels of detail in each of their E&E reports.

22. Maud Couvé was a Frenchwoman whose husband was serving in the Royal Air Force. Alice Brouard and her husband, John, were both British subjects, having been born in the Channel Islands. John Brouard was at that time still confined in an internment camp outside Paris, so after their own release from internment Alice and her elder daughter, Marguerite, had moved in with Maud. Alice's second daughter, thirteen-year-old Christine, was living with her grandparents in Normandy. Details on the two women and their activities as helpers are drawn from Marguerite Brouard-Miller's delightful unpublished 2002 memoir, *The World War II Years of Marguerite,* and from the author's January 2017 interviews with her. Details on Davitt's stay with the women are drawn from *E&E 99.*

23. Mme. Melot was arrested by the Germans on November 13, 1943, and deported to Ravensbrück. She survived, and was liberated in April 1945. Dickson, the RNZAF pilot, had previously made it safely to Spain as part of the group that included Kee Harrison.

24. In his E&E report Joe simply identifies the location as "a place where Capt. [Kee] Harrison later stayed." Harrison only sheltered at two locations during his time in Paris: the first was the home of Jean and Laure de Traz on rue de Miromesnil, where he lodged from July 20 to August 8, and the second was with

Mme. Rospape, from August 8 to August 17. Joe never stayed with the de Trazes, which leaves Mme. Rospape's apartment as the only logical location for his sojourn after leaving rue de Madrid. Harrison arrived at rue du 29 Juillet on Sunday the eighth, which was the day after Joe left to return to Invalides. *E&E 91* and *E&E 125.*

CHAPTER 6

1. Some sources have indicated that the "Germaine" Joe Cornwall refers to in his *E&E 125* as being part of his escort to Gare d'Austerlitz on August 17 was Germaine Bajpai, the elegant and very attractive forty-seven-year-old chief of the Comète network's chain of safe houses. This is unlikely, in that Mme. Bajpai was careful never to use her real name when dealing with evaders, instead going by the code names "Francoise" or "Madame Haurfoin" (unlike Maud Couvé, who tended to tell evaders her real name rather than giving them her nom de guerre, "Margie"). Since in his E&E report Cornwall says that Yvette Morin also accompanied him to the train station that day, it is logical to assume that the "Germaine" he refers to was Mme. Mercier, whom he already knew through the Morins.

2. *E&E 125.*

3. No evidence survives to explain the suspicions the Morins and others in Turma-Vengeance briefly harbored against Gabrielle Wiame, though it may have stemmed from the fact that her husband, Charles, was a policeman. After the war both the Wiames were widely lauded for their work with several evasion networks, and Gabrielle was credited with aiding more than one hundred evaders. She was ultimately awarded the U.S. Medal of Freedom with Gold Palm.

4. *E&E 125.*

5. Ibid.

6. While submarines were often used to put spies, saboteurs, and other covert operatives ashore in Occupied France, such vessels were considered far too valuable to the Allied war effort to be risked just to retrieve evaders and therefore almost never did so.

7. In the week following his landing just northwest of Paris, Bieger walked almost two hundred miles south. After finally being found by résistants he spent time in a camp in the mountains before being moved to Lyon. On October 1 he was escorted to Paris, where he was turned over to Jean-Claude Camors, head of a network known as BCRA-Camors (BCRA was Charles de Gaulle's London-based organization). On October 2 he was moved to Brittany. Bieger's story is detailed in *Escape and Evasion Report No. 133,* and in the March 8, 2012, edition of the U.S. Air Forces Escape & Evasion Society newsletter.

8. Despite its purposely innocuous-sounding name, the OSS was the United States' primary interservice intelligence and covert-action organization for much

of the latter part of World War II. Created in the summer of 1942 under the leadership of William J. "Wild Bill" Donovan, the organization operated in both the Pacific and European theaters, conducting espionage and sabotage missions, organizing and training local guerrilla groups, and orchestrating the sort of propaganda and misinformation campaigns that are now referred to as "information warfare." The OSS's chief of operations in Switzerland was the professorial Allen W. Dulles, who later became head of the postwar Central Intelligence Agency, itself an outgrowth of the wartime OSS.

9. Known as the División Azul (Blue Division) and designated by the Germans as the 250. Infanterie-Division, the unit consisted of some sixteen thousand officers and men. The division distinguished itself in action against the Soviets, but political pressure from the Allied governments forced Franco to recall the unit to Spain in the fall of 1943. Most of the several thousand men who chose to ignore the order were absorbed into regular German units and the Waffen-SS, though some were massed into the regimental-size Legión Azul (Blue Legion). Spanish pilots also served Nazi Germany, flying fighters in action against the Soviets.

10. Many of the routes through the mountains had been pioneered by Spanish Republicans seeking to flee Spain following the victory of Franco's fascist forces in the 1936–1939 Spanish Civil War. The flow of people reversed following the 1939 outbreak of war in Europe, with troops of the defeated armies, Jews, and general refugees streaming south.

11. Headed by Vice Admiral Wilhelm Canaris, the Abwehr was primarily responsible for gathering intelligence on the organization, equipment, and effectiveness of Germany's military opponents. The organization also had a counterintelligence branch, which among other tasks was charged with penetrating foreign intelligence agencies and groups. As part of that latter mission the Abwehr sought to penetrate Britain's SIS and SOE, as well as anti-German resistance movements in the occupied countries, and turn their members into witting or unwitting assets. This often brought the Abwehr into direct competition with the Gestapo, whose primary purpose was to eliminate résistants rather than turn them into double agents.

12. Created in 1939, MI9 was officially Section 9 of Britain's Directorate of Military Intelligence. Its mission was to facilitate the escape of Commonwealth prisoners of war from Axis captivity, to support existing evasion organizations, and create and support new ones, and to produce and distribute items that would aid escapers and evaders. MIS-X was organized within the U.S. War Department in October 1942 to undertake the same operations for American military personnel as MI9 did for Commonwealth service members. MIS-X was modeled on MI9, and the two organizations cooperated closely.

13. Two members of the 94th Bomb Group who managed to make it to Paris were unable to complete their home runs. Staff Sergeants Richard Lewis and Eino

Asiala, the right waist and tail gunner, respectively, on Kee Harrison's aircraft, were arrested by the Germans in late August as they arrived in the capital by train. They and another of their crewmates who had been captured, left waist gunner Staff Sergeant Earl Porath, spent the remainder of the war in German POW camps.

14. The post–Bastille Day activities of Turner, Polk, McNemar, and Eastman are drawn from, respectively, *E&E 98, E&E 109, E&E 110,* and *E&E 112.*

15. Like John Harding—the English sports promoter who was good friends with Jeff and Louise Dickson—Don Harding is not related to the author, though he and the author's father both came from Kansas.

16. Broussine had escaped to England in 1940 to join de Gaulle and parachuted back into France early in 1943 to establish the Bourgogne network. For an in-depth and fascinating account of the formation and operations of the Bourgogne line, see Broussine's excellent *L'Evadé de la France Libre.*

17. The Germans had confiscated much of France's better rolling stock in the months following the armistice, leaving the SNCF and local railways to make do with older and far less reliable equipment.

18. Both Americans and the RCAF gunner, Sergeant David McMillan, all eventually made it safely back to England. See Harding's *Escape and Evasion Report No. 111.*

19. In one of those coincidences that are so unexpected yet so oddly common in wartime, Munday's Fortress bore the serial number 42-3330, one numeral off *Salty's Naturals'* 42-3331. Both aircraft had come off the same Douglas Aircraft assembly line in Long Beach, California, likely within hours of each other, and both had gone down on the same day, likely within minutes of each other. On top of that, all available sources indicate that Munday's aircraft was shot down by none other than Egon Mayer.

20. Details regarding the journey to Spain undertaken by Davitt, Carpenter, and Potvin are drawn from, respectively, *E&E 99, E&E 100,* and *E&E 101.*

21. After resting up for several days, Munday joined a later group of evaders and eventually made it to Gibraltar, and from there back to England.

22. Davitt's E&E report says the man, F/O Peter Ablett of the RAF's 78 Squadron, stayed in Andorra. But Ablett's own account says that he was captured while still in France after becoming separated from the group. He spent the remainder of the war in a German POW camp.

23. Harding-Higgins 2017.

24. The general account of the time Roy Scott and Tony Trusty spent at Invalides is based on their escape and evasion reports, *MI9/S/PG(-)1566* and *MI9/S/PG(-)1449,* respectively. Scott's impressions of Joe Cornwall and Yvette Morin are contained in his 1996 interview with Canadian researcher Michael LeBlanc. Scott's Halifax bore the serial number B8334 and wore the individual squadron code NF-X.

25. Interestingly, the false papers provided to both Dick Davitt and Harry Eastman had carried the same incorrect stamp, but they got to Spain nevertheless.

26. The author can personally attest that though the letters of Trusty's inscription have been somewhat softened by weather and the passage of more than seventy-five years, they remain clearly legible.

27. The organization was known to the Germans as the Französischer Infanterie-Regiment 638, and is most often referred to in English as the French Volunteer Legion.

28. The phrase appears in Trusty's *MI9/S/PG(-)1449.*

29. In addition to Joe Cornwall's *E&E 125,* details on the events of September 16–18 are drawn from Andrew Lindsay's *Escape and Evasion Report No. 389* and Percival "Vic" Matthews's *MI9/S/PG(-)1559.* Lindsay was the copilot of a 386th Bomb Group B-26 shot down on August 22, 1943. Matthews was the pilot of a Lancaster of the RAF's 61 Squadron, which was brought down by a German night fighter on August 15.

30. Vic Matthews returned to the United Kingdom on November 12, 1943. It took Andrew Lindsay a bit longer—he finally made his home run on February 6, 1944.

31. As in the case of Gabrielle Wiame, the suspicions about Andrzej Wyssogota-Zakrzewski turned out to be entirely unfounded.

32. An outspoken critic of the Nazis and their French collaborators throughout the occupation, Chevrot was also a member of the resistance organization known as the Front national de l'independence de la France.

33. Among those swept up was Noor Inayat Khan, a British SOE operative of Indian and American descent who was arrested on October 13, just three days before Joe Cornwall left Paris. The first female radio operator sent into Occupied France as part of Britain's support for the resistance movement, she was betrayed by someone within her network. After harsh interrogation she was executed at Dachau concentration camp on September 13, 1944.

34. Hampton-Claerebout 2017.

35. There is some confusion about the identity of the third passenger. Though Cornwall said he was British and named Louis, Colonel Brosse identified him as a French captain named Bernard. (See *Témoignage de M. le Colonel Brosse.*) One possible explanation is that the third person was indeed a British SIS officer, but one who had grown up completely bilingual and while operating in France had for security purposes let his compatriots believe he was French. This is not as unlikely as it might seem: British agent John Goldsmith—author of the delightful memoir *Accidental Agent: Behind Enemy Lines With the French Resistance*—had grown up splitting his time between England and France, and his Parisian accent was so authentic that his French comrades were later stunned to discover he was British.

36. McBride's Lysander carried the serial V9367 and was coded MA-B. Details of Operation Primrose are drawn from McBride's own mission notes in *Report on Lysander Operations Undertaken by No. 161 Squadron on the Night of 18/19 October, 1943*; the *Operations Log, No. 161 (Special Duties) Squadron, Oct. 1943*; Hugh Verity's excellent history of the RAF's secret landings in wartime France, *We Landed by Moonlight*; *Agents by Moonlight* by Freddie Clark; and Pierre Hentic's *Agent de l'Ombre*.

37. Sadly, James McBride was killed almost exactly two months after flying Joe Cornwall to freedom. The RAF pilot was returning to RAF Tangmere from an agent pickup mission in France on the night of December 17, 1943, and found the airfield shrouded in thick fog. He aborted his first landing attempt when he lost sight of the field, and on his second approach crashed about a mile short of the runway, possibly as the result of fuel starvation. The Lysander immediately caught fire, and though the two agents McBride was carrying—Léon-Marcel Sandeyron of the Azur network and a female member of the Amarante *réseau* known by the code-name "Atlas"—were able to escape, the pilot himself was trapped in the cockpit and died in the fire. A second 161 Squadron Lysander also crashed that night, again during a landing attempt. The second aircraft was on approach to fog-shrouded Ford airfield when it dove into the ground, killing the pilot and both passengers.

38. The USAAF did not provide Joe Cornwall with a car, driver, and escort for his journey to London as a courtesy—it was done entirely for security purposes. MIS-X and MI9 did not want newly returned evaders to speak to anyone about their experiences in France, so as not to inadvertently compromise the evasion networks or their members. Evaders who reached England by sea or by air from Gibraltar or North Africa normally traveled to London by train, seated in sealed compartments and escorted by armed guards. That Joe Cornwall made the trip to the capital by car was apparently due to the fact that he arrived in the United Kingdom in the middle of the night and by unusual means, and that MIS-X officials were eager to hear the reasons for his lengthy stay in Paris.

CHAPTER 7

1. The location, wartime operations, and administrative procedures of the U.S. Special Reception Center are detailed in sources including *Military Intelligence Service in the European Theater of Operations* (hereafter cited as *MIS-X in the ETOUSA*) and *The Escape Factory: The Story of MIS-X*. The townhouse at 63 Brook Street is still there, though as part of extensive renovations in the early 2000s its interior was completely gutted. During the reconstruction process No. 63 was joined to the much larger No. 61 next door, to form an office complex totaling more than thirty thousand square feet. On the other side of the townhouse, at No. 65, is the embassy of Argentina.

2. MACR 116 pertaining to *Salty's Naturals* was issued late on July 14, 1943. It lists Clara B. Cornwall as Joe Cornwall's wife—the same personnel clerk obviously having assumed that Clara's middle name was Brawner (her actual maiden name).

3. Clara Gypin married Clarence Wester "Smokey" Rebuck in the spring of 1943. It is unclear why she was living in Raceland in the summer of that year.

4. The two newspapers known to have run notices regarding Joe Cornwall's MIA status were *The Times* of Shreveport, Louisiana, and the *Clarion-Ledger* in Jackson, Mississippi. Both papers ran the piece on Tuesday, August 3.

5. The general nature of Joe Cornwall's MIS-X interviews is extrapolated from descriptions of such sessions in sources including *MIS in the ETO; M.I.S.-X Manual on Evasion, Escape, and Survival;* and *The Escape Factory.* Specific aspects of the interviews are based on *E&E 125.*

6. Details on exactly how the message was passed are unclear, but it is likely that the news was included in one of the regular radio transmissions between SOE and Pierre Hentic, who then passed the information through André Schoegel.

7. Joe Cornwall was the 125th USAAF returned evader to be debriefed by MIS-X in the European Theater, hence the number of his report.

8. The standard nondisclosure form is coded AG 383.6 and carries the subject line "Safeguarding of P/W Information." Joe Cornwall actually signed his on October 19, 1943, the day of his arrival at 63 Brook Street.

9. *Company Morning Report, 331st Bomb Sq., Station 468, October 28, 1943,* notes "Cornwall, Joseph E., S/Sgt., asgd [assigned] and jd [joined] 25 Oct, per par [paragraph] 5, SO [special order] #292, HQ, Eighth AF."

10. The crews of three B-17s were rescued after ditching in the English Channel or North Sea on the return flight, and the crew of one aircraft survived a crash-landing near Dover. *The Big Square A,* 358.

11. Joe Cornwall's promotion was authorized by Paragraph 11, Special Order 83, HQs. USAAF Station 468, as noted in *Company Morning Report, 331st Bomb Sq., Station 468, October 29, 1943.*

12. Joe Cornwall was actually issued two forty-eight-hour passes for his trip to London. The first (marked C-38288) covered the period from midnight on November 21 through midnight on the twenty-third, and the second (J-63548) from midnight on the twenty-third to midnight on the twenty-fifth. Both passes specified Cornwall was to stay at the Columbia Club.

13. Information on Joe Cornwall's return flight to the United States is drawn, in part, from the *Entry Declaration of Aircraft Commander (Entry Immigration and Customs)* filed by Captain C. B. Springer of TWA upon the arrival of C-54A serial 41-37283 at Washington National Airport on December 5, 1943. The C-54 was the military variant of Douglas's DC-4 airliner. The C-54A had airline-style seats for 22 passengers, as well as a large loading door and a cargo hoist.

14. *The Army Air Forces in World War II: Volume 7, Services Around the World*, 551. Hereafter cited as *Services Around the World.*

15. *Services Around the World,* 525. Also see *Psychiatric Experiences of the Eighth Air Force: First Year of Combat (July 4, 1942—July 4, 1943)* for a more complete explanation of the mental-health issues specific to combat aviators in Europe and the way in which those issues were handled both overseas and once the individual returned to the United States.

16. Redistribution Center No. 3 eventually grew to encompass five hotels and an apartment complex, as well as gas stations and an Elks Club. Most of the facilities were on Ocean Avenue, just to the north and south of the Santa Monica Pier and where today the Pacific Coast Highway intersects the Santa Monica Freeway. A satellite facility of the Redistribution Center known as Castle Hot Springs was located some fifty miles northwest of Phoenix, Arizona.

17. Letter, Louise M. Dickson to Lawrence H. Templeton, October 25, 1943.

18. Letter, Lawrence H. Templeton to Louise M. Dickson, n.d.

19. Letter, Louise M. Dickson to Joseph E. Cornwall, March 31, 1944.

20. In an April 18, 1944, letter written while she was still in Fort Myers, Louise Dickson gave a detailed account of her conversation with Joe Cornwall. The letter has no addressee, but was apparently intended for John Harding, the Dicksons' longtime friend at the National Sporting Club in London.

21. It has proven impossible to determine who the three other people were, and "Roger," "Bob," and "Paul" are almost certainly noms de guerre.

22. The story of how the letter came into the author's possession—and its surprising importance—is told in the following chapter.

23. See *La Régiment de Sapeurs-Pompiers de Paris, 1938–1944,* 61. The Durins' presence at the Morins' home is also documented in *Liste des Français Hébergés Pour un Temps Assez Long, Par la Famille Morin.*

24. The Corsican-born radio operator's last name is sometimes rendered in official documents as Mario. He also occasionally used the nom de guerre "Robert."

25. The Paris Gestapo was subordinate to the Befehlshaber der Sicherheitspolizei (BdS), the commander of the security police and security service in the city, himself a representative of the Reich Security Main Office in Berlin.

26. Dupont was interrogated by the Belgian-born collaborator and Abwehr agent Georges Delfanne (alias "Christian Masuy"), who was infamous for his ingenious torture methods. Dupont was ultimately sent to Konzentrationslager (KZ) Buchenwald, where he used his medical skills to care for other prisoners. Dupont survived, and was freed on April 11, 1945, when the U.S. 6th Armored Division liberated the camp. Delfanne, for his part, was captured at the end of the war, tried for his crimes, and executed by firing squad on October 1, 1947.

27. Wyssogota-Zakrzewski spent time in the Buchenwald, Dora, and Bergen-Belsen concentration camps, but survived.

28. Mme. Melot was deported to Ravensbrück, the concentration camp for women located some ninety miles north of Berlin, but survived.

29. Germaine Bajpai and Fernande Onimus were both likely betrayed by Comète member Maurice Grapin, who had been turned by SS-Major Hans Josef Kieffer, deputy head of the Paris SD. Sadly, both Bajpai and Onimus died in Ravensbrück.

Cécile Durin also ended up in Ravensbrück, but survived and returned to Paris on May 16, 1945. Her husband never joined her, however. Paul Durin was initially sent to Buchenwald, near Weimar, but when advancing American forces neared the camp in April 1945 he was among the thousands of prisoners the Germans forced to march eastward. Many of the prisoners, including Durin, were put aboard the ocean liner–turned–prison ship *Cap Arcona* in the Bay of Lübeck. On May 2, 1945, the ship and others nearby were attacked by Typhoon fighter-bombers of the Royal Air Force; the British pilots had been told the vessels were carrying German troops and VIPs attempting to escape to Norway. Nearly five thousand prisoners, including Paul Durin, died in the assault or when *Cap Arcona* capsized and sank. See *La Régiment de Sapeurs-Pompiers de Paris, 1938–1944*, op. cit.

30. The family name is also given as Lérida in some documents. Details on the brothers and their activities are drawn from Harding-Claerebout 2017. The men are also mentioned in several postwar MIS-X documents pertaining to the Morins.

31. Sources indicate that one of the Dérida brothers was located and executed after the end of the war by a group of French Resistance fighters who had just returned from a concentration camp. The other brother was tried in 1946 and sentenced to twenty years in prison, though nothing more is known about him.

32. After the war the building reverted to the Sûreté Nationale, and is currently home to the Direction générale de la police nationale (DGPN), part of France's Ministry of the Interior.

33. Surviving records indicate that the arrests among the Paris-based evasion organizations between June and August 1944 were almost certainly the result of information provided by a coterie of informers, including—among others—the brothers Dérida; a man named André Baveau (or Baveaux or Raveau); the well-known, Belgian-born traitor Jacques Desoubrie; and Roger Leneveu (known as Roger the Legionnaire). In postwar reports, both Andrzej Wyssogota-Zakrzewski and Gabrielle Wiame said they believed it was Baveau/Baveaux who specifically informed on the Morins. For more on these individuals and the damage they caused, see Patrice Miannay's excellent *Dictionnaire des Agents Doubles dans la Résistance* and J. M. Langley's *Fight Another Day*.

34. Michel Bourgeois was deported to Bergen-Belsen, but survived. After the war, transformed by his experience in the concentration camp, he became a priest

and spent twenty-three years as the chaplain to the fishermen of Saint-Vaast-la-Hougue, on the English Channel. Gustave Salomon was sent to Buchenwald, but also survived. Joseph and Yvonne Gorjux were deported on the same day and aboard the same train as Georges, Denise, and Yvette Morin. Yvonne Gorjux died at Bergen-Belsen, but Joseph survived. Their daughter, Pierrette, also survived the war.

35. German records indicate that the people aboard the August 15 train represented twenty-six nationalities—the most numerous were French (1,867), American (83), and British (57), but there were also Poles, Swiss, Danes, Belgians, and a host of others. While the majority of the Americans were aviators and others POWs, one was an American-born woman who had married a Frenchman and joined the French Resistance against the Nazis. Her name was Virginia d'Albert-Lake, and her fascinating story is detailed in *An American Heroine in the French Resistance*. It is interesting to speculate whether d'Albert-Lake may have come into contact with Yvette and Denise Morin on the deportation train, or even at Ravensbrück.

36. The tunnel episode is recounted by both Virginia d'Albert-Lake and Émile Bollaert, a decorated World War I veteran, interwar politician, and member of the Comité français de la Libération nationale who, like Georges Morin, was being transported to Buchenwald aboard the train.

37. Georges Morin's journey from Paris to Buchenwald is recorded in *Effeckten an KZ Buchenwald, Morin, Georges, Kriegswehrmachtgefängnis Paris-Fresnes, 10.8.1944*. Details of his classification upon arrival at Buchenwald appear in *Häftlings-Personal-Karte KZ Buchenwald, Georges Morin*.

38. Mittelbau-Dora was originally a Buchenwald subcamp, but was designated a camp in its own right in the summer of 1944. Fabrication of the V-1 and V-2 was transferred to Mittelbau-Dora after Allied air raids on the research center at Peenemünde prevented continued missile construction operations there.

39. *Veränderungsmeldung KZ Mittelbau, 26.12.44, Morin, Georges*. The document states that Georges Morin—who, according to his SS death certificate, died in the early morning hours of December 23, 1944—was one of 46 prisoners whose bodies were cremated on December 25. However, because the *Veränderungsmeldung KZ Mittelbau* is dated December 26, many of the memorial plaques honoring Georges—including the two that grace the halls of Invalides—cite the 26th as the date of his death.

CHAPTER 8

1. *An American Heroine in the French Resistance*, 156.

2. *Häftlings-Personal-Karte KZ Ravensbrück, Denise Morin* and *Häftlings-Personal-Karte KZ Ravensbrück, Yvette Morin*.

3. Harding-Claerebout 2017. Yvette Morin-Claerebout also spoke about conditions in Ravensbrück in a 2016 video interview with the Fondation pour la mémoire de la déportation titled *Témoignage CNRD 2016/2017 Morin, Yvette*.

4. Harding-Claerebout 2017.

5. Some of the French female prisoners who were transferred from Ravensbrück to Torgau cite the date of the movement as September 11. But most German records—including *Überstellungsliste von KL Ravensbrück nach KL Buchenwald (Arbeitslager Torgau), Morin, Denise; Morin, Yvette*—list the date as September 21.

6. Torgau was home to a POW camp known as Stalag IV-D, which housed some eight hundred French and British enlisted men who worked in various labor camps in the region.

7. *American Heroine*, 164.

8. Harding-Claerebout 2017.

9. *American Heroine*, 165. One of the key leaders of the women's revolt at Torgau was Jeannie Rousseau, a French intelligence agent who had been providing vital information to the Allies regarding German efforts to develop and deploy the V-1 flying bomb and V-2 ballistic missile. Arrested just days before the June 1944 Allied landings in Normandy, she ultimately survived Ravensbrück, Torgau, and the "punishment camp" at Königsberg. Her crucial role in alerting the Allies to the dangers of the German V-weapons did not come to light until the 1970s, and she was always dismissive of her important contributions to the Allied war effort, saying many others did far more. She died in August 2017 at the age of ninety-eight.

10. Harding-Claerebout 2017.

11. The village is often confused with the much larger town of Abterode, some 22 miles to the northwest in Hesse. Indeed, even the bureaucrats who managed Nazi Germany's vast concentration-camp system used the incorrect "Abterode" on official documents, including those that recorded the transfer of Yvette and Denise Morin to the camp, which is often referred to as Abteroda-Berka because of its proximity to the town of Berka/Werra.

12. Other production sites for the BMW 003 axial flow turbojet engine included salt mines in Heiligenrode, Ploemintz, and Stassfurt. The 003 was used in prototypes of the Me 262 fighter, and in production models of the Arado Ar 234 bomber and Heinkel He 162 fighter.

13. Working around Torgau's acid baths was so debilitating that the women were completely replaced by new groups of female prisoners sent every six weeks from Auschwitz and other camps. Surviving records indicate that more than half of the women sent back to Ravensbrück from Torgau did not survive the war. Hermann Pister, for his part, was arrested by American troops and ultimately tried and convicted for his crimes at Buchenwald. He was sentenced to

death, but died of a heart attack in Landsberg Prison before the sentence could be carried out.

14. *Individuelle Dokumente KZ Buchenwald, Morin, Denise (Besondere Borfommnisse)* (the latter phrase is usually translated as "special activities"); *Individuelle Dokumente KZ Buchenwald, Morin, Yvette (Besondere Borfommnisse)*. These documents carry the Buchenwald identification because Abteroda was an *Aussenkommando* of that larger camp. Each document indicates that the subject was actually located at Abteroda (though the word is incorrectly spelled on both as Abterode).

15. Harding-Claerebout 2017.

16. Why Abteroda's SS commander believed that starving slave laborers from any camp in the Nazi system might be expected to perform error-free technical work for the regime that was working them to death is unclear.

17. Details on the layout, organization, and conditions at Markkleeberg are drawn largely from two excellent books: Susan Ottaway's *A Cool and Lonely Courage: The Untold Story of Sister Spies in Occupied France*, and *Snow Flowers: Hungarian Jewish Women in an Airplane Factory, Markkleeberg, Germany*, by Zahava Szász Stessel.

18. Their arrival was documented on the same *Individuelle Dokumente KZ Buchenwald, Morin, Denise (Besondere Borfommnisse)* and *Individuelle Dokumente KZ Buchenwald, Morin, Yvette (Besondere Borfommnisse)* as cited above.

19. *KL Buchenwald Arbeitseinsatz, Häftlingskommando für Junkers, Markkleeberg*.

20. Harding-Claerebout 2017.

21. Ibid.

22. *Snow Flowers*, 168.

23. Harding-Claerebout 2017. The Jewish prisoner's name has sadly been lost to history. Yvette described her as an "angel," and remembered the woman telling her that when the SS arrested her they nailed her nine-month-old baby to a door and then executed her husband on the spot.

24. Yad Vashem—the Israel-based Holocaust Martyrs' and Heroes' Remembrance Authority—estimates that up to a quarter-million concentration camp prisoners died or were murdered on the forced death marches conducted during the last ten months of World War II in Europe.

25. The Nazis referred to the region as the Protectorate of Bohemia and Moravia. The route of the Markkleeberg death March was Meissen-Niederau-Dresden-Freital-Tharandt-Höckendorf-Dippoldiswalde-Theresienstadt. The latter is now Terezín in the Czech Republic.

26. The Line of Contact was simply the demarcation between the Soviet forces and those of the American, British, and French armies, and in many areas was far to the east of the occupation zone boundaries agreed to by the Allies at the Yalta Conference in February 1945. Following the German surrender on May 8,

1945, the western armies withdrew to the stipulated areas. The new line ultimately became the border between East and West Germany.

27. Located at 19 avenue Kléber in Paris's 16th arrondissement, the building was occupied by the Germans' Militärbefehlshaber Frankreich (Military Commander in France) until the liberation. It then housed various Allied organizations, and is now the luxury hotel Peninsula Paris. The MIS-X office was usually entered through the rear of the building, at 30 rue La Perouse, which is now a separate establishment known as the Majestic Hôtel-Spa Paris.

28. *Visit of Madame and Mademoiselle Morin.*

29. *Declarations, Morin, Madame Denise.*

30. *MIS-X to IS9 (Donald Darling, Awards), Ref: Mme and Mlle Morin.* The sum of FF 22,000 would be worth approximately $6,000 in 2018 dollars.

31. Madame Gladys Oriot had given Yvette English lessons after Joe left Paris. The missive was sent via Major John F. White's office at MIS-X in Paris, with a foreword by Madame de Larminat asking the officer to forward the letter to Joe, "of whom no one of us has any news."

32. *Deportee Questionnaire, Subject Georges Julien Morin.*

33. It remains unclear exactly who authored the letter, though it may have been either Germaine Mercier or André Schoegel.

EPILOGUE

1. *Final Payment Roll, USAAF Separation Center, Roster No. 15, Group D, Cornwall, Joseph E.*

2. Letter, M. J. Furness, U.S. Fish & Wildlife Service, to Joseph E. Cornwall.

3. Details on Joe Cornwall's USAF service are drawn from his Official Military Personnel File and his National Archives Form 13164.

4. Harding-Gypin 2017. See also *State of Colorado, County of El Paso, Marriage License 44008.*

5. *Death Certificate, Joseph Ellison Cornwall, Adams County Colorado, February 2, 1993.*

6. Letter, Major John F. White to Madame Veuve Denise Morin, May 14, 1946.

7. General Order 362, HQs., U.S. Forces European Theater, December 26, 1946.

8. General Order 364, HQs., U.S. Forces European Theater, December 27, 1946.

9. The award grades and dates of presentation are detailed on MIS-X (Paris) copies of IS9 note cards "Morin, Denise," "Morin, Yvette," and "Morin, Georges." Why Georges could not have been posthumously awarded a decoration of higher grade is unclear.

10. France's highest order of civilian and military merit has five grades of increasing distinction, with progression through the first three normally based on the time an individual has held each grade. According to records provided to the author by the Legion's Grande Chancellerie, Denise Morin was created a chevalier (knight) by decree on July 13, 1961, an officier (officer) on October 30, 1963, and a commandeur (commander) on July 9, 1981. The most recent was bestowed on Denise by General Albert Marie Gabriel de Galbert, who was at that time the governor of the Invalides. Yvette Morin-Claerebout was created a chevalier by decree on January 25, 1967, and an officier by decree on December 4, 1975. Note that several months can pass between the time of the decree and the actual presentation of the award.

11. Harding-Claerebout 2017.

12. The description of Raoul Claerebout is based directly on his daughter's memory of him. In a 2017 interview Ellen Hampton conducted on the author's behalf with Yvette Morin-Claerebout and her daughter, Denise Weil, the latter described her father as "a gambler, a cheat and a violent drunkard." Moreover, Mme. Weil remembered Raoul's mother as "a monster" who abused everyone and tried to get any money coming to Denise Morin and Yvette from war benefits.

13. *Justification du Projet et Définition des Travaux Proposes.*

APPENDIX

1. Details drawn from the May 14, 1945, letter to Louise M. Dickson from John Harding.

Bibliography

ARCHIVES AND ABBREVIATIONS

Documents were obtained from the following sources, which are attributed as cited.

UNITED STATES:
AFHRA: U.S. Air Force Historical Research Agency, Maxwell AFB, Alabama.
AFHSO: U.S. Air Force Historical Studies Office, Anacostia Naval Annex, Washington, D.C.
AFSRC: U.S. Air Force Albert F. Simpson Historical Research Center, Maxwell AFB, Alabama.
AHEC: U.S. Army Heritage and Education Center, Carlisle, Pennsylvania.
CIA: Central Intelligence Agency, Langley, Virginia.
CMH: U.S. Army Center of Military History, Fort McNair, Washington, D.C.
DTIC: Defense Technical Information Center, Fort Belvoir, Virginia.
NARA-MMRC: National Archives and Records Administration, Modern Military Records Center, College Park, Maryland.
NARA-NPRC: National Personnel Records Center, St. Louis, Missouri.

UNITED KINGDOM:
IWM: Imperial War Museum, London.
RAFM: Royal Air Force Museum, London.
UKNA: National Archives, Kew, Richmond, Surrey.

FRANCE:
BDIC: Bibliothèque de documentation internationale contemporaine, Nanterre.
FR: Fondation de la Résistance, Paris.

MAI: Musée de l'Armée Invalides, Paris.
SHD: Service historique de la défense, Vincennes.

GERMANY:
BA-B: Bundesarchiv, Berlin.
BA-F: Bundesarchiv-Militärarchive, Freiburg.
ITS: International Tracing Service, Bad Arolsen.

Official Documents

Aircraft Flight Characteristics, B-17. Boeing Aircraft Co., Seattle, Washington, June 1, 1944. Air Corps Library.

Attestation d'Appartenance aux F.F.C.: Georges Morin. Secretariat d'Etat aux Forces Armees (Guerre), Direction du Personnel Militaire de l'Armee De Terre, 6ème Bureau, December 14, 1949. SHD.

Attestation d'Appartenance aux F.F.C.: Yvette Morin. Secretariat d'Etat aux Forces Armees (Guerre), Direction du Personnel Militaire de l'Armee De Terre, 6ème Bureau, December 13, 1949. SHD.

Awards Fiche: Morin, Georges Julie [sic] and Famille [sic]. Military Intelligence Service, MIS-X, Awards Branch, HQs., European Theater of Operations (ETOUSA), April 19, 1948. NARA-MMRC.

Bombing Data, 102nd & 103rd Combat Wings, 14 July 1943. HQs., VIII Bomber Command, July 18, 1943. AFHRA.

Bulletin de Décès: Morin, Georges Julien. Ville de Paris, État Civil, Mairie du 7 Arrondissement, December 10, 1946. SHD.

Carte de Combattant Volontaire de la Resistance: Denise Laure Marie Morin. SHD. Office National des Anciens Combattants et Victimes de Guerre, December 6, 1949. SHD.

Case Files Relating to French Citizens Proposed for Awards for Assisting American Airmen, Container 1118, Names Moreau–Morin. Military Intelligence Service, MIS-X, Awards Branch, HQs., European Theater of Operations (ETOUSA), June 1946. NARA-MMRC.

Case Files Relating to French Citizens Proposed for Awards for Assisting American Airmen, Container 1167, Names Schnerb–Seiler. Military Intelligence Service, MIS-X, Awards Branch, HQs., European Theater of Operations (ETOUSA), June 1946. NARA-MMRC.

Certificat de Validation des Services, Campagnes et Blessures des Déportés et Enternés de la Résistance: Claerebout, née Morin, Yvette Edmée. October 3, 1950. SHD.

Certificat de Validation des Services, Campagnes et Blessures des Déportés et Enternés de la Résistance: Georges Julien Morin. January 17, 1951. SHD.

Certificat de Validation des Services, Campagnes et Blessures des Déportés et Enternés de la Résistance: Yvette Edmée Morin. September 14, 1950. SHD.

The Combined Bomber Offensive, April Through December 1943. Historical Office, HQs., Army Air Forces, Washington, D.C., 1946. AFHRA.

Company Morning Reports, 331st Bomb Squadron (H), 94th Bomb Group (H), for the Month of July 1943. NARA-NPRC.

Company Morning Reports, 331st Bomb Squadron (H), 94th Bomb Group (H), for the Month of August 1943. NARA-NPRC.

Company Morning Reports, 331st Bomb Squadron (H), 94th Bomb Group (H), for the Month of September 1943. NARA-NPRC.

Company Morning Reports, 331st Bomb Squadron (H), 94th Bomb Group (H), for the Month of October 1943. NARA-NPRC.

Consolidated List of French Helpers Proposed for Award to Date. Morin, Denise, Morin, Yvette. 7709 MIS-X Detachment, HQs. Command, U.S. Forces, European Theater, July 1946. NARA-MMRC.

Death Certificate, Joseph Ellison Cornwall, Adams County Colorado, February 2, 1993. Office of the County Clerk, Adams County, Colorado.

Declarations, Morin, Madame Denise. 6801 MIS-X Detachment, HQs. Command, U.S. Forces, European Theater, June 20, 1945. NARA-MMRC.

Demande d'Attestation d'Etat de Services, Mouvement de Résistance "Vengeance," Denise Laure Marie Morin. June 1948. SHD.

Demande d'Attestation d'Etat de Services, Mouvement de Résistance "Vengeance," Georges Julien Morin. June 1948. SHD.

Demande d'Attestation d'Etat de Services, Mouvement de Résistance "Vengeance," Yvette Edmée Eugénie Morin. June 1948. SHD.

Demande d'Attestation d'Etat de Services, Mouvement de Résistance "Vengeance," André Auguste Schoegel. June 1948. SHD.

Deportee Questionnaire, Subject Georges Julien Morin. IS9 Awards Branch, Paris. July 9, 1945. NARA-MMRC.

The Early Operations of the Eighth Air Force and the Origins of the Combined Bomber Offensive. Historical Office, HQs., Army Air Forces, Washington, D.C., 1946. AFHRA.

Effeckten an KZ Buchenwald, Morin, Georges, Kriegswehrmachtgefängnis Paris-Fresnes, 10.8.1944. 1.1.5.1/5299149/ITS Digital Archive, Bad Arolsen.

Enlisted Record and Report of Separation, Templeton, Lawrence H. Separation Center, Camp McCoy, WI, November 24, 1945. NARA-NPRC.

Entry Declaration of Aircraft Commander, C-54 137283, Prestwick, Scotland, to Washington, D.C., Dec. 5, 1943. NARA-MMRC

Erection and Maintenance Instructions for Army Model B-17F. Boeing Aircraft Co., Seattle, Washington, December 1, 1942. Air Corps Library.

Escape and Evasion Report No. 52, S/Sgt. Lester Brown Jr. Office of ACS, G-2, MIS Detachment, HQs, ETOUSA, August 9, 1943. NARA-MMRC.

Escape and Evasion Report No. 53, S/Sgt. John H. Houghton. Office of ACS, G-2, MIS Detachment, HQs, ETOUSA, August 9, 1943. NARA-MMRC.

Escape and Evasion Report No. 54, 2d Lt. Joseph Rosio. Office of ACS, G-2, MIS Detachment, HQs, ETOUSA, August 15, 1943. NARA-MMRC.

Escape and Evasion Report No. 55, 2d Lt. George W. Evans. Office of ACS, G-2, MIS Detachment, HQs, ETOUSA, August 15, 1943. NARA-MMRC.

Escape and Evasion Report No. 56, S/Sgt. John H. Kuberski. Office of ACS, G-2, MIS Detachment, HQs, ETOUSA, August 15, 1943. NARA-MMRC.

Escape and Evasion Report No. 71, S/Sgt. Anthony F. Cucinotta. Office of ACS, G-2, MIS Detachment, HQs, ETOUSA, August 31, 1943. NARA-MMRC.

Escape and Evasion Report No. 86, S/Sgt. Lawrence H. Templeton. Office of ACS, G-2, MIS Detachment, HQs, ETOUSA, September 11, 1943. NARA-MMRC.

Escape and Evasion Report No. 87, 2d Lt. Roscoe F. Greene. Office of ACS, G-2, MIS Detachment, HQs, ETOUSA, September 12, 1943. NARA-MMRC.

Escape and Evasion Report No. 88, 1st Lt. William C. Wetzel. Office of ACS, G-2, MIS Detachment, HQs, ETOUSA, September 9, 1943. NARA-MMRC.

Escape and Evasion Report No. 91, Capt. Kee H. Harrison. Office of ACS, G-2, MIS Detachment, HQs, ETOUSA, April 9, 1943. NARA-MMRC.

Escape and Evasion Report No. 92, 1st Lt. Floyd B. Watts. Office of ACS, G-2, MIS Detachment, HQs, ETOUSA, September 17, 1943. NARA-MMRC.

Escape and Evasion Report No. 98, 2d Lt. David H. Turner Jr. Office of ACS, G-2, MIS Detachment, HQs, ETOUSA, September 20, 1943. NARA-MMRC.

Escape and Evasion Report No. 99, S/Sgt. Richard S. Davitt. Office of ACS, G-2, MIS Detachment, HQs, ETOUSA, September 20, 1943. NARA-MMRC.

Escape and Evasion Report No. 100, S/Sgt John L. Carpenter. Office of ACS, G-2, MIS Detachment, HQs, ETOUSA, September 26, 1943. NARA-MMRC.

Escape and Evasion Report No. 101, T/Sgt. Samuel E. Potvin. Office of ACS, G-2, MIS Detachment, HQs, ETOUSA, September 26, 1943. NARA-MMRC.

Escape and Evasion Report No. 111, T/Sgt. Donald E. Harding. Office of ACS, G-2, MIS Detachment, HQs, ETOUSA, October 6, 1943. NARA-MMRC.

Escape and Evasion Report No. 112, S/Sgt. Harry L. Eastman. Office of ACS, G-2, MIS Detachment, HQs, ETOUSA, October 10, 1943. NARA-MMRC.

Escape and Evasion Report No. 125, S/Sgt. Joseph E. Cornwall. Office of ACS, G-2, MIS Detachment, HQs, ETOUSA, October 19, 1943. NARA-MMRC.

Escape and Evasion Report No. 355, 2d Lt. Sidney Casden. Office of ACS, G-2, MIS Detachment, HQs, ETOUSA, January 30, 1944. NARA-MMRC.

Escape and Evasion Report No. 389, 2d Lt. Andrew C. Lindsay. Office of ACS, G-2, MIS Detachment, HQs, ETOUSA, February 7, 1944. NARA-MMRC.

Escape and Evasion Report No. 531, 1st Lt. William B. Lock. Office of ACS, G-2, MIS Detachment, HQs, ETOUSA, March 26, 1944. NARA-MMRC.

Etat des Lieux de Hotel des Invalides (Justification du projet et definition des travaux proposés). Agence de l'Architecte en Chef des Invalides, 1988. MAI.

Extract of French Declaration, Joseph Gorjux. 6801 MIS-X Detachment, HQs. Command, U.S. Forces, European Theater, February 28, 1945. NARA-MMRC via Michael LeBlanc.

Extract of French Declaration, Pierrette Gorjux. 6801 MIS-X Detachment, HQs. Command, U.S. Forces, European Theater, November 20, 1945. NARA-MMRC via Michael LeBlanc.

Final Payment Roll, USAAF Separation Center, Roster No. 15, Group D, Cornwall, Joseph E. NARA-MMRC.

Flexible Gunnery Training in the AAF. Assistant Chief of Air Staff, Intelligence, Historical Section, March 1945. AFHRA.

Fonds Turma-Vengeance. Réseau Turma-Vengeance. Listes, Rapports et Comptes-rendus des Activiteés des Membres du Réseau. N.D. BDIC.

Fonds Turma-Vengeance. Réseau Turma-Vengeance. Région II: Paris et la Seine: Listes des Membres des Réseaux, Attestations d'Appartenance aux Réseaux. N.D. BDIC.

For U.S. Armed Forces in U.K.—Bury St. Edmunds. British Council, London, 1943.

General Order No. 102, Awards of Distinguished Flying Cross; 1st Lt. Edward A. Purdy. HQs., Eighth Air Force, July 15, 1943. AFHRA.

General Order No. 226, Awards of Distinguished Flying Cross; Capt. Edward A. Purdy (Missing in Action). HQs., Eighth Air Force, December 16, 1943. AFHRA.

General Order No. 362, Citation for Medal of Freedom With Bronze Palm: Yvette Morin. HQs., U.S. Forces, European Theater, December 26, 1946. NARA-MMRC.

General Order No. 362, Citation for Medal of Freedom With Silver Palm: Denise B. Morin. HQs., U.S. Forces, European Theater, December 26, 1946. NARA-MMRC.

General Order No. 364, Citation for Medal of Freedom With Silver Palm (Posthumous): Georges Morin. HQs., U.S. Forces, European Theater, December 27, 1946. NARA-MMRC.

The German Intelligence Service and the War. Office of Strategic Services, Washington, D.C. N.D. CIA.

Häftlings-Personal-Karte KZ Buchenwald, Denise Morin. 1.1.5.4/7663042/ITS Digital Archive, Bad Arolsen.

Häftlings-Personal-Karte KZ Buchenwald, Georges Morin. 1.1.5.3/6658071/ITS Digital Archive, Bad Arolsen.

Häftlings-Personal-Karte KZ Buchenwald, Yvette Morin. 1.1.5.4/7663071/ITS Digital Archive, Bad Arolsen.

Häftlings-Personal-Karte KZ Ravensbrück, Denise Morin. 1.1.5.4/7663043/ITS Digital Archive, Bad Arolsen.

Häftlings-Personal-Karte KZ Ravensbrück, Yvette Morin. 1.1.5.4/7663072/ITS Digital Archive, Bad Arolsen.

Helpers and Betrayers. MIS Detachment, HQs., ETOUSA, May 16, 1945. NARA-MMRC.

History, 6th Photographic Group, Reconnaissance. Monthly Reports, 1 March 1944 through 30 September 1945. NARA-NPRC.

Individual Deceased Personnel File, Russell E. Crisp. The Adjutant General's Office, U.S. Army, Washington, D.C., 1948. NARA-NPRC.

Individual Deceased Personnel File, Jefferson D. Dickson. The Adjutant General's Office, U.S. Army, Washington, D.C., 1948. NARA-NPRC.

Individual Deceased Personnel File, Carroll T. Harris Jr. The Adjutant General's Office, U.S. Army, Washington, D.C., 1948. NARA-NPRC.

Individual Deceased Personnel File, Edward B. Jones. The Adjutant General's Office, U.S. Army, Washington, D.C., 1948. NARA-NPRC.

Individual Deceased Personnel File, Charles W. Lichtenberger. The Adjutant General's Office, U.S. Army, Washington, D.C., 1948. NARA-NPRC.

Individual Deceased Personnel File, Richard J. Marquardt. The Adjutant General's Office, U.S. Army, Washington, D.C., 1948. NARA-NPRC.

Individual Deceased Personnel File, Edward A. Purdy. The Adjutant General's Office, U.S. Army, Washington, D.C., 1948. NARA-NPRC.

Individual Deceased Personnel File, Francis J. Santangelo. The Adjutant General's Office, U.S. Army, Washington, D.C., 1948. NARA-NPRC.

Individual Deceased Personnel File, John W. Smith. The Adjutant General's Office, U.S. Army, Washington, D.C., 1948. NARA-NPRC.

Individual Deceased Personnel File, Charles M. Sprague. The Adjutant General's Office, U.S. Army, Washington, D.C., 1948. NARA-NPRC.

Individuelle Dokumente KZ Buchenwald, Morin, Denise. 1.1.5.4/7663039/ITS Digital Archive, Bad Arolsen.

Individuelle Dokumente KZ Buchenwald, Morin, Denise (Besondere Borfommnisse). 1.1.5.4/7663039/ITS Digital Archive, Bad Arolsen.

Individuelle Dokumente KZ Buchenwald, Morin, Yvette. 1.1.5.4/7663068/IST Digital Archive, Bad Arolsen.

Individuelle Dokumente KZ Buchenwald, Morin, Yvette (Besondere Borfommnisse). 1.1.5.4/7663070/ITS Digital Archive, Bad Arolsen.

KL Buchenwald Arbeitseinsatz, Häftlingskommando für Junkers, Markkleeberg, 10.3.1945. NARA-MMRC.

L'Affaire Andre Raveaux. N.D. FR via Michael LeBlanc.

Liste de Pilotes Americains et Anglais Hébergés par la Famille Morin. 7709 MIS-X Detachment, HQs. Command, U.S. Forces, European Theater, July 1946. NARA-MMRC.

Liste des Français Hébergés Pour un Temps Assez Long, Par la Famille Morin. 7709 MIS-X Detachment, HQs. Command, U.S. Forces, European Theater, July 1946. NARA-MMRC.

Lysander and Hudson Pick Up Operations: Execution of Operations—Notes for Pilots. S/Ldr Hugh Verity, 1944. UKNA via Robert Body.

Lysander and Hudson Pick Up Operations: Preparation Instructions for Pilots. S/Ldr Hugh Verity, 1944. UKNA via Robert Body.

Memoire de Proposition Pour l'Attribution de Medaille de la Resistance: Yvette Morin. Ministere de la Guerre, Réseau Action Vengeance, February 24, 1947. SHD.

MI9/S/PG(-)1449. Evaded Capture in France: Sgt. James George Antony Trusty, RAF. IS9(W), London, October 6, 1943. UKNA via Michael LeBlanc.

MI9/S/PG(-)1559. Evaded Capture in France: Sgt. Percival Victor Matthews, RAF. IS9(W), London, November 12, 1943. UKNA via Michael LeBlanc.

MI9/S/PG(-)1566. Evaded Capture in France: W/O Roderick Alexander Scott, RCAF. IS9(W), London, November 7, 1943. UKNA via Michael LeBlanc.

Military Intelligence Service in the European Theater of Operations. HQs., U.S. Forces, European Theater, N.D. CIA.

M.I.S.-X Manual on Evasion, Escape, and Survival. The War Department, Washington, D.C., 1944. NARA-MMRC.

Missing Aircrew Report #114. HQs., Army Air Forces, Washington, D.C., July 14, 1943. NARA-MMRC.

Missing Aircrew Report #115. HQs., Army Air Forces, Washington, D.C., July 14, 1943. NARA-MMRC.

Missing Aircrew Report #116. HQs., Army Air Forces, Washington, D.C., July 14, 1943. NARA-MMRC.

Missing Aircrew Report #161. HQs., Army Air Forces, Washington, D.C., August 10, 1943. NARA-MMRC.

MIS-X to IS9 (Donald Darling, Awards), Ref: Mme and Mlle Morin. 6801 MIS-X Detachment, HQs. Command, U.S. Forces, European Theater, July 11, 1945. NARA-MMRC.

MIS-X to IS9 (Darling, Lefort), Ref: Mme Morin. 6801 MIS-X Detachment, HQs. Command, U.S. Forces, European Theater, N.D. NARA-MMRC.

Narrative Mission Report, VIII Bomber Command Mission 72. Office of the S-2, 331st Bombardment Squadron, July 11, 1943. NARA-MMRC.

Narrative Mission Report, VIII Bomber Command Mission 73. Office of the S-2, 94th Bombardment Group, July 15, 1943. NARA-MMRC.

Narrative Mission Report, VIII Bomber Command Mission 73. Office of the S-2, 331st Bombardment Squadron, July 17, 1943. NARA-MMRC.

Narrative Unit History, 331st Bombardment Squadron, July–August 1943. Office of the S-2, 331st Bombardment Squadron. AFHRA.

Neuzugänge KL Buchenwald vom 3.9.44 (mit Personalbogen), Morin, Georges. 1.1.5.1/5363114/ITS Digital Archive, Bad Arolsen.

Neuzugänge KL Buchenwald vom 19.10.44 (von KL Ravensbrück nach Akdo Abterode [sic] *Über Akdo Torgaü, eingetroffen am 6.10.44), Morin, Denise; Morin, Yvette*. 1.1.5.1/5290022/ITS Digital Archive, Bad Arolsen.

Operations Log, No. 161 (Special Duties) Squadron, Oct. 1943. UKNA via Robert Body.

Origins of the Eighth Air Force: Plans, Organization, Doctrines. Assistant Chief of Air Staff, Intelligence, Historical Division, Washington, D.C., 1944. AFHRA.

Pilot Training Manual for the B-17 Flying Fortress. Office of Assistant Chief of Air Staff, Training, Army Air Forces, May 1945. Air Corps Library.

Pilot's Flight Operating Instructions for Army Models B-17F and G. Office of Assistant Chief of Air Staff, Training, Army Air Forces, August 1, 1943. Air Corps Library.

Politische Französinnen, Neuzugänge, 19 Oktober 1944. Morin, Denise (57616/31904); Morin Yvette (57615/31903). Politische Abteilung, KL-Weimar-Buchenwald Standesbeamte. BA-F.

Psychiatric Experiences of the Eighth Air Force: First Year of Combat (July 4, 1942–July 4, 1943). Office of the Air Surgeon, Army Air Forces, August 1944. AFHRA.

Questionnaire Concernant l'Aide Apportee Aux Evades Allies: Gorjux, Joseph. 6801 MIS-X Detachment, HQs. Command, U.S. Forces, European Theater, June 28, 1946. NARA-MMRC.

Recommendation for a Donation in Favor of Madam Veuve Denise Morin. 6801 MIS-X Detachment, HQs. Command, U.S. Forces, European Theater, May 14, 1946. NARA-MMRC.

Recommendation for a Pension in Favor of Madame Veuve Denise Morin. IS-9 (Awards Bureau), Paris, April 29, 1946. UKNA.

Recommendation for Award of Medal of Freedom With Bronze Palm: Yvette Morin. 6801 MIS-X Detachment, HQs. Command, U.S. Forces, European Theater, May 2, 1946. NARA-MMRC.

Recommendation for Award of Medal of Freedom With Silver Palm: Denise Bourinet Morin. 6801 MIS-X Detachment, HQs. Command, U.S. Forces, European Theater, May 1, 1946. NARA-MMRC.

Recommendation for Award of Medal of Freedom With Silver Palm: Georges Julien Morin. 6801 MIS-X Detachment, HQs. Command, U.S. Forces, European Theater, May 1, 1946. NARA-MMRC.

Recommendation for Payment, Mme and Mlle Morin. 6801 MIS-X Detachment, HQs. Command, U.S. Forces, European Theater, July 11, 1945. NARA-MMRC.

Renseignements d'Etat Civil Concernant Le Deporte ou l'interne: Claerebout, Yvette, Née Morin. N.D. BDIC.

Report Brought In By Miss Pierrette Gorjux. 6801 MIS-X Detachment, HQs. Command, U.S. Forces, European Theater, July 24, 1945. NARA-MMRC via Michael LeBlanc.

Request for Interview: Madame Denise Morin. 7709 MIS-X Detachment, HQs. Command, U.S. Forces, European Theater, March 19, 1946. NARA-MMRC.

Résumé d'Activité de Madame Morin. N.D. BDIC.

Roster of Officers—Dickson, Captain Jefferson D. HQs., 452nd Bombardment Squadron, 322nd Bombardment Group, October 24, 1942, via Christine Hilger.

SIPO & SD Kommandos in France: Personnel and Chief Groups of Agents. Supreme HQs., Allied Expeditionary Force, April 1945. CIA.

Special Order 292, Return of MIA Personnel: Cornwall, S/Sgt. Joseph E. NARA-NPRC.

Statement by Sgt. Percival Victor Matthews, RAF, Evaded Capture in France. M.I.9/S/P.G. (-) 1559, November 12, 1943. UKNA.

Statement by WO Roderick Alexander Scott, RCAF, Evaded Capture in France. M.I.9/S/P.G. (-) 1566, November 8, 1943. UKNA.

Statement by Sgt. James George Antony Trusty, RAF, Evaded Capture in France. M.I.9/S/P.G. (-) 1449, October 5, 1943. UKNA.

Statistical Mission Report, VIII Bomber Command No. 73. HQs., 94th Bomb Group, July 14, 1943. AFHRA via George Saltsman.

Sterbebuch Standesamt Sangerhausen, III/160, Georges Morin. 1.1.27.1/2538504/ITS Digital Archive, Bad Arolsen.

Tactical Mission Report, Mission No. 73, 14 July 1943. HQs., VIII Bomber Command, APO 634, August 9, 1943. AFHRA.

Tactical Report, Form 103A Statistical, Mission No. 73. HQs., 94th Bomb Group, July 14, 1943. AFHRA.

Tactical Report of Mission, Le Bourget, 14 July 1943. HQs., 4th Bombardment Wing, July 18, 1943. AFHRA via George Saltsman.

Témoignage de M. le Colonel Brosse, 28/8/48. SHD.

Totenschein, Beamter Georges Morin. Konzentrationslager-Sangerhausen Standesbeamte, December 25, 1944. BA-F.

Überstellungsliste von KL Ravensbrück nach KL Buchenwald (Arbeitslager Torgau), Morin, Denise; Morin, Yvette. 1.1.35.1/3760958/ITS Digital Archive, Bad Arolsen.

Überstellungsliste zum Aussenlager Dora, Morin, Georges. 1.1.5.1/5363099/IST Digital Archive, Bad Arolsen.

Veränderungsmeldung KZ Mittelbau, 26.12.44, Morin, Georges. 1.1.27.1/2534339/ ITS Digital Archive, Bad Arolsen.

Visit of Madame and Mademoiselle Morin. 6801 MIS-X Detachment, HQs. Command, U.S. Forces, European Theater, June 14, 1945. NARA-MMRC.

Visit of Mme. Paul Durin. 6801 MIS-X Detachment, HQs. Command, U.S. Forces, European Theater, November 21, 1945. NARA-MMRC.

Voucher for Pay and Allowances of Individual Enlisted Men—S/Sgt. Jesse Gypin Sr., Fitzsimons General Hospital, September 29, 1942. NARA-NPRC.

War Diary, 331st Bomb Squadron, 94th Bomb Group, May 1943. AFHRA.

War Diary, 331st Bomb Squadron, 94th Bomb Group, June 1943. AFHRA.

War Diary, 331st Bomb Squadron, 94th Bomb Group, July 1943. AFHRA.

Weekly Status and Operations Report, 94th Bomb Group, July 11-17, 1943. NARA-MMRC.

Interviews

Brouard-Miller, Marguerite. Audio-recorded by the author, January 25 and 30, 2017.

Gypin, Nathaniel. Audio-recorded by the author, February 8 and August 25, 2017.

Higgins, Byron. Audio-recorded by the author, March 12, 2017.

Hilger, Christine Dickson. Audio-recorded by the author, December 14, 2016.

LeBlanc, Michael. Audio-recorded by the author, February 7 and 10, 2017.

Lynch, Roger. Audio-recorded by the author, March 12, 2017.

Morin-Claerebout, Yvette. "Témoignage CNRD 2016/2017 MORIN Yvette." Video-recorded by La Fondation pour la Mémoire de la Déportation, released September 2016.

———. Audio-recorded by Ellen Hampton, February 10, 2017.

———. Audio-recorded by the author, June 5, 2017.

Saltsman, George. Audio-recorded by the author, March 15, 2017.

Scott, Roderick A. Audio-recorded by Michael LeBlanc, June 1996.

Templeton, Bruce. Audio-recorded by the author, July 13, 2017.

Correspondence

Begg, 2nd Lt. Joseph R., to Louise Dickson, February 7, 1946.

Brainerd, I. M., to Effie B. Belcher, June 22, 1944.

Burnett, Thurman D., to Ralph H. Saltsman Jr., April 5, 1976.

Callon, Sim C., to Lawrence Templeton, April 27, 1987.

Cornwall, Joseph E., to "Whom It May Concern," September 2, 1945.

Dickson, Jefferson Davis, Jr., to Louise M. Dickson, June 20, 1943.

Dickson, Louise M., to Lawrence Templeton, October 25, 1943.

———, to Joseph E. Cornwall, March 31, 1944.

———, to John Harding [?], April 18, 1944.

Doyle, David F., to Louise M. Dickson, March 26, 1945.

Dunlop, Brigadier General Robert H., to Lieutenant Colonel Carroll T. Harris Sr., April 12, 1944.

Frank, Mrs. Willis T., to Louise M. Dickson, August 10, 1943.

Furness, M. J., U.S. Fish & Wildlife Service, to Joseph E. Cornwall, May 20, 1946.

Harding, John, to Louise M. Dickson, December 23, 1943.

———, to Louise M. Dickson, May 14, 1945.

Hilger, Christine Dickson, to the author, February 27, 2017.

Horkan, Brigadier General G. A., to Louise Dickson, May 2, 1947.

LeBlanc, Michael Moores, to Ralph H. Saltsman, October 19, 1999.

Lefort, Captain, to Major Donald Darling, April 21, 1945.

Mercier, Madame Germaine, to Joseph Cornwall (via Major John F. White Jr., MIS-X Paris), June 4, 1945.

Olynik, Michael, to Dr. Joseph Gorjux, January 4, 1946.

Pasco, Jean, to Ralph H. Saltsman Jr., June 28, 1993.

Purdy, Ann L., to Major W. F. Heyman, QMC, September 11, 1944.

Saltsman, Ralph H., Jr., to Dr. Eugene M. Emme, October 5, 1981.

———, to Lawrence H. Templeton, July 26, 1993.

———, to Claude-André Simoneau, December 30, 1997.

———, to Lawrence H. Templeton, February 14, 1998.

Templeton, Lawrence H., to Louise M. Dickson, n.d.

———, to Ralph H. Saltsman Jr., February 22, 1998.

Unknown, to Louise M. Dickson, April 18, 1944.

Warner, Captain J. W., to Effie B. Belcher, July 24, 1944.

White, Major John F., to Major Donald Darling, March 19, 1945.

———, to Madame Veuve Denise Morin, May 14, 1946.

Memoirs

Miller, Marguerite Brouard. *The World War II Years of Marguerite*. Self-published, 2002.

Saltsman, Ralph H., Jr. *My Story*. Unpublished typescript. 1945.

———. *Good Time Cholly II*. Self-published, 1993.

———. *Return to Normandy*. Self-published, 1993.

SECONDARY SOURCES

Books

Bachelier, Christian. *La SNCF sous l'Occupation Allemande, 1940–1944: Rapport Documentaire.* 2 vols. Paris: Institut d'Histoire de Temps Présent-CNRS, 1996.

Berlière, Jean-Marc. *Au coeur de la Préfecture de Police: de la Résistance à la Libération: 1ère partie.* Paris: Editions BLM, 2009.

Blandford, Edmund L. *SS Intelligence: The Nazi Secret Service.* Shrewsbury, UK: Airlife Publishing, 2000.

Bodson, Herman. *Downed Allied Airmen and Evasion of Capture: The Role of Local Resistance Networks in World War II.* Jefferson, NC: McFarland, 2005.

Bowers, Peter M. *Fortress in the Sky.* Granada Hills, CA: Sentry Books, 1976.

Bowman, Martin. *B-17 Flying Fortress Units of the Eighth Air Force, Part 1.* Botley, Oxford, UK: Osprey, 2000.

———. *We Were Eagles: The Eighth Air Force at War.* Vol. 1, *July 1942 to November 1943.* Stroud, UK: Amberley Publishing, 2014.

Breker, Arno. *Paris, Hitler et Moi.* Paris: Presses de la Cité, 1970.

Broussine, Georges. *L'Evadé de la France Libre: Le Réseau Bourgogne.* Paris: Tallander, 2000.

Bruning, John R. *Bombs Away! The World War II Bombing Campaigns Over Europe.* Minneapolis, MN: Zenith Press, 2011.

Carruthers, Bob. *Hitler's Propaganda Pilgrimage.* Barnsley, North Yorkshire, UK: Pen and Sword Books, 2015.

Chevrot, Jean. *Une figure influente de l'église parisienne du XXe siècle: Georges Chevrot, 1879–1958.* Paris: Éditions Publisud, 2002.

Clark, Freddie. *Agents by Moonlight: The Secret History of RAF Tempsford During World War II.* Stroud, Gloucestershire, UK: Tempus Publishing, 1999.

Craven, Wesley F., and James Lea Cate, eds. *Plans and Early Operations January 1939 to August 1942.* Vol. 1 in the series *The Army Air Forces in World War II.* Chicago: University of Chicago Press, 1948.

———. *Europe: Torch to Pointblank, August 1942 to December 1943.* Vol. 2 in the series *The Army Air Forces in World War II.* Chicago: University of Chicago Press, 1948.

———. *Men and Planes.* Vol. 6 in the series *The Army Air Forces in World War II.* Chicago: University of Chicago Press, 1955.

———. *Services Around the World.* Vol. 7 in the series *The Army Air Forces in World War II.* Chicago: University of Chicago Press, 1957.

D'Albert-Lake, Virginia. *An American Heroine in the French Resistance: The Diary and Memoir of Virginia d'Albert-Lake.* Edited by Judy Barrett Litoff. New York: Fordham University Press, 2008.

Darling, Donald. *Sunday at Large: Assignments of a Secret Agent.* London: William Kimber, 1977.

Delarue, Jacques. *Histoire de la Gestapo.* Paris: Librarie Arthème Fayard, 1962.

Douglas, Graeme. *Boeing B-17 Flying Fortress: Owner's Workshop Manual.* Minneapolis, MN: Zenith Press, 2011.

Drake, David. *Paris at War, 1939–1944.* Cambridge, MA: Harvard University Press, 2015.

Foot, M. R. D. *SOE in France.* London: Her Majesty's Stationary Office, 1976.

Foot, M. R. D., and J. M. Langley. *MI9: Escape and Evasion, 1939–1945.* London: Bodley Head, 1979.

Freeman, Roger A. *The Mighty Eighth: A History of the U.S. Eighth Air Force.* Garden City, NY: Doubleday. 1970.

———. *B-17 Fortress at War.* New York: Charles Scribner's Sons, 1977.

———. *U.S. Strategic Airpower in Europe, 1942–1945.* London: Arms and Armour Press, 1989.

Generalstab des Heeres (Kriegswissenschaftliche Abteilung). *Kampferlebnisse aus dem Kriege an der Westfront 1940.* Berlin: Mittler Verlag, 1941.

Giesler, Hermann. *Ein Anderer Hitler: Bericht Seines Architekten.* Stegen am Ammersee, Germany: Druffel & Vowinckel Verlag, 2005.

Gildea, Robert. *Marianne in Chains: Daily Life in the Heart of France During the German Occupation.* New York: Metropolitan Books, 2003.

———. *Fighters in the Shadows: A New History of the French Resistance.* London: Faber & Faber, 2015.

Glass, Charles. *Americans in Paris: Life and Death Under Nazi Occupation.* New York: Penguin Group, 2009.

Goldsmith, John. *Accidental Agent: Behind Enemy Lines With the French Resistance.* London: Leo Cooper, 1971.

Hansell, Haywood S., Jr. *The Strategic Air War Against Germany and Japan: A Memoir.* Washington, DC: Office of Air Force History, 1986.

Hentic, Pierre. *Agent de l'Ombre.* Paris: Éditions de La Martinière, 2012.

Hope, Bob. *I Never Left Home.* New York: Simon & Schuster, 1944.

Isby, David C., ed. *Fighting the Bombers: The Luftwaffe's Struggle Against the Allied Bomber Offensive.* Barnsley, South Yorkshire, UK: Frontline Books, 2016.

Jablonski, Edward. *Flying Fortress.* New York: Doubleday, 1965.

Johnson, Frederick A. *Boeing B-17 Flying Fortress.* North Branch, MN: Specialty Press, 1997.

Katsaros, John. *Code Burgundy: The Long Escape*. Norwalk, CT: Oakford Media, 2010.

Kershaw, Alex. *Avenue of Spies*. New York: Crown Books, 2015.

Koreman, Megan. *The Escape Line: How the Ordinary Heroes of Dutch-Paris Resisted The Nazi Occupation of Western Europe*. New York: Oxford University Press, 2018.

Kozak, Warren. *LeMay: The Life and Wars of General Curtis LeMay*. Washington, DC: Regnery Publishing, 2009.

L'Amicale de Ravensbrück et l'Association des Déportées et Internées de la Résistance. *Les Françaises à Ravensbrück*. Paris: Éditions Gallimard, 1966.

Langley, J. M. *Fight Another Day*. London: Collins, 1974.

Lasseter, Don. *Their Deeds of Valor*. Bloomington, IN: Xlibris Publishing, 2002.

Leixner, Leo. *Von Lemberg bis Bordeaux*. Munich: Verlag Franz Eher Nachfolger GmbH, 1941.

Lemarchand, Loïc. *Bel atterrissage capitaine!* Le Coudray-Macouard, France: Cheminements, 2008.

Lewis, Richard L., and William R. Larson. *Hell Above and Hell Below: The Real Life Story of an American Airman*. Wilmington, DE: Delapeake Publishing, 1985.

Miannay, Patrice. *Dictionnaire des agents doubles dans la Résistance*. Paris: Le Cherche Midi, 2005.

Miller, Donald L. *Masters of the Air: America's Bomber Boys Who Fought the Air War Against Nazi Germany*. New York: Simon & Schuster, 2006.

Mitchell, Alan. *Nazi Paris: The History of an Occupation, 1940–1944*. Oxford, UK: Berghahn Books, 2008.

Morris, Craig F. *The Origins of American Strategic Bombing Theory*. Annapolis, MD: Naval Institute Press, 2017.

Muratori-Philip, Anne. *L'Hotel Des Invalides (La memoire des lieux)*. Paris: Complexe, 1992.

Nauroth, Holger. *Jagdgeschwader 2 "Richthofen."* Altglen, PA: Schiffer Publishing, 2004.

Neave, Airey. *Saturday at MI-9*. London: Trinity Press, 1969.

———. *The Escape Room*. New York: Doubleday, 1970.

Nijboer, Donald. *Gunner: An Illustrated History of World War II Aircraft Turrets and Gun Positions*. Erin, ON: Boston Mills Press, 2001.

Oehmichen, Hermann, and Martin Mann. *Der Weg der 87: Infanterie-Division*. Self-published, 1969.

Ottaway, Susan. *A Cool and Lonely Courage: The Untold Story of Sister Spies in Occupied France*. New York: Little, Brown, 2014.

Ottis, Sherri Greene. *Silent Heroes: Downed Airmen and the French Underground.* Lexington, KY: University Press of Kentucky, 2009.

Overy, Richard. *The Bombers and the Bombed: Allied Air War Over Europe, 1940–1945.* London: Penguin Books, 2013.

Rist, Charles. *Une saison gâtée: Journal de la Guerre et de l'occupation (1939–1945).* Paris: Fayard, 1983.

Rossiter, Margaret L. *Women in the Resistance.* New York: Praeger, 1986.

Sautreuil, Henri-Alexandre. *Les Invalides: Ou La Mémoire Vivante de la Seconde Guerre Mondial.* Saint-Cyr-sur-Loire: Editions Alan Sutton, 2005.

Shneck, Donald R., and Ralph H. Shneck. *Cheerio and Best Wishes.* West Lafayette, IN: Purdue University Press, 2013.

Shoemaker, Lloyd. *The Escape Factory: The Story of MIS-X.* New York: St. Martin's Press, 1990.

Slater, Harry E. *Lingering Contrails of the Big Square A.* Self-published, 1980.

Speer, Albert. *Inside the Third Reich.* New York and Toronto: Macmillan, 1970.

Spiller, H. J. *Ticket to Freedom.* London: William Kimber, 1988.

Stessel, Zahava Szász. *Snow Flowers: Hungarian Jewish Women in an Airplane Factory, Markkleeberg, Germany.* Vancouver, Canada: Fairleigh Dickenson University Press, 2009.

Umbreit, Hans. *Der Militärbefehlshaber in Frankreich 1940–1944.* Boppard am Rhein, Germany: Harald Boldt Verlag, 1968.

United States Strategic Bombing Survey. *Summary Report (European War).* Washington, DC: U.S. Government Printing Office, 1945.

Vaughan, Hal. *Doctor to the Resistance: The Heroic True Story of An American Surgeon and His Family in Occupied Paris.* Washington, DC: Brassey's, 2004.

Verity, Hugh. *We Landed by Moonlight.* Shepperton, UK: Ian Allen, 1978.

Wake-Walker, Edward. *Westland Lysander, 1936–46 (All Marks).* Yeovil, Somerset, UK: Haynes Publishing, 2014.

Weal, John. *Fw 190 Aces of the Western Front.* London: Osprey, 1996.

———. *Jagdgeschwader 2 "Richthofen."* Botley, Oxford, UK: Osprey, 2000.

Wetterwald, François. *Vengeance: Histoire d'un Corps Franc.* Paris: Imprimerie J. Téqui, 1946.

Wieviorka, Olivier. *The French Resistance.* Cambridge, MA: Belknap Press of Harvard University Press, 2016.

Williamson, Gordon. *World War II German Police Units.* Botley, Oxford, UK: Osprey, 2006.

Woodrum, Henry C. *Walkout.* Bloomington, IN: iUniverse, 2010.

Zaloga, Steven J. *Liberation of Paris, 1944.* Oxford, UK: Osprey, 2008.

———. *Defense of the Third Reich, 1941–1945.* Oxford, UK: Osprey, 2012.

Newspaper Articles

Baltimore Sun. "General Forrest Lost in U.S. Raid on Kiel June 13." June 25, 1943.

Bend (OR) Bulletin. "Redmond Flier Gets Air Medal." August 14, 1943.

"Funeral Sunday for Redmond Man." April 22, 1949.

Chicago Tribune. "Hitler at Tomb of Napoleon, a Conqueror, Too." June 27, 1940.

Daily Mail (London). "Beat 25 Fighters at Kiel." June 14, 1943.

Daily Sketch (Manchester, UK). "Fortresses Smashed Suicide Squadrons." June 20, 1943.

Daily Times-News (Burlington, NC). "Captain Dickson Aims for Paris and Sports Arena." August 8, 1942.

Daily Tribune (Greeley, CO). "Five Coloradoans Get Flying Cross." September 10, 1943.

Daily Variety (Hollywood, CA). "Film Men Made Military History in World War I." January 7, 1942.

Decatur (IL) Herald. "When Jeff Dickson Died . . . " June 18, 1944.

Oakland (CA) Tribune. "Yanks Weather Kiel Ack-Ack, But Bike Handlebars Too Tough." August 6, 1943.

St. Petersburg (FL) Times. "Shot Down in France, Dodges Nazis, Escapes, Tells Story." November 6, 1943.

Sandusky (OH) Register. "Jefferson Davis Dickson Is Missing in Action." March 22, 1944.

Tampa (FL) Tribune. "Wife Says Dickson Died in Air Battle." June 13, 1944.

The Times (Shreveport, LA). "Raceland Sergeant Lost in European Battle Area." August 3, 1943.

Times Herald (Olean, NY). "Lucky Finding of Napoleon Relics Cited—Scattered Along Roadway." October 18, 1940.

Monographs

"It's the Little Things: Escape and Evasion in World War II." Oron P. South, U.S. Arctic, Desert, Tropic Information Center, Maxwell Air Force Base, Alabama, n.d.

"Were They Prepared? Escape and Evasion in Western Europe, 1942–1944." Major Laura C. Counts, USAF Air Command and Staff College, April 1986. DTIC.

Magazine/Journal Articles

Armstrong, James E. "The Voyage of the Suzanne-Renne." *The Communicator* (newsletter of the U.S. Air Forces Escape & Evasion Society), March 8, 2012.

Beatty, Jerome. "Ringmaster of Paris." *American Magazine*, February 1939.

———. "Ringmaster of Paris" (condensed). *Reader's Digest*, June 1939.

Coté, Amy. "Wehrmacht Perceptions of Paris and the French During the Second World War." *The Corvette: The University of Victoria Undergraduate Journal of History* 1, no. 1 (2013).

Grant, Rebecca. "Escaping the Continent." *Air Force*, October 2014.

Paine, Ralph Delahaye, Jr. "France Collapsed From Internal Decay." *Life*, July 8, 1940.

Rossiter, Margaret L. "Le Rôle Des Femmes Dans La Résistance En France." *Guerres Mondiales et Conflits Contemporains*, July 1989.

Saltsman, Ralph H., Jr. "Air Battle at Kiel." *Air Power History*, Summer 1989.

Seiss, Karlheinz. "Jäger und Ihre Beute." *Luftflotte West: Herausgegeben von Der Luftflotte* 3, no. 30 (July 30, 1943).

Slater, Harry. "That's the Way It Was: Eight Over Kiel." *Nostalgic Notes* (94th Bomb Group Association newsletter), March 1977.

Templeton, Lawrence E. "If Memory Serves Me Correctly." *Nostalgic Notes*, March 1980.

Unknown Author. "Hitler and Napoleon: Two 'Little Corporals' Meet in Paris." *Life*, August 15, 1940.

Unknown Author. "Mission: Le Bourget—14 July 1943." *Nostalgic Notes*, March 1976.

Unknown Author. "Mr. Five By Five." *Nostalgic Notes*, December 1988.

Miscellaneous

Ranvoisy, Emmanuel, Odette Christienne, and Frédéric Plancard. "Le Régiment Sapeurs-Pompiers de Paris, 1938–1944." Organizational history produced by the Office of the Mayor of Paris, 2011.

Index